the author

EDWARD E. THORNTON is Professor of Pastoral Theology and Clinical Pastoral Education at Crozer Theological Seminary in Chester, Pennsylvania. He is a graduate of Oklahoma Baptist University (B.A.), University of Oklahoma (M.A.), and Southern Baptist Theological Seminary (B.D. and Th.D.).

While employed as supervisor of clinical pastoral education in the Texas Medical Center, Dr. Thornton began work on this history. His work answers the need for perspective on the contending theories of clinical training. Most of his information came from interviews with those who were involved in making the history.

Dr. Thornton is the author of numerous magazine articles and one other book, *Theology and Pastoral Counseling*.

professional
education
for ministry

professional education for ministry

A HISTORY OF CLINICAL PASTORAL EDUCATION

EDWARD E. THORNTON

ABINGDON PRESS ♪ Nashville and New York

PROFESSIONAL EDUCATION FOR MINISTRY

Standard Book Number: 687-34329-1
Library of Congress Catalog Card Number: 79-97569

The quotations from Richard C. Cabot, M.D.,
"Clinical Training on the Earhart Foundation," in
*The Institution Bulletin: Andover Newton Theo-
logical School,* Oct., 1935, are used by permission
of *The Institution Bulletin.*

Selections from Fred Eastman, "Fathers of the
Clinical Training Movement," in *The Journal of
Pastoral Care,* Spring, 1951, and Paul W. Pruyser,
"Anton T. Boisen and the Psychology of Religion,"
in *The Journal of Pastoral Care,* December, 1967,
are used by permission of *The Journal of Pastoral
Care.*

The quotation from Anton T. Boisen, "Clinical
Training in Theological Education: The Period
of Beginnings," in *The Chicago Seminary Register,*
Jan., 1951, is used by permission of the *CTS Register.*

The quotations from "Man of the Month: Donald
C. Beatty," in *Pastoral Psychology,* Feb., 1955, and
from Harry Emerson Fosdick, "The Minister and
Psychotherapy," *Pastoral Psychology,* Jan., 1960, are
used by permission of *Pastoral Psychology.*

The quotation from Charles R. Feilding, "Education for Ministry," in *Theological Education,* Autumn, 1966, is used by permission of *Theological
Education.*

SET UP, PRINTED, AND BOUND BY THE
PARTHENON PRESS, AT NASHVILLE,
TENNESSEE, UNITED STATES OF AMERICA

TO MY FATHER

EVERETT WHITFIELD THORNTON
a missionary, educator, and historian from
whom I learned to value history, to be an
educator, and to seek the frontiers of life
and ministry

contents

PREFACE 9

Part I
Beginnings, 1923-1930

1. THE TWENTIES 23
2. THE FATHERS: KELLER, CABOT, AND BOISEN ... 40
3. ANTON T. BOISEN 55

Part II
The Era of Separatism, 1930-1946

4. THE COUNCIL'S STORY 75
5. THE NEW ENGLAND GROUP 99

Part III
The Era of Unification, 1947-1967

6. A BEACHHEAD ON STANDARDS, 1947-1953 113
7. THE FAILURE OF FEDERATION, 1953-1960 140
8. THE BREAKTHROUGH TO UNION, 1960-1967 172

Part IV
Beyond Unification

9. DYNAMICS AND DEVELOPMENT 199
10. PROFESSIONAL EDUCATION FOR MINISTRY 213

APPENDIXES

A. *Clinical Pastoral Education's Genealogical Chart* 237
B. *Standards for Clinical Pastoral Education, 1953* 239
C. *Standards for Clinical Pastoral Education, 1968* 242
D. *Constitution and Bylaws, The Association for Clinical Pastoral Education, Inc., 1967* 250

NOTES 265

BIBLIOGRAPHY 285

INDEX 295

PREFACE

This book is about clinical pastoral education. It is part history; part propaganda; part analysis, interpretation, and critique. The first question a book presents to the reader is how to sift what it contains, how to determine the author's angle. Why did he write it? Does he have a hidden agenda? I want, at the outset, to do what I can to make these questions easy to answer. I should like to level with you as to my personal bias with respect to clinical pastoral education.

My first brush with clinical pastoral education occurred in 1950 when I became an aide in a psychiatric hospital in the context of a seminary-endorsed training program. Under the tutelage of able supervisors my awareness of myself expanded as I became aware of the experiencing of the patients. In retrospect the big feelings I associate with this experience were surprise and joy. I entered clinical training looking for a pastoral identity. I found myself in the process. Since becoming a supervisor I have seen this happen over and over again to others. I am prepared to generalize on the matter and say that clinical pastoral education does this to one. If it does not, the trainee has been shortchanged; or perhaps he has not put out enough.

My search for pastoral identity began in reaction against the pastoral models I had known in youth. It was as if I had been looking into a three-faced mirror such as are found in clothing stores, had twisted and turned for many years wondering how I would look in this fashion or that, and then bolted out of the store. By 1947 I had decided not to buy any of the merchandise I had been trying on. Then in the pulpit of the First Baptist Church of Shawnee, Oklahoma, a new

9

model appeared. R. Lofton Hudson was one of the few clergymen in my acquaintance to offer an emotionally honest relationship. He was psychologically informed and relevant. I responded heartily. In order "to try it on for size" I moved to Louisville, Kentucky, to study with Wayne E. Oates at the Southern Baptist Theological Seminary.

The models against which I was reacting were the premillenial "seer" of mysteries; the pietistic "man of God"; and the evangelistic, "soul winning" preacher. The first model was incarnate in my maternal grandfather who spread his charts outlining the end of time before my impressionable eyes and confidently predicted the end of the world in 1947. I remember as a boy thinking, "In 1947 I will just be graduating from college. So why sweat an education? Why not live it up while I can—and repent in 1946 just in case." Recently it occurred to me that senility had advanced so far in both of my grandparents that the world did come to an end for grandfather by 1947. (He would have exploded in rebuttal of this kind of psychologizing had he heard it.)

The pietistic model of the man of God who was kind but incompetent in the face of human needs predominated during my elementary and high school years in Iowa and South Dakota. One pastor saw himself as a prophetic voice, but he was the most incompetent of all in human relationships. When our family moved to Oklahoma in 1942, I was assaulted by the evangelistic, soul winning type known as "preacher." And these are the images I saw in the three-faced mirror of ministerial models. These are the images I rejected.

I have opted for a professional, "person-centered" model of ministry that is informed by the behavioral sciences and shaped in the fire of human crises. Instead of the premillenial stance of seer, the psychologically sophisticated minister seeks to discover the predictability of behavior on the basis of dynamic patterns of energy transformation within man. He makes discriminating use of the man sciences with undiminished concern for theological goals in the study and service of man. While the pietistic man of God is above all in pursuit of spiritual perfection, the professional minister develops new "disciplines" of the inner life. The disciplines of the professional model foster the expansion of conscious awareness, interpersonal sensitivity, emotional honesty, spontaneity, and authenticity.

The soul winning evangelist aspires to create an ideological empire, to homogenize differences. A dominant element in revivalism has been the desire to conquer men's minds, to win adherents in ever-increasing numbers, and to install the combustible power of emotionality in the chasis of the church—to make it go. The trouble is that once the thing gets rolling it runs some people down. And some it runs over. Clinical pastoral education is clearly on the side of appreciating rather than obliterating differences among poeple. Unhappily some cripples may be found in the wake of the new professional model of ministry, too, but the differences in priority are clear. The professional model unambiguously seeks the fulfillment of persons above any kind of ideological conformity.

The professional, person-centered model is as obsolete to some social actionists as the models in my three-faced mirror are to me. According to sociologist Paul Halmos, the polarity between personal and political solutions to human problems is root deep. Halmos says the counseling field in its totality arose out of disillusionment with political ways of coping with man's predicament.[1] In his Welsh way, Halmos sees two kinds of "betterers": "those who would first rectify the anomalies of society before giving a personal helping hand to the individual, and those who would consider the personal assistance of the individual as more urgent and potent than the bettering of society." [2]

Social actionists are stimulating a revival of faith in political solutions. In their zeal and their frustration they sometimes fail to appreciate the complementary and potentially reinforcing character of both kinds of "bettering."

As I see it, the dispossessed of a society suffer from a profound sense of powerlessness and rejection. In response to the enormity of their need, the ministering method of choice is political. As basic human needs are met—needs for food, clothing, shelter, and for hope in the possibility of belonging to the human family with dignity and respect—the ministering method of choice becomes personal. Much of the misery of those whose human rights are secure arises from a neurotic nucleus: mis-perceiving oneself as powerless, unloved, and even unlovable. So long as a people are, in reality, politically powerless and socially unloved, even outcast, it is as frustrating to invest our resources in counseling services as it is inhumane to deny such services. As the realities change, the methods of ministry must change. A new priority is required for ministry among the franchised. To be sure, the need for political action continues, because some of the prerequisites of a creative human community are undeniably political in

11

nature. But the wholesale waste of human potential and the emotional crippling of even the world's favored children before they enter kindergarten are problems that have personal origins and require solutions on a personal level. Inauthentic, alienated man is in part the product of industrialization, urbanization, and mass culture, but more immediately he is the creation of frightened people in flight from the shadows of their own psychic life. His needs require of us the courage to commit ourselves to the building of a health-giving community in the home, the church, and the school.

Another polarity within which clinical pastoral educators function is the tension between the seminaries and institutions of health, welfare, and rehabilitation. The research out of which this book has come was begun in an effort to understand the conflict between supervisors of clinical pastoral education and seminary deans and professors. In 1958 I joined the faculty of the Institute of Religion in the Texas Medical Center of Houston. Our faculty was perennially strung between the academic demands of a graduate program in pastoral counseling and the clinical demands of the hospitals and chaplain supervisors responsible for the clinical training of our students. Educationally we were answerable to deans and a committee of professors from five theological schools in Texas; professionally we had to prove ourselves to medical and paramedical personnel and to chaplain supervisors who were not immediately answerable to seminary deans. One of the amusing ironies of that situation was to discover that some of our seminary committee members were more anxious to have proof of our clinical competence than of our theological sophistication, while many of our medical colleagues distrusted us for fear that we would abandon our religious identity. My own churchly identity was suspect by some seminary officials because of the ecumenical and clinical context of the Institute of Religion. My professional competence was questioned by some fellow supervisors because I took my training in the context of a graduate theological degree.

My slant on the matter is to affirm the tension between seminary and hospital, but to do so on the basis of a primary commitment to theological education. On this issue, as on the previous issue concerning personal and political solutions, I believe that my own bias reflects that of the majority within the clinical pastoral education enterprise. The history of the movement bears this out in ample detail as we shall see.

In 1966-67 I was part of a committee engaged in the final stages of preparing a constitution and bylaws for the new Association for Clinical Pastoral Education. Four organizations were shifting from competition to cooperation in forming the Association. Chaplain supervisors and seminary professors of pastoral care and counseling were working side by side. Then a debate arose over the phrasing of the Preamble to the Constitution and the statement of purpose. The working document contained a page and a half of copy on these two items. The statements were replete with references to "the good of the church and the education of her clergy," "the mission of the church," and the like. Concern arose because no mention was made of the health and welfare goals of clinical pastoral education. Phrases like "the mission of the church" do not communicate as convincingly to hospital administrators as to seminary deans. Anxieties about the priority of commitment to theological education were ventilated. A year later the section on purpose that was proposed by the committee to the newly elected House of Delegates was a single sentence: "The general purpose of this Association is to facilitate the mission of the churches in the field of clinical pastoral education." That sentence stirred another debate and was amended to read simply: "The general purpose of this Association is to facilitate clinical pastoral education." Aside from illustrating the beauty of multiple rewriting in the preparation of copy for a constitution, this process reflects the tension between seminary and hospital perspectives that continuously blurs in and out of focus for the clinical pastoral educator.

A curious situation has occurred in the relationship of chaplain supervisors and pastoral counselors. For years the leaders of clinical pastoral education have sponsored counseling centers in relation to their hospital programs of supervised pastoral ministry. The two functions overlap in many ways. Today, however, we have both an Association for Clinical Pastoral Education and an American Association of Pastoral Counselors. Many of us are active in both; the seminaries have a stake in both. The relationship between the two functions has been an uneasy one, however, from the early thirties to the present.

I am committed to the essential unity of pastoral care and counseling as subspecialties within the field of pastoral theology. The former is more appropriate to "general practice" in the ministry, and the later

13

to specialization as things now stand. This seems to me an unhappy situation, but I do not see a clear alternative.

We are groping toward a more comprehensive concept of professional pastoral ministry than is provided by either the hospital chaplain or the psychotherapist in a clinic practice. The model of community mental health centers is instructive. More useful, in my experience, is the model of the psychological consultant. James Dittes in *The Church in the Way* (New York: Scribner's, 1967) has sketched the outlines of a ministry within traditional structures that is informed by highly sophisticated psychological theory and is supposedly to be performed by ordinary pastors. The promise of Dittes' model of ministry is limited by one fact to which he gives little attention. His ordinary pastor cannot function in the way described without extraordinary personal and professional training in the realm of interpersonal relationships. And so we are back with the problem to which clinical pastoral education has addressed itself for nearly a half-century: how shall seminarians and clergymen gain the personal maturity, the conceptual sophistication in the area of human behavior, and the professional competence needed to meet the demands of their office with a sense of adequacy and fulfillment?

Charles Feilding, in "Education for Ministry" (*Theological Education,* Autumn, 1966), suggests reorganizing all pastoral training around an organizing and administering perspective rather than the shepherding perspective so well interpreted by Hiltner and others. Niebuhr's model is the "pastoral director." Today we speak more often of the pastor as an "enabler," serving his laymen as a consultant, a teacher, a supervisor, and a facilitator of their ministry in the world. Whatever the language that finally emerges and whatever the model that becomes normative (if, indeed, any model becomes normative for more than a minority among the clergy), I see clinical pastoral education and the more specialized forms of pastoral counseling performing an indispensable service, though probably within an overarching concept and style of ministry that has not yet clearly appeared.

The prophecy I have just made arises not from clairvoyance but from an analysis of the developmental process normal to professional groups. Freeman studied law, medicine, and ministry, and proposed the following sequence as a guide for measuring the growth of any profession:

1. a social problem emerges

14

2. it is treated by the most available unspecialized persons responding to the need
3. a grouping of pertinent skills emerges
4. recognized procedures and theoretical foundations are formulated
5. some form of group consciousness and apprenticeship occurs
6. education centers on theory and skills
7. services become marketable and codes and standards develop
8. specialization comes in
9. a synthesis of specializations is devised
10. the profession has to determine whether to surrender a part of
    its function to others or encompass a new social problem (where-
    upon the process repeats) [3]

According to this outline, clinical pastoral education has just completed stage eight and is already grappling with the issues of stages
nine and ten. In my opinion the incorporation of a united Association for Clinical Pastoral Education (1967) embodied the recognition by many people in the field that a single specialization had developed; that our similarities as specialists in clinical pastoral education were more binding than parochial, regional, or other interests
that formed the basis of previous affiliations. Stage nine, "a synthesis
of specializations," will be accomplished as the Association for Clinical
Pastoral Education becomes linked in functionally meaningful ways
with groups who come at the same issues from other approaches. Some
of the obvious candidates for such a synthesis are the American Association of Pastoral Counselors, the Society for the Advancement of
Continuing Education for the Ministry, the Association of Seminary
Professors in the Practical Fields, the Academy of Parish Clergy, the
Association of Religion and the Behavioral Sciences, and groups yet
to emerge, such as those involved in action training.

The great enticement at the stage of synthesis is that of new breakthroughs in the relief of human suffering and the actualizing of human potential. Dramatic leaps forward have occurred when a mature
synthesis of professions has become linked with a different discipline
altogether. We see in the marriage of physical medicine and rehabilitation to physics and electronic engineering, for example, a healthy off-
spring of both diagnostic and treatment tools. Education and cybernetics promise a welcome progeny, as do psychiatry and the chemistry
of the brain. Similarly the many groups in the study of ministry may

be happily impregnated (as some have already been) in liaison with social psychology, family therapy, communication theory, cybernetics, and the computer. I am dreaming of a future that I believe to be already present within the profession.

A sober assessment requires scrutiny of the profession's past. The history of clinical pastoral education contains clues to the profession's future. While I shall concentrate on the history in the pages that follow, I hope that the story of clinical pastoral education will stimulate a regular alternation of attention from the past to the future. I hope, too, that the experience of clinical pastoral educators will prove instructive for those concerned with other focuses of theological education and for those concerned generally with innovation in professional education.

Little doubt could remain that I have large personal investments in the profession whose history I am writing. It is this very sense of having a stake in the field, however, that urges me to seek by means of history a new objectivity, to correct old biases, and to discern and appreciate more fully the differences within the broad field of professional education for ministry.

The history of clinical pastoral education has been ten years in the writing. It was begun in 1959 as a doctoral dissertation under the title, "A Critique of Clinical Pastoral Education." My critique was based on a historical examination of the field from the perspective of the profession's relation to theological education. I quickly discovered that the history of clinical pastoral education was still walking around in the persons who made it. Little had been written. News of the death of Helen Flanders Dunbar, M.D. in 1959 galvanized my resolution to gather the history while many of the principals were still available. Financial resources as a doctoral candidate did not permit the travel that would have been required to secure personal interviews with all those who played leading roles in the clinical training drama. I solved the problem by developing a separate list of questions for each person whom I wished to interview. I then called each one long distance to make a proposal: would you spend an hour at a tape recorder freely talking about your involvement in the clinical training movement in response to a forthcoming list of questions? The response was gratifying. Others were asked to add bits and pieces of vital information by mail. With tape recordings, correspondence, and a few personal interviews providing the input, I gained an intimate acquaintance with the personalities and events of the movement. Much of this information was assimilated so thoroughly that it is now impossible to sort it out and assign footnote credits to this man for one bit of information and to that one for another. At some points, therefore, a reference will simply read "communication with leaders of clinical pastoral education." Wherever exact quotations appear and wherever my materials enable me to offer more precise documentation, I do so, of course. In some instances, however, my own assimilative processes and nearly two decades of immersion in clinical pastoral education constitute the only known source for factual information as well as for interpretative comments.

A few respondents gave their information under strict conditions that it not be used in publication. These stipulations have been observed scrupulously. The confidential nature of all information received in 1959-60 was protected with the help of the Librarian of the Southern Baptist Theological Seminary. I filed a separate bound volume entitled "Experience Survey Supplement" in a locked file in the library. The Supplement may be examined only upon written permission from me or from a professor of the psychology of religion at the Southern Baptist Theological Seminary. It contains a transcript of tape-recorded interviews and historically relevant excerpts of all correspondence gathered in my original research. (One contributor did not give permission for his material to be included in the Supplement, and this material is available only from the contributor, himself, whose name and address appear in the Supplement.) Materials gathered since 1960 are in my personal possession and are available only upon written consent from the respective contributors during their lifetimes.

Anton T. Boisen's personal library and papers have been deposited in the Archives of the Chicago Theological Seminary Library. Historical records of the Council for Clinical Training, Inc., remain in the former Council office, which is now the headquarters of the Association for Clinical Pastoral Education, Inc., 475 Riverside Drive, New York City 10027. Institute of Pastoral Care, Inc., materials are housed in the Archives of the Boston University School of Theology Library. Minutes of the former Southern Baptist Association for Clinical Pastoral Education are being put on microfilm by the Historical Commission of the Southern Baptist Convention, Southern Baptist Convention Building, Nashville, Tennessee. Records of the Lutheran Advisory Council and subsequent developments among Lutheran denominations at the national level are to be found in the Division of Chaplains and Clinical Pastoral Education, Lutheran Churches of U.S.A., 315 Park Avenue, South, New York City 10010.

A major disappointment in my data-gathering efforts during the past three years concerns the Guiles correspondence and records of the New England programs deposited at Andover Newton Theological School. Guiles's successor at Andover Newton felt that insufficient time had elapsed for the full story to be known. He ruled, therefore, that historical materials in his care could not be used for this study. While understandable from one perspective, this decision imposed rather severe limits on the historical reconstruction of the New England group in general and of the career of A. Philip Guiles in particular. Since Guiles was a key person in the history of the movement, the history of the first three decades may need to be rewritten after the Guiles materials become available to historical research.

Seward Hiltner reconstructed the history of clinical pastoral education from the perspective of his involvement in its organizational life during the thirties and forties. More than one hundred pages of copy have been deposited in the Menninger Foundation Archives by Hiltner. This material was made available to me, but much of it must remain "classified," as it were, for the time being. Very little of it is incorporated into the present work. It is available only upon written permission from Hiltner, who continues to be actively engaged in the verification and correction of crucial matters of fact and of interpretation.

Debts of gratitude to those who have contributed to my historical research and writing extend back, therefore, to the fifties. The faculty of the Southern Baptist Theological Seminary provided my first experience of clinical pastoral education in the context of graduate theological education. Research on the history of clinical pastoral education for the doctoral dissertation was completed under the supervision of professors Henlee Barnette, C. Penrose St. Amant, Samuel Southard, and Wayne E. Oates. As major professor and supervisor of much of my clinical work, Oates contributed immeasurably not only to this research but also to my development as a clinical pastoral educator.

It was Seward Hiltner who activated my interest in publishing a history of clinical pastoral education. In the summer of 1965 Hiltner had occasion to read my doctoral dissertation. He began at once to urge its publication and introduced me in the fall of 1965 to Abingdon Press. It would be hard to say whether Hiltner's help was more substantial in providing historical data or in encouraging persistance in the task of publishing. He gave generously in both respects.

Major chunks of historical data were provided during 1959-60 by the following persons: John M. Billinsky, Anton T. Boisen, Ernest E. Bruder, Dawson C. Bryan, Russell L. Dicks, Seward Hiltner, Reuel L. Howe, Leroy Kerney, Frederick C. Kuether, Edward Mahnke, Wayne E. Oates, Robert A. Preston, W. C. Seitz, and the Advisory Committee of the National Conference on Clinical Pastoral Education. Others who made significant contributions by means of interview or correspondence were Charles C. Bachmann, Malcolm Ballinger, Clarence Y. Barton, A. Donald Bell, Conrad Bergendoff, Ralph D. Bonacker, Alfred Carpenter, Lennart Cedarleaf, Maurice C. Clark, Merrimon Cuniggim, T. Sloane Guy, Jr., Herbert W. Hillebrand, I. Fred Hollander, Homer Jernigan, Armen D. Jorjorian, Thomas W. Klink, Knox Kreutzer, Earl Loomis, Carl A. Plack, John M. Price, Emily Spickler, Samuel Southard, John R. Thomas, and Richard K. Young.

Between 1966 and 1968 additional data were gathered. Charles E. Hall, Jr., who was then President of the Council for Clinical Training, Inc., presented my request to the Board of Governors for access to the Council's files. I am grateful to Hall in particular for his endorsement of my request and to the entire Board of Governors for permission to draw freely from their official records. The Institute of Pastoral Care, Inc., established their official archives in the library of the Boston University School of Theology. Being one of the first persons to make extensive use of these archives, I want to express my profound appreciation to Dean Walter G. Muelder of Boston University School of Theology. Dean Muelder persisted in a campaign that led to the establishment of the archives on February 2, 1960. Emil M. Hartl, a veteran supervisor of the Institute of Pastoral Care, organized the minutes of the Board of Governors for filing. Paul E. Johnson was the principal contributor of the several file drawers of material available in 1967 when I was privileged to use the archives. To each of these men the profession of clinical pastoral education owes a debt, as do I. It is a debt I am most pleased to acknowledge personally.

A special delight during the second phase of data-gathering was my interview with Robert E. Brinkman. My appreciation goes out to him and also to Fred Kuether, who introduced us in the spring of 1968. To Charles V. Gerkin I am indebted for extensive information and an interpretation of events related to the Georgia Association for Pastoral Care, Inc. Innumerable details concerning recent developments were confirmed or supplied by John I. Smith, formerly Executive Director of the Institute of Pastoral Care, Inc., and first President of the Association for Clinical Pastoral Education. The story of clinical pastoral education at Worcester State Hospital in 1928 and 1968 was made possible also by generous assistance from John Smith. Among the many others who supplied firsthand information incorporated in the history are the following: Henry Cassler, Stewart G. Cole, Dwight W. Cumbee, Gaines S. Dobbins, Emil M. Hartl, Robert Leslie, W. Clinton Powers, Leon R. Robinson, Jr., Thompson L. Shannon, Kenneth R. Strom, and E. A. Verdery.

All the help of all the people named above might well have been lost so far as publication is concerned except for the consideration of my Dean at Crozer Theological Seminary, R. Melvin Henderson. Dean Henderson provided assistance with some of the expenses of data-gathering, protection from excessive demands for professsional involvement in institutional maintenance, and personal encouragement of a most genuine order. President Ronald V. Wells and my colleagues on the faculty of Crozer Theological Seminary have made possible the story told in the final chapter by their personal support of professional education for ministry. Those directly engaged in the program of clinical pastoral education at Crozer merit special thanks in this regard. They are chaplain supervisors E. Dean Bergen, J. Richard Flowers, William J. Jackson, Albert L. Meiburg, and Kent D. Smith; assistant supervisors David Canady, Ray Cooley, Ralph Lebold, Dale MacTavish, and Rodney J. R. Stokoe; Director of Field Education Robert S. Lowndes; professors of Old Testament and Systematic Theology respectively, Jesse H. Brown and W. Kenneth Cauthen (who made clinical pastoral education at Crozer Theological Seminary interdepartmental); and consultants Charles D. Flory, Ph.D., psychologist, and Richard Cole, M.D., psychoanalyst.

Last in this recital of gratitude and first in affection is my wife, Betty. Her understanding of the profession and her interest in the writing of its history have been matched by her perseverance at the typewriter as my very private secretary.

Part I

Beginnings, 1923-1930

1

THE TWENTIES

I have two reasons for beginning the history of clinical pastoral education in the decade of ballyhoo, jazz, Bruce Barton, and Al Capone, rather than in ancient history. Clinical pastoral education is a twentieth-century phenomenon, and the continuities between the twentieth-century and previous centuries have been documented thoroughly in the historical work of McNeill, Kemp, Niebuhr and Williams, Clebsch and Jaekle, and Hiltner.

Hiltner's formula for relating pastoral theology to its heritage is a sound one. He found continuity in the pastor's attitudes and motivations, discontinuity in method and in cognitive formulations about the pastor's shepherding functions.[1] An example of the tendency to ignore the discontinuities created by clinical pastoral education and to distort history accordingly is the work of William Goulooze.[2] Goulooze devoted a section to historical analysis of pastoral theology from 1850 to 1950 and made a case for unbroken continuity in pastoral care traditions. His thesis is convincing until one notices that he has not made a single reference to pastoral care since 1925 as it has been developed by leaders in clinical pastoral education. One must conclude, therefore, that he has established only this: that the pastoral care tradition is marked by continuity more than by discontinuity from 1850 until the early twenties. In the twenties education for the ministry began to change in a radical way.

23

The immediate context in which clinical pastoral education arose consisted of reaction against traditional theological education and attraction for medical psychology and social work. The new and revolutionary action called clinical training occurred in the midst of a decade of social revolution—the twenties. These themes will be discussed in turn.

Reaction Against Traditional Theological Education

Clinical training began as a reaction against traditional theological education, but it was a reaction at the periphery of seminary life. More important to an assessment of beginnings is the fact that the reaction was occurring at significant points in the center of the religious establishment. In 1918 the first Conference of Theological Seminaries and Colleges in the United States and Canada (the forerunner of the American Association of Theological Schools) was planned by President Lowell of Harvard. The third and fourth sessions of the Conference were devoted to consideration of the obligation of seminaries to provide professional education for the parish minister, the religious education specialist, the prospective seminary teacher, and specialists in social service and in missions. The fifth and final session asked to what extent the "Case system" or the "Clinical Method" could be used in practical training for the ministry.[3]

Luther A. Weigle of Yale urged the 1926 Conference to re-evaluate theological curricula in accordance with the principles of functional education. A professional model of theological education had been conceived in imagination if not in practice. Others were calling for exploration of the new "mental therapy" for the practical task of the minister. Some called for more field work and some for more integration of theory and practice. Many lamented the minister's ineffectiveness, but no one suggested taking seminarians into health and welfare institutions under theological supervision to begin the process of integration and the development of adequacy for pastoral ministry.[4]

The ambivalence of theological educators about the relation of the theological education to behavioral science is seen in an address by Dean D. L. Ritchie of the United Theological College, Montreal. He bewailed the addiction of thelogical educators to the fads of religious education, psychology and sociology, but before concluding his address, he said:

Is it possible that the principles that underlie the rapidly growing science of mental therapathy (*sic*) may have to be made part of an effective course in Pastoral Theology? I do not mean that pastors should set up as psychiatrists, . . . but are there no highways of knowledge there, which, carefully taught, would help the pastor to avoid mistakes and render more effective service to troubled souls? [5]

As the decade of the twenties closed, Dean W. L. Sperry of Harvard and Dean Shailer Mathews of Chicago were unequivocal in rejecting the traditional, classical model and embracing a professional model for theological education. They agreed that precision was required, especially in sociological and psychological sciences.

Mathews observed, "If one is to deal with personality he must understand the pathology as well as the normal elements in personal experience." Recognizing that the methods of psychiatry and social work are each partial, that the conventionally trained minister is also equipped only partially, Mathews concluded, "There must be developed an inclusive technique." To this end he favored the rise of supervised field work and urged that evaluation of students center on what he called "personal efficiency" rather than on credit hours and grades. The center of integration for all departments ought to be personality and vocational effectiveness, urged Matthews. Only at the Ph.D. level should the major focus include skills in research.[6]

More widely read and discussed than the speeches cited above was the Kelley study, *Theological Education in America*, published in 1924. Kelley reported on his survey of 161 theological schools. Social surveys were much in vogue among denominations and among other professions at the time. They were a popular instrument for effecting institutional change.

Kelley was not bashful about stating his own educational bias. He concluded that according to prevailing educational standards, half the seminaries could not qualify as educational institutions. He recommended (1) standardization; (2) clarification of types and aims of seminaries, with some schools specializing in certain areas such as the rural church; (3) the study of the actual job of ministers as a basis for curriculum revision; (4) the use of teaching methods of the functional type being developed in medical, legal, and social work education.[7]

Kelley lamented the avoidance of science in most seminaries but praised the increasing number that were "formally committed to the scientific procedure, whose teachers know and speak the language of science, use its methods in the classroom and the laboratory, and undertake to interpret the life of the individual, the community and the world in terms of principles found in harmony with scientific theories and discoveries." His most insistent recommendation concerned educational philosophy and methodology. In the language of progressive education, he argued: "Whatever the type of seminary, under whatever auspices it is conducted, upon whatever academic grade the work is carried on, the seminary should *teach students.*" To this end professors were encouraged to make more use of "the seminar, the library, the laboratory and the field." Receiving a special accolade were those few seminaries offering "supervised field work, in which observation-visits under supervision are made to social service and human welfare agencies, and in which supervision is given to practice service with specific groups and individuals, and to field work of student pastors." [8]

The intellectual basis for these judgments against traditional theological education was experimentalism in philosophy and its educational expression, progressivism. William James and John Dewey are the best known architects of experimentalism. Experimentalism was not the product of speculation but rather a rationalization of the Western world's way of living for the past three to four hundred years. It was pragmatic, depending upon empirical inquiry under the discipline of the scientific method. It was a striking example of men living their way into a system of thinking, rather than the reverse.[9]

In 1919 the Progressive Educational Association was formed to advance Dewey's ideas. Progressivism assumed that reality was what it seemed to be and that the good for man was based on what was best for the group, judged if possible by scientific investigation. Pedagogically, learning began with "felt needs, curiosities, interests, problems." Engagement with problem situations led to problem-solving, and problem-solving actualized one's selfhood as a responsible, deciding person. Self-actualization and socialization were prime goals in progressive education. Since learning at all levels was thought to occur "through living," the teacher must surrender the logical organization of his materials to the psychological principle of organization. The growing edge of a student's experience was of more consequence than the proven verities of his culture in teaching the student to

26

find and solve problems and to cope constructively with change. Teaching how to think was more important than teaching what to think. Progressive education, therefore, required an open rather than a closed curriculum, and involvement in the whole community rather than isolation in an academic "ivory tower." [10]

Dewey and his disciples gave a strong impetus to the scientific movement in education, but progressivism and the teaching of science were not identical causes. The battle of science vs. liberal arts anticipated Dewey by a full half-century. The Flexner Reports disclosed in 1910 and 1912 that the major medical schools in America were fifty years behind scientific developments in the universities. The use of the stethoscope and the microscope were not mentioned in the Harvard Medical School catalogue until thirty years after they had been developed for the general use of physicians.[11] Dr. Samuel Cabot, uncle of Richard C. Cabot, who will be discussed subsequently, fought the majority of the medical staff of the Massachusetts General Hospital in mid-nineteenth century to obtain the admission of nurses in training, and was told that "only a medically trained man could be trusted to carry out such delicate scientific procedures as taking a patient's temperature with a clinical thermometer." [12] In 1905, Richard Cabot fought another battle on behalf of introducing and maintaining social workers in the same hospital.[13]

The point of these stories is to say that all professional education was in a low estate at the beginning of the present century. Reform in theological education waited upon reform in professional educational generally. When we see how long medical education resisted the claims of science, we realize that some theological educators were remarkably open to change when confronted subsequently with the claims of progressivism. It is entirely possible that those theological educators who incorporated the scientific method in linguistic, biblical, and historical studies during the half-century prior to the twenties were educationally more contemporary than many of their counterparts in medicine and law.

Theological liberalism prepared the way for the initial acceptance of clinical pastoral education in seminaries such as Chicago Theological Seminary, the University of Chicago Divinity School, Union, Yale, and the major schools of Boston. American liberalism took many forms, but, according to Cauthen, it found its identity as a movement within theology at three points: (1) an emphasis on continuity rather than discontinuity in the world, (2) a focus on the autonomy of human reason and experience rather than on an authoritative divine revelation, and (3) a stress on the dynamic rather than the static nature of life and the world.[14] Congruence between the views of early clinical training leaders is greater with those whom Cauthen calls the "evangelical" liberals than with "modernistic liberalism." At the point of theological method, the founders of clinical pastoral education were dedicated in their own way to the development of an empirical theology. The more radical liberals such as MacIntosh rejected the psychology of religion as it was being done by Boisen and others,[15] and Wieman told Boisen to his face that theologians have no obligation to study the religious ideas and experiences of the mentally ill.[16] Similarities were greater than differences, however. Clinical pastoral education never could have taken root in theological education without the development of positive attitudes toward science, trustful attention to individual and social experience, and openness to the evidences of dynamic process in both nature and history.

The initiative in professional education shifted dramatically from theology to medicine in 1910-12. Upon publication of the Flexner Reports, an aroused public demanded legislation raising the standards of medical education and effectively closing large numbers of substandard schools. Laboratory equipment and hospital affiliations were required for scientific research and clinical supervision. Lecture methods were minimized in favor of methods that fostered student initiative—seminars, tests, laboratory, and case studies.[17]

From 1924 to 1970 leading theological educators have been attempting to do for the seminaries, by surveys and persuasion, what was done for medical education by legal coercion in 1912. One difference is that today the scientific challenge to theological education comes not only from the natural sciences but also from the behavioral sciences, and not only from science but also from progressive education. It is in this context that clinical pastoral education has played a key role during its history to date. Clinical pastoral educators have been the allies, sometimes wittingly but often unwittingly, of those educational statesmen who have decided that the ministry ought to be a profession as well as a calling, that theological education must become professional education incorporating the sciences, just as centuries ago it expanded to include the humanities.

The historian John T. McNeill wrote in 1934, "We are evidently at the opening of a new era in the history of the cure of souls. The ministry to personality will be at once scientific and religious." [18] Most Protestant clergymen implicitly agreed with McNeill as the twenties came to a close. Most seminary presidents were blind to the new reality. The contrast between attitudes of seminary alumni and seminary administrators is strikingly drawn in the May studies published in three volumes in 1934. Alumni rated seminary training for "the practical problems of the minister" first in importance; seminary presidents listed practical problems fifth.[19] It is no wonder that large numbers of seminarians and alumni shared a mood of discontent, if not of active rebellion, toward theological education.

The inadequacies described in the May studies were largely overcome in clinical pastoral education. May urged (1) that theological education needs a comprehensive re-study of its goals and methods, and this study needs to be conducted *with an eye to the quality of work done in medicine and law;* (2) since the minister's field of specialization has been invaded by two professions that are more competent and successful than the ministry, i.e. psychiatry and social work, these areas need special attention; (3) the times require more functional education.[20] The Kelley and May studies span the decade of the twenties, pointing in the same direction—toward a functional curriculum. But resistance to change was deep-seated in the seminaries. Discontent among students continued. Clinical training remained on the periphery, providing a haven or perhaps a guerrilla hangout for those who were in reaction against traditional theological education.

Clinical pastoral educators were not alone in their discontent with traditionalism, and neither were they the first to launch progressive educational innovations within seminary curricula. Among the most vigorous intellectual disciplines at the turn of the century was sociology. Its influence upon Protestant churchmen in America is well known in terms of the social gospel. None of the many gifted leaders of the social gospel movement was more significant as a forerunner of clinical pastoral education than Graham Taylor.

Prior to World War I, Taylor was called to the chair of practical theology at Hartford Theological Seminary. He accepted on the condition that he could remain with the Fourth Congregational Church of Hartford, of which he was pastor. This downtown church became for Taylor "a clinic where the students could come in contact with actual human need." Kemp reviews his career:

Later, he went to the Chicago Theological Seminary, where he held the first chair of Christian Sociology in the United States. In his inauguration address, he told the students that their chief textbooks would be people, the men and women of the shops, the factories, the street. He said he would establish a clinic similar to those used by medical students, where they would study the cause and cure of poverty, intemperance and crime, and the relationship of heredity and environment and their influence on the making of character. When the school was unable to raise the funds for this clinic which he wanted, he did so himself by renting an old house out of his own salary in a congested part of the city. It was cleaned up and christened "Chicago Commons." . . . Here his students met with him and his staff and compared notes on their week's activities. One such evening is described. One recounts what he has seen and heard visiting jails that day, another his experience in a hospital, a third his interviews with employers and labor leaders, a fourth his observation in the courts and at probation agencies, a fifth his studies of child life in the neighborhood, a sixth his survey of health and sanitary conditions, a seventh a report of the churches of the district, and an eighth his impressions of social conditions in the ward. Discussion follows each student's presentation of his facts gathered at first hand, questions are raised, the next steps planned, and Professor Taylor draws the meeting to a close by showing the relation of their work to the up-building of the kingdom of God on earth.[21]

The work of Graham Taylor and his students gives evidence both of the seriousness with which they took the ministry of social work and of the emergence of a full-blown "clinical" program built to please any progressivist in education.

Classical curricula were invaded by the psychology of religion and religious education as well as Christian sociology. By the early twenties, the studies of Starbuck and Coe, of Ames, Stratton, Leuba, and Pratt had stimulated a vigorous movement within seminary circles, both theoretically and practically.[22] The core concern of these men was to apply empirical methods to the study of religious experience and to assimilate the insights of educational psychology into the programming of religious education. As early as 1912 at least one student of religious education, Karl Stolz, saw the relevance of empirical methods for theological education and anticipated the rise of clinical training. He said:

The time is near, when minister and theological students will study the man in a human laboratory. . . . In the same way as medical students have a clinical year, theological students should take a clinical internship in hospitals, where together with doctors they will study the man as he is.[23]

The seminaries turned most often to fieldwork in seeking a more professional and more functional education in the early twenties. Fieldwork programs appeared at such widely separated schools as Union Theological Seminary in New York City and Southwestern Baptist Theological Seminary in Fort Worth, Texas. Two Methodist schools, Garrett and Boston, developed the supervision of fieldwork more fully than any others described in the Kelley study of 1924.[24]

The push behind fieldwork programs was articulated as early as 1913 by the Reverend William Palmer Ladd. Addressing the General Convention of the Protestant Episcopal Church, he said:

The theological courses in our seminaries need to be supplemented by some kind of practical training. We all know how we found ourselves the week after our graduation and ordination face to face with problems with which our seminary course had not prepared us to deal. Most of us floundered across the gulf and sooner or later got on our feet, but with some of us it was later rather than sooner, and only after costly and perhaps bitter experience. Can we not do something to eliminate this waste? [25]

Episcopal seminaries were virtually unanimous in adopting fieldwork programs in the twenties. General Theological Seminary in New York City placed students under the supervision of their City Mission Society. Virginia Theological Seminary used rural church placements with periodical faculty supervision.[26] A small seminary in southern Ohio, Bexley Hall, created the most original experiment from the standpoint of the clinical training enterprise. The Bexley Hall Plan merits title as the first clinical pastoral education program in history.

Clinical training's mother was traditional theological education. She was impregnated by a rejuvenated medical profession and the two of them set up housekeeping in a new suburb developed by the progressivists in education.

Attraction to Medicine and Social Work

Social work was initially more attractive to the innovators in theological education than medicine. Psychosomatic medicine was believed to be more relevant to a minister's education than psychoanalysis. Actually social work and medical psychology came close to each other in the twenties. Together they offered hope of relevance and professional competence to ministers disillusioned with the traditional in their own discipline. Medicine and social work together constituted the positive pole, and traditional theological education the negative pole in a new field of force known as clinical training for theological students.

It may come as a surprise to learn that the first steps toward clinical pastoral education were not informed by Freudian psychoanalysis. The Bexley Hall Plan was the result of creative interaction between a seminary dean and a physician, William S. Keller, M. D., in Cincinnati, Ohio. In 1923 Keller put theological students to work in social agencies under social casework supervision. Boisen could certainly be claimed as a contradiction of the view that the sources of clinical training were non-Freudian. Yet Boisen had no knowledge of Freud prior to his illness. During his first hospitalization he discovered Freud, but he decided not to risk entering treatment in a psychoanalytically oriented center. We shall go into the peculiarities of Boisen's contributions in the next chapter, but at this point simply claim that he is at most an exception rather than a contradiction to the point. Richard C. Cabot was almost irrationally opposed to psychiatry; he saw no use whatsoever for the use of mental hospitals in the clinical training of theological students. The three founding fathers are akin, therefore, in their detachment from psychoanalytic theory.

The social work supervision of the Cincinnati program was compatible with the medical orientation of Cabot and the Boston group in the early years of clinical training. It took two decades for their compatibilities to become clear to those involved, but I am anticipating the story of a later chapter.

The history of social work shows an alternation of emphasis from mass betterment to individual betterment. According to Stroup, the trend toward mass betterment continued from approximately 1880 to 1910. Evidences of the swing toward mass betterment are the settlement movement and Consumer's League begun in 1889, Housing Reform in 1901, Anti-Tuberculosis in 1902, the Child Labor Movement in 1904, and the Association for Labor Legislation in 1906. The pendulum swung back toward individual betterment from about 1905 to 1920, including the development of medical social work in 1905, Visiting Teachers in 1906, Child Welfare and Mental Hygiene in 1909, Social Hygiene in 1912, Red Cross Home Service in 1917, Psychiatric Social Work from 1918, and Family Welfare from 1919.[27] The focus remained on the individual, with increasing reliance upon psychiatric theory, in the thirties and forties. Not until the sixties have we seen the pendulum beginning to swing back again toward mass betterment.

Medicine first challenged theological education overtly in the person of Richard C. Cabot, M.D., a liberal, socially conscious, and imaginative physician. Cabot burst into the spotlight of the seminary world with his now-famous article published in December, 1925, "A Plea for a Clinical Year in the Course of Theological Study." The idea of a clinical year in the course of theological study was formed during the academic year 1924-25. The Dean of the Episcopal Theological School invited Cabot to meet a class of senior students once a week and discuss the clinical dimensions of their ministry. Alfred Worcester, M.D., a general practioner, collaborated with Cabot in developing a course that is surprisingly contemporary. The course contained the following topics: visiting of the sick, care of the dying and the bereaved, advice as to marriage and parenthood, visiting the aged, dealing with sex problems, use of praise and blame, ways of meeting misfortune, delinquency in children and adults, the problem of alcoholism and drug addiction, the problem of the neurasthenic, insanity and feeblemindedness, the art of conversation, avoidance of gossip, the differences between men and women, race traits and race psychology.[28]

Cabot was surprised to learn that theological schools provided students with no training and no practice in pastoral work. He was even more incredulous to discover that theological educators assumed it "could not be taught." Cabot was certain it could be taught and equally certain that such training and practice ought not "to draw theological students away from theology and into medical or social work." By analogy with medical students, who learn the art of personal ministries from their medical teachers, Cabot reasoned that theological students could learn to be more effective ministers if they were given "a clinical year as a part of theological study." [29]

Cabot was committed to a mechanistic, organic approach to medicine. He stood firmly within the scientific tradition in this respect. He shared the view that man's mastery over nature began only when supernatural explanations of man and society gave place to natural

33

ones. He was a rationalist who abhored the magical approach where-ever it appeared.

Cabot, like many physicians of his day, was in reaction against the Vitalism of the nineteenth century. Vitalism threatened to bind science once again to the principle of "purpose"; it was perceived as a revival of prescientific animism. Physics and chemistry held the secrets to life phenomena, and they alone could liberate science from magic. The concept of stability or *homeostasis* as developed by Cabot's colleague at Harvard, Walter B. Cannon, resolved a major medical dilemma of the time. *Homeostasis* "attributes to the organism a tendency to maintain within itself certain constant conditions necessary to perpetuate its life." [30] The concept of stability accounted for the instinct of self-preservation without attributing to it any teleological significance. *Homeostasis* described goal-oriented behavior but not a manifestation of purpose. On this foundation Cabot and others were able to hold a psychosomatic viewpoint without being indebted either to religion or to psychoanalysis for their holistic concepts.

The attraction of psychologically oriented ministers and socially concerned physicians for each other is seen in a headline phenomenon known as the Emmanuel Movement. The Emmanuel Episcopal Church of Boston opened a clinic for spiritual healing in 1904 under the leadership of two gifted ministers and several prominent physicians. Their collaborative work became statistically impressive and sky-rocketed into national attention almost overnight. The movement died with its original creators in 1940, but it was significant for clinical pastoral education not only in shaping public opinion toward favoring an alliance of clergy and physicians but also as a specific training ground for Cabot and Boisen.

Cabot became active in the movement in its first few years. His idea for a clinical year in theological education began to germinate out of these early experiences with the Emmanuel Movement. On December 27, 1908, Cabot was quoted in the Boston Post as advocating cooperation between physician and ministry in the "cure" of the sick. Cabot said, "There ought to be a school where training for such work is given." [31]

The conduct of tuberculosis classes brought Cabot into alliance with Joseph H. Pratt, M.D., as well as the ministers Worcester and McComb. On the basis of his work with the tuberculosis classes Pratt has been called the founder of group psychotherapy in the United

States.[32] Cabot would have wanted no part of such an appellation. Boisen joined the team in the early twenties. He said that by the twenties a shift of attitude had already occurred in the thinking and practice of Worcester and McComb. Whereas they had made extensive use of hypnosis in their early healing efforts, they came to deal more and more with the underlying difficulties in the personal and social environment and to look with misgiving on attempts at healing that relied either on these manipulations or on suggestion or upon "faith alone." [33] Whatever the special emphases of the Emmanuel clinics in 1904 and 1921, respectively, both Cabot and Boisen saw the healing effect of a medico-religious ministry, and both experienced the possibility of cooperative interdisciplinary functioning for the benefit of the patient.[34]

The Emmanuel Movement ultimately failed. Both Cabot and Boisen were instructed by its failure as they had been by its successes. At least three factors contributed to its failure: (1) its leaders failed to train other ministers, (2) Worcester himself did not grow with his movement. He remained authoritarian to the end, even when the defects of his approach became obvious through psychiatric research;[35] and (3) doctor-clergy relationships broke down. Worcester advised his patients to leave their doctors and work with those who supported his efforts. Much of the hostility of medical men was rooted in this fact rather than in their rejection of the value of spiritual healing.[36] Cabot and Boisen benefited from these lessons and consistently advocated close relationships between the clinical training movement and theological education. They were open to the latest thought in medical research. They were sensitive to the prerogatives of the medical staff in the care of the patient. The failures of the Emmanuel Movement, then, became part of the foundation on which a more durable structure was built in clinical pastoral education.

The mental hygiene movement was well underway in the twenties. The National Committee on Mental Hygiene embodied humanistic concern to reform mental hospitals initially. Superintendents of asylums were stung into awareness of the nonmedical needs of their patients, and the public was educated to support programs for the prevention of mental illness. From 1922 to 1927 the National Committee's new Division on the Prevention of Delinquency explored the problems of establishing and improving child guidance clinics. In 1927, a demonstration period (supported by the Commonwealth

Fund) ended, and the number of child guidance clinics then expanded rapidly. The mental hygiene movement worked consistently for the upgrading of mental health professions, supporting the establishment of training programs for psychiatric social work in 1918 and for psychiatrists in 1923, and agitating for the certification of psychiatrists. The certification goal was achieved in 1934 with the creation of the American Board of Psychiatry and Neurology.[37]

Mental hygiene enthusiasts achieved impressive results in shaping public opinion, in stimulating the maturation of mental health professions, and in establishing patterns of professional development that were to be followed in successive decades by clinical pastoral educators in their own development as a mental health profession. The mental hygience movement contributed an intangible but important attitude of exuberant optimism to the mental health field. The influence of these attitudes cannot be overestimated. They sustained the morale of those chaplain supervisors (as well as the more established professionals) in mental hospitals who were supported not infrequently out of such unreliable sources as the "canteen fund."

The attraction of medicine for clinical training leaders became stronger than the appeal of social work early in the history of the movement. One factor was that physicians and psychiatrists took more initiative toward the rebel ministers who were seeking opportunity for clinical training than did the social workers. Discussions between a group of physicians and clergymen in New York City beginning in 1923 resulted in the formation in 1925 of a Joint Committee on Religion and Medicine within the Public Health Relations Committee of the New York Academy of Medicine. It was this group that selected Helen Flanders Dunbar, M.D. to make a special study of the psychosomatic relations between religion and medicine in 1929.[38] Dunbar became Director of the Joint Committee in 1931. In 1937 the functions and many of the members of the Joint Committee, including Dunbar, moved into the Federal Council of Churches of Christ in America as its first Commission on Religion and Health. Chaired by Howard Chandler Robbins, former Dean of the Cathedral of St. John the Divine, this Commission and its successor Commissions and Departments of the National Council of Churches continued to function significantly in the nurture of clinical pastoral education as a profession linking religion and medicine.

How shall we interpret the attraction of medicine and social work

36

for clergymen in the twenties? I find merit in an interpretation Dunbar offered in making her first annual report as Medical Director of the Council for the Clinical Training of Theological Students, September 29, 1930. She said:

Today, it is the priest who is coming to be suspect and ostracized from increasingly large social groups. This would seem to be taking place after the manner of the old legend of the king, all of whose subjects imbibed insanity from a magic well and thenceforth termed their monarch a madman, and harkened no longer to his words. As they were about to put him away, the king in self-defense drank from the same well, whereupon the populace rejoiced because their king had recovered his sanity. If the priest is to be restored to his place in a populace which has imbibed deeply the scientific method, he must drink at the same well.[39]

We might interpret the rise of clinical pastoral education in the twenties in terms of the contest between Elijah and the prophets of Baal. Using the biblical account as a paradigm of contemporary events, we could say that the scientific community threw down the challenge: "The God who answers by healing, he is God." Medicine invoked science; theology invoked religion. The people hesitated, then turned to medicine. For it was the god Science who answered with healing. The great temples of America became her medical centers devoted to the god of health. The high priests became physicians and psychiatrists. Clinical pastoral education may be said to be an effort by the religious community to secure the fire of healing for the altars of church and synagogue. Most clinical pastoral educators have been convinced that without effectively meeting the needs of people for psychic wholeness, the altar fires will go out and the houses of worship will go dead.

A Decade of Social Revolution

A revolution began in theological education during the twenties because it was a decade of social revolution. The poets and composers of the lost generation sensed that they were at the end of an age. Their innards gnawed at them with the starvation of a whole civilization. As Archibald MacLeish observed, "The starvation of a whole civilization was a new idea in 1923." They wrestled with the evidence that the old world was no longer there; they created "the metaphor for our experience of our lives." [40]

On the surface of American society, in full view of all, a revolution in morals occurred; obsession with sex became conscious. Women gained their suffrage and strode into full economic independence. Youth went on a rampage. Judge Lindsey proposed in 1927 to establish "companionate marriage" on a legal basis. The flappers set the pace for millions in smoking cigarettes, and when women dared smoke in the company of men a formidable barrier between the sexes had been breached. The painted woman became respectable even as her skirts went up, her breasts went flat, and her hair was bobbed.[41]

The social revolution was fed by political disillusionment following World War I. Americans acted out their disillusionment by withdrawing from Europe and rejecting the League of Nations. At home the nation fell ill with hysterical hate. Red-hunting was matched in its irrationality and cruelty only by the tactics of a revived Ku Klux Klan. And then the prophets of America's rural and urban gods met, not on Mount Carmel, but in Dayton, Tennessee, for the Scopes trial. Legally the fundamentalists won, but morally they lost. The pious were free to keep their religion locked in a science-proof compartment, but the drift away from Fundamentalism continued. As Frederick Lewis Allen said of the twenties, "the prestige of science was colossal" and "psychology was king." Freud had been popularized. affording ample rationalization for the sophisticated. Clergymen pled the authority of ancient tradition and practical usefulness, but in Fosdick's words, "one query could prick all such bubbles: Is it scientific?" Science became the arbiter of the generation's thought, "until to call even a prophet and a seer scientific is to cap the climax of praise." [42]

Prohibition became one of the most striking ironies of the twenties. At the historical moment that sobriety became a legal requirement the nation began to stagger with speculation intoxication. The thirst for easy money was well publicized in the scandals of the Harding administration. The tragic consequences of intemperate speculation were acted out in Miami, Florida. Miami bank clearings that exceeded one billion dollars in 1925 slid to just over one-half billion in 1926 and to a mere 142 million in 1929. In spite of sober advice, federal controls were defeated in 1928 and speculation zoomed on. Speculation on the market was congrunt with the American illusion of an unlimited frontier. It provided compensation for the collapse of spiritual foundations. The new prosperity matched the nation's intoxication with the new science.[43]

The crash was both financial and psychological. As the market toppled in, so did the glib faith of the twenties—the faith in *laissez faire* and Republicanism, in science and psychology. The moment of truth came, and it proved to be the truth of which Karl Marx and Sigmund Freud were the prophets: economic and biological determinism and the triumph of the irrational over the mechanisms of repression.

The enduring achievements of the twenties were on as grand a scale as the failures were colossal. MacLeish found the twenties to be "the greatest period of literary and artistic innovation since the Renaissance." [44] Both architecture and music in America expressed an "infinitely extendible" quality. The New York City skyline and American jazz had this in common: they could go on and on. They were "processes pure and simple." [45]

The vogue in education during the twenties was Jacksonian. America was more in love with process than with product, with method than with result, with means than with ends. And progressivism in education went on and on through the decades of the thirties, the forties, and the fifties. Challenged by essentialism though it has been, and modified by reconstructionism in the sixties, the spirit and form of progressivism in education is more alive and durable than ever. Like the architecture of our center cities, the visions of Montessori and Dewey continue an upward thrust. They nourish a well-rooted faith—faith in the futue of the secular city and of the self-actualizing citizen.

In such an era as the twenties it would have been remarkable if no new movement had surged out of the times and into the theological schools. Clinical pastoral education rode the tides of social and educational revolution washing around the foundations of traditional theological education.

History is shaped by sociological processes but also by the individuality of particular men. From this point on the history will be told primarily in terms of charismatic personalities and the groups that formed around them. I shall begin with three men who in my judgment deserve to be known as the fathers of clinical pastoral education.

2

THE FATHERS: KELLER, CABOT, AND BOISEN

Two physicians and a minister stand as the progenitors of clinical pastoral education. Each had his own cause, his own dream, his own expectation of a return on his investment in the clinical training of theological students. Keller wanted to train social engineers equipped "to create a new world, not alone to hand on a religion." [1] Cabot sought for the clergy the achievement of professional competence in their pastoral ministry. Boisen was centered on research in the psychology of religious experience.

Each had his own sphere of influence, his own following, and eventually his own organizational self-extension; yet no one of them would be known today as father of a new profession without the interaction with certain contemporaries whose names remain "lower case" in the history of clinical pastoral education. We would not have Keller without Dean Mercer of Bexley Hall; we would not have Cabot without A. Philip Guiles at Andover Newton Theological School; and we would not have Boisen without William A. Bryan, M.D., Superintendent of Worcester State Hospital. In each instance the new profession emerged as a result of the creative interaction of a theological educator and a concerned medical doctor. This pattern in clinical training's beginnings is repeated over and over again in subsequent history. Men of medicine and men of theology become cooperatively engaged in the education of ministers for the work of healing both in the personal and the societal spheres of life.

Leaders cannot be leaders without followers. As Boisen has shown in his study of *Religion in Crisis and Custom*, "men of force, of vision, of singleness of purpose do not always get a following." The ground for any social and religious movement must be prepared, and a group of people must be ready to respond to the leaders who arise. The reverse is also true that "without leadership social movements can hardly get under way." [2] I shall tell the story of Keller, Cabot, and Boisen, therefore, with the spotlight playing across several factors, particularly the goals of each and how these goals were received by the early participants in clinical training; their personalities insofar as they are known and have a bearing on the movement; and, with less illumination, the people who formed an inner circle around them. Their disciples will remain shadowy in this chapter, but some of them will come into center stage in later chapters.

William S. Keller, M.D., Cincinnati, Ohio

The clinical training of theological students began in Cincinnati, Ohio, in the summer of 1923. William S. Keller, M.D., a member of the Episcopal Church, received as house guests for the summer five Middlers from Bexley Hall, an Episcopal seminary in centrol Ohio. The Bexley Hall Plan, as the program was called, grew into the Graduate School of Applied Religion. It was the first clinical training program, and in many ways it was and is unique.

Keller dreamed the dream of political liberals like John Dewey and Herbert Croly, that social engineering on a national scale held the greatest promise for America. Disillusioned with Theodore Roosevelt and Wilson even prior to Harding-style Republicanism, the political liberals of the early twenties adopted a strategy of social education through "the experimental method and creative experience." [3] Keller's political affiliations are not known, but his social vision and the educational philosophy he articulated place him in the liberal minority of the early twenties.

Keller was convinced that "ministry in the modern community had much to learn, both factually and in terms of skills, from social work, medicine and community organization." [4] His hunch was confirmed by students who reported, subsequently, that the chief defect of the social gospel was that it was heard as pious hot air by those actually involved in social work and community organization. They saw the

41

Cincinnati program dedicated to putting *"Christian love in action* in the observable social situation." [5]

Social vision was matched in Keller by the physician's sense of the value of learning by doing. "In every profession," Keller said, " 'doing it' has been the method of 'learning it.' " He saw that theological education consisted of three years of theory and no laboratory training except for the "ceremonies and functions," which, said Keller, "are not his main work and take but a small part of his time." Keller's diagnostic skills penetrated the personal and social consequences of these deficiences in theological education. In the only extant writing from his own hand, Keller diagnosed the situation as follows:

Many clergy as a means of escape go into teaching; while others try spiritual healing because of its supposed kinship to their training. The far greater number who do not succeed in breaking through the barrier develop a mild melancholia and disappointment from which they may not emerge. Not a few good men have lost heart and some times give in to an honest sense of futility. . . . There is nothing wrong with the ministry except for the fact that we have too frequently been guilty of training men for canonicals rather than for life work.[6]

Opportunity to prescribe and treat the ailments he saw so clearly came during the spring of 1923. The Very Rev. Samuel A. B. Mercer, Dean of Bexley Hall, entered into conversations with Keller prompted by an educational innovation at Bexley Hall. Dean Mercer had arranged a series of lectures by the Rev. Floyd Van Keuren, assistant minister at Trinity Church, Columbus, and lecturer in sociology at Ohio State University, "dealing with the social problems of contemporary urban life and agencies dealing with them." Seminary upperclassmen spent several days in Columbus with Dr. Van Keuren making a study of these agencies. Student reaction was so positive that Dean Mercer was moved to explore with Dr. Keller the possibility of a summer placement in Cincinnati for a select group.[7]

The students who entered Keller's clinical training program were men who had lived in a scholastic environment almost entirely. They were "from small cities or even villages, most of them graduates of Kenyon College, a small school in a village of 500." They then attended seminary at Bexley Hall in the same village. Because of a "consideration of facts such as these," Dr. Keller "hoped through the Summer School to contribute to the social understanding and maturity of the students of Bexley Hall." [8]

The Bexley Hall Plan was simple in design and inexpensive in execution, but it depended almost entirely upon Keller's hospitality, planning, and funding during the first few summers. The students lived in Keller's home. "Each was assigned to one social agency to which he devoted the entire summer." Assignments included social casework in a mental hospital, a human relations court, a public welfare program, and a social hygiene society.[9] On weekends the group gathered in Keller's home "to report on their work for the week and to discuss the relevance to the work of the parish priest." [10]

When the Bexley Hall Plan began its second summer in 1924, its complexion was slightly different. Dean Mercer had left Bexley Hall, and Keller had recruited students from two other seminaries in addition to Bexley Hall—the Episcopal Theological School of Cambridge and Berkeley Divinity School of New Haven. Responsibility for housing and placing students continued to rest upon Dr. Keller entirely.[11] Agency placements were greatly expanded. By 1929, Keller reported 36 cooperating social agencies. The report for that summer shows 1,200 families contacted; 160 staff meetings attended by one or more men; 175 court sessions attended by one or more men; 310 religious services in 20 parishes, missions, and institutions in the Dioceses of Southern Ohio and of Lexington; 2 corporate communions; and one quiet day with meditations. Group meetings included lectures on casework and the methods of various agencies, and the relation of the church to these problems; seminar discussions and reports focused on the correlation of lectures and direct experiences in the community.[12]

In 1927, Keller's program appeared in a new dress with solid denominational support. Named the Summer School in Social Service for Theological Students and Junior Clergy, the school was organized under the Department of Social Service of the Protestant Episcopal Church in the Diocese of Southern Ohio. Keller was chairman of the Department.[13] A significant new dimension of the school in 1927 was the addition of a theological supervisor. The Rev. Gilbert P. Symonds, Rector of Christ Church, Glendale, assisted Keller in the supervision of eight students. This addition of pastoral to medical and social work supervision brings the Keller program into the pattern of interdisciplinary supervision that was soon to become standard for all programs of clinical pastoral training. The fact of sponsorship by a single denomination is a characteristic not shared by the early programs in hospital settings, but the close cooperation between the center and a theological seminary in 1923 was duplicated two years later by Boisen and became a familiar feature of the new educational enterprise in succeeding years.

A new phase began in 1935-36. The Summer School expanded into a year-round program and became the Graduate School of Applied Religion. It acquired two buildings of its own for classes, offices, and dormitories. Joseph F. Fletcher became Dean in 1936 and remained with the school until 1944 when both he and the school were assimilated into the faculty and curriculum of the Episcopal Theological School of Cambridge. Fletcher defined the goal of the Graduate School of Applied Religion as developing "a rational pattern of the Good Life." By a rational pattern he meant the "integration of the spiritual and the scientific," and by "the Good Life" he meant, as Keller did in 1923, the results of social engineering guided by Christian principles at the national as well as local levels of political organization.[14]

The Graduate School was not an action training group in the contemporary sense of the term. The course of study involved clinical work concentrated largely in Cincinnati's Family Society where students functioned as social caseworkers and carried small case loads under social work supervision. Seminars encouraged the students to interpret their experience in religious frames of reference. In this sense, the year's internship was regarded as "a part of, not apart from theological education." Fletcher helped his students seek "the apologetic witness" of clinical experience.[15] They were concerned to reclaim for the church "the full allegiance of the scientists who have the necessary technique at their fingertips for working out social and psychological problems." To achieve the apologetic goal they struggled to develop "a statement of religion which will win them back" to the church. Their method, lifted from the pages of the liberalism of the time, was to articulate "a full integration of spiritual and scientific truth, a 'single rational pattern of the Good Life.' "[16]

The school was interdenominational and related academically to the University of Cincinnati for the exchange of credits. Students lived the common life and engaged in corporate worship as they would have done in the seminaries from which they came. The Graduate School prospered until World War II cut into its supply of students. Fletcher favored the alternative of assimilating into theological education, provided a seminary could be persuaded to make clinical training a regular part of its curriculum—on a full-time summer and graduate basis. Just such an offer was received from the Episcopal Theological School of Cambridge, and on May 5, 1944, the change became official.[17]

The use of clinical training to equip ministers for social engineering was the first but it has not been the main task of clinical pastoral educators during the last four decades. The mainstream of the clinical training movement flowed into the channel of individual healing. Keller's program is linked in purpose to that of Graham Taylor in the World War I era. It is a forerunner of the action training programs that have mushroomed into being during the sixties. For two decades, though, it was identified with the clinical pastoral education movement. In the Graduate School of Applied Religion, it moved rapidly out of the "movement" stage toward identification as a new profession. Fletcher and his staff never quite turned the corner from the training of pastors for parish functioning to the education of specialists in community organization. The Graduate School did not reproduce itself in other communities. Two more decades had to pass before clinical methods would be applied extensively to the training of ministers for political action. The transplanting of Fletcher and his program from Cincinnati to Boston, necessitated by World War II, was a historical accident that stunted the development of clinical training as a tool of social engineering.

Even had the Graduate School of Applied Religion not been terminated, the relationship between advocates of the two styles of human improvement would have been strained. In the thirties students in hospital centers were made to feel distrustful of the Keller program. They felt that supervision was not adequate. Hiltner made a study of the program while serving as Executive Secretary of the Council for the Clinical Training of Theological Students, Inc. He concluded that it was creative in design and execution. Supervision left something to be desired, but in terms of social outreach and of ethical and theological undergirding, the Cincinnati program was superior to those in the Boisen orbit.[18] Keller's program probably would not have found itself altogether at home within the framework of clinical pastoral education as it developed out of the vision of Cabot and Boisen. It stands as a reminder, however, to those who work in the public and the private sectors that each may learn from the other and find common cause as educators and as persons concerned to improve the human situation.

Richard C. Cabot, M.D., Boston, Massachusetts

To understand Richard C. Cabot, one must understand what it means to be a Cabot. The Cabots are an old New England family who have produced a succession of distinguished citizens. Cabots have been in the vanguard of medicine for several generations. Consistent with this heritage, Richard C. Cabot made history by introducing social workers into Massachusetts General Hospital in 1905. Twenty years later at age 57 he confronted theological education with his case for the introduction of a clinical year into theological study. Russell Dicks observed that "the Cabots were reputed to have a private line of communication with God. I always suspected," Dicks said, "that Richard Cabot really believed that." [19]

Richard Cabot was born May 21, 1868, in Brookline, Massachusetts. He graduated *summa cum laude* from Harvard in 1889. He continued in medicine, specializing in internal medicine and becoming professor of clinical medicine at Harvard Medical School. Cabot served in World War I and returned with an inner restlessness. Feeling that he had made his contribution to medicine, he wanted to tackle something new. It was to the treatment of the moral fiber of mankind that he turned. Rollin Fairbanks reported that Cabot believed firmly that a man should seek a new vocation when he was fifty. In 1920, therefore, Cabot accepted a chair at Harvard in the field of ethics. He retired from the Medical School in 1929 at age 60. He participated in the incorporation of the Council for the Clinical Training of Theological Students in January, 1930, and served as its president until 1935. He retired from Harvard's chair of Social Ethics in June, 1934. In September, 1934, he became professor of Sociology and Applied Christianity at Andover Newton Theological School. [20] Not long before his death he asked to be transferred to the Department of Theology, and his request was granted. His career ended with his students continuing to gather about him at his home. During his final illness in the spring of 1939, they met at his bedside working out "a theology by which one should face the solemn and inevitable experience of death." [21]

Cabot's character blended the pride of stoic discipline with the

46

humility of paying careful attention to his failures, even risking the exposure of his errors before his peers and students. Of his stoicism, no more characteristic act is known than one reported by Anton Boisen. In September, 1934, Cabot was to give the keynote paper for the Fall Conference of the Council for the Clinical Training of Theological Students. The supervisors were told on their arrival in New York that Cabot would be unable to attend because of the serious illness of his wife. "That evening," wrote Boisen, "he was there and gave his paper. His wife had died that morning, but he had immediately left for New York, saying that was what she would have him do." [22]

Cabot's teachability is dramatically revealed in the Clinical Pathological Conference, which he inaugurated at Harvard Medical School. As Cabot told it himself, he would read aloud the written "histories" of patients who had died and on whose bodies an autopsy had been performed. Each student would hand in a card containing the student's diagnosis based on the written record, which he had studied in advance. Cabot would then develop his own diagnosis on the spot as he read the record. No one in the group knew what diagnosis the attending physician had made during the patient's life nor what had been found at the autopsy. Once Cabot had committed himself publicly, along with his students, the pathologist who had done the autopsy told the group what had "in very truth been found." [23]

Cabot's Clinical Pathological Conferences pulled down the facade of professorial impregnability with one methodological stroke. His rigorous search for a differential diagnosis and his bold self-exposure as a diagnostician provided a model for the clinical teaching of seminarians and clergy as well as of medical students. Instead of an autopsy, clinical pastoral educators substituted the verbatim transcript of pastoral conversations. As developed by Dicks and Fairbanks the verbatim was clearly an adaptation of the Clinical Pathological Conference. It was designed for those whose primary method of treatment is conversation. Supervision of pastoral ministry has evolved several models since Cabot and Dicks, but always it has affirmed the value of diagnostic thinking and of the teacher being teachable enough to expose his own fallibility to his students.

In the Clinical Pathological Conferences Cabot acted out his creed that "the only absolute need of a human soul" is the need to grow. In *The Art of Ministering to the Sick,* Cabot said of this learning process:

For twenty-three years the growing edge of my medical knowledge stretched itself out each week to receive its food. Thus far and no farther went my diagnostic fitness. But it was sure of its chance to grow. Groping, stumbling, I was each week a little less of a groper and stumbler. Sure, clear gain. More gain when I failed, and so located a dangerous weakness, than when I succeeded. For success, though it increases the confidence which we all need for our next job, does not stimulate growth so much, and growth, I take it, is the only absolute need of a human soul.[24]

How inevitable it was that Cabot should find the central goal of ministry to be the cultivation in patients of "a new sensation, the *sense of growth*." [25] The minister functions at his best when he helps people move beyond their preoccupation with failure and success into a new concentration upon what they may learn from their experiences or how they may grow. "Regret for failure is close to self-pity and so to self-destruction," Cabot reasoned; "content with success melts into self-indulgence and self-annihilation. . . . The soul of man lives by its awareness of growth." The decisive mark of the Divine in man is the need to grow; hence the minister has no more important task than to stimulate growth and to help people expand their awareness of growth as it occurs.[26]

We begin now to see the shape of Cabot's dream for the clinical training of theological students. He was consistently more interested in health and in growth than in the distortions of growth. Cabot was optimistic about man. His optimism rested upon his confidence in the "wisdom of the body," which he occasionally described as the activity of God in healing. Consistent with his Unitarian upbringing, Cabot spoke of the healing power of nature and of God interchangeably. He was as comfortable with the language of theology as of medicine. In this context, then, he defined the task of the Christian minister: "to nourish the consciousness of God in the life of man." For the accomplishment of this task, the minister "needs unusual intimacy with God and rare understanding of man." Theological education was credited by Cabot with paying attention to the former but charged with the neglect of the latter.[27]

Cabot urged theological educators to develop what he called a clinical theology. Clinical theology is "theology brought to the bedside, to the bereaved, to the dying, to the invalid, to the aged and to the delinquent." Clinical teachers should be clinical theologians, according to Cabot, and "every theologian should be able to apply his theology for the assistance of those who need God to help them face their sufferings." While theological schools should have some research men who do not apply their knowledge, "the majority who teach religion . . . should be able to show their students how to do the things they teach and to prove their worth." [28]

Cabot saw beyond clinical training as it was then operating—supported by private individuals, foundations, and by the hospitals, themselves. He saw that "in the long run the seminaries should themselves draw into their service as professors men who can apply their knowledge to help people in trouble." He sought to allay the fear that a clinical approach to education would compromise intellectual standards. "Theology needs hard thinking and intimate knowledge of the Bible," but he insisted that "it needs also the enrichment that comes to any study when it is applied to the needs of men and tested by the difficulties of making it prevail in the midst of affliction and doubt." Cabot had no patience with those who would "socialize" or "psychologize" the gospel or transform the work of ministry into social work or psychiatry. "We want no minister to compete with physicians in the task of healing or with social workers in the work of rehabilitating the needy. Those two great professions have their work," and ministers have theirs. Theological schools "mean to train pastors," Cabot acknowledged, "but in fact we train preachers and leave them to pick up the mastery of their pastoral duties without adequate *instruction on the job.*" [29]

In a word, Cabot was pleading in these statements, published in 1935, for a thoroughly professional model of theological education. His goal for ministers: competence in pastoral work. His final plea to theological educators rested on his faith that ministers trained in "clinical theology"

shall reinvigorate the ministry and reinforce the preacher. So we shall deepen our theology and revive our intimacy with Jesus Christ. So we shall give new impetus to the life of the Christian church. So we shall deepen the community's respect for the clergy. So we shall make our students welcomed in their parishes because the people will see their ministers doing the work of Jesus Christ seven days in the week, not only in the honorable distinction of preaching, but in the humble services of the home. Individual service brings Christianity home to men's hearts. They see the minister in the thick of the fight against despair and temptation. They see him suffer. They sometimes see him fail as the doctor often fails, and they esteem him all the more because he has given his best and made a good fight.

When the Christian minister fills that position in his parish, when he is known by his deeds, he will be listened to in the pulpit as he has never been listened to in our time.[30]

Russell Dicks assessed Cabot's role in launching clinical training for theological students by saying "in my opinion [clinical training] would never have gotten started had it not been for Cabot." [31] Others would make the same claim for Boisen. I am inclined toward Philip Guiles as the keystone in the arch, or more precisely, the Cabot-Guiles alliance. However the credits are distributed, Cabot's role in the genesis of clinical pastoral education is substantial. He performed a service beyond that of prophet and interprter of the meaning of pastoral ministry. Additional factors were his financial support and his cultivation of new leadership for the cause.

Three of the men who got their start with a big assist from Cabot were Anton Boisen, Philip Guiles, and Russell Dicks. Boisen and Guiles will be discussed more fully in later sections, but a few words are in order at this point. Almost immediately after his discharge from Westboro State Hospital in late January, 1922, Boisen enrolled in a course in social ethics at Harvard Divinity School under Cabot. Boisen wrote, "Dr. Cabot was much interested in my story, and although he himself did not accept the psychogenic interpretation of mental disorder, he gave stanch support to my project." Cabot was again Boisen's teacher in the academic year 1922-23. Boisen's chief project during the year was the preparation of case records for teaching purposes, using the model learned from Cabot in what Boisen called "one of the best courses I have ever had." Continuing to study part-time with Cabot in 1923-24, Boisen invested his major time in the Boston Psychopathic Hospital. He did research involving psychometrics and sociological surveys while waiting for a decision from the Institute for Social and Religious Research. Boisen had sought funding of a project "for the study of the interrelationship of religious experience and mental illness." When word finally came that the project was rejected, Cabot "came to the rescue" by offering to back the project himself. Before this could be launched, however, Cabot learned that Dr. William A. Bryan of the Worcester State Hospital was "willing to try a chaplain." [32] Cabot offered to recommend Boisen for the position. During the first two and a half years post-hospital, Boisen's rehabilitation was accomplished with a generous investment of interest, respect, and tender care from Cabot. Cabot contributed both to Boisen's developing identity as a professionally trained minister and to his competence as an educator.

No sooner had Boisen become settled at Worcester than the idea of providing clinical training for theological students was born. On December 24, 1924, a few students from the Episcopal Theological School in Cambridge came to talk with Boisen about becoming attendants at Worcester State Hospital as a form of summer employment. Boisen said, "That gave me the idea." His plans for clinical training in the summer of 1925 formed rapidly. He learned later that "it was Cabot's idea that they look into this." The students were enrolled, in fact, in the course that inspired Cabot to publish his "Plea For a Clinical Year in the Course of Theological Study" (1925) .[33]

Cabot's support for clinical training was continuous and financially substantial. In 1929 Boisen joyfully told Cabot that Philip Guiles had decided to give himself to the cause of clinical training. Boisen reported that Cabot "was as pleased as I was and promised to back our budget to the extent of eighteen hundred dollars." [34] One year later Cabot withdrew his support of Boisen. By 1930, however, Boisen was securely established as a mental hospital chaplain and a clinical pastoral educator.

The rupture in the relationship with Cabot was due to Boisen's second psychiatric hospitalization (subsequent to his mother's death in June, 1930). It was to Cabot that Boisen finally turned for help in being hospitalized. But Cabot had been, as Boisen said, "aroused." "He had throughout been opposed to the psychogenic interpretation of mental illness." "My views," Boisen added, "now became abhorrent to him. He decreed that I must have nothing to do with the program of instruction." [35]

Cabot's negative bias toward psychiatry was recognized by all who knew him. He shared the view widespread among the medical profession that most psychosis is organically based. While he recognized functional illness, he did not take seriously the psychoanalytic view of unconscious motivation. Writing on "Psychotherapy and Its Relation to Religion" in 1908, Cabot said that people are sick from functional illnesses because they do not know how to behave themselves—for example, poor scheduling, compulsive overactivity, and the like. He advocated a didactic approach to treatment such as helping patients make a realistic schedule. He believed in "work cures" more than in "rest cures," and most of all in a kind of positive thinking that discriminates fear of pain from fear of death, worry from thinking, and the like.[36] In 1936, Cabot strongly advised ministers to leave mental problems to the medically trained. He warned that the treatment of "insanity" by ministers is done "at the peril not only of their patients but of their own position in the community." He conceded that a minister ought to know enough about "insanity" to recognize the symptoms and make appropriate referral to psychiatrists.[37] Cabot's attitude toward psychiatry was a factor in the split between the Boston group and the New York group, who gathered around Helen Flanders Dunbar, Boisen, and others, but this is a story for another chapter.

Back to Cabot's most notable protégés, we turn next to Austin Philip Guiles. Guiles entered clinical training with Boisen in the summer of 1928, but by 1930 he was standing with Cabot opposed to Boisen's further engagement in the clinical training of theological students.[38] It is not clear why Guiles sided with Cabot against Boisen at this point. Guiles did not share Cabot's negative attitude toward psychiatry. On the contrary, Guiles was enthusiastic in his treatment of psychiatric patients as a minister. Russell Dicks said that in spite of this, Cabot "was fascinated and intrigued by Guiles and his crazy schemes."

Just how devoted Cabot was to Guiles can be seen in a crisis that occurred in 1932. Guiles had gone to the Massachusetts General Hospital as chaplain. On the basis of his mental hospital experience he worked in the out-patient department interviewing psychiatric patients. "As there were few psychiatrists around, he would actually take psychiatric consultations and write in the histories giving his opinion concerning the mental condition of the patients." Dicks added that this behavior on the part of a non-medic at the Massachusetts General Hospital "would be like a Jew saying Mass at St. Peters. To understand the seriousness of that action one has to understand the rigidities of medical protocol as practiced in Boston." Guiles was not permitted to return to the hospital in any capacity, Cabot's continued sponsorship notwithstanding.[39]

Russell Dicks entered the picture at this point. He was sent to the Massachusetts General Hospital in 1933 by Dunbar "to hold it for the Council." Conflict had already broken out between Dunbar and Guiles, and Dicks was Dunbar's pawn in the contest. The nature of the conflict will be examined in Chapter 4. Cabot was not highly partisan at this point. Cabot's attitude was "work with everybody—it does not matter what the organization is." As matters turned out, Dunbar had no money in the treasury to pay Dicks the promised salary of $150 per month. When Dicks got down to less than fifty cents in his pocket, he was willing for Cabot to take over. Dicks recalled that when Cabot came to take over his support, he said, " 'providing you help Guiles get his program on its feet.' " Dicks attempted a dual role for awhile, seeing himself allied with both Dunbar and Guiles, but he felt that the Council for Clinical Training supervisors became suspicious of him. Before long he "moved over into the Guiles camp." [40]

The story of Guiles-Cabot collaboration in the development of clinical training in the Boston area will be told more fully later. Suffice it to point out here that they climaxed their cooperative efforts in 1934 when Cabot joined Guiles on the faculty of Andover Newton Theological School. They taught "clinical theology" together until Cabot's death in 1939.

What remains to be said about Russell L. Dicks in relation to Cabot is that he, too, was "crazy" enough to excite Cabot's interest and affection. Dicks wrote a long report of his first summer's work at Massachusetts General in 1933. After Cabot read it, he said to Miss Ida Cannon, the medical social worker who was on the team, "Here's a man who writes down the prayers he has with a man who is dying. We'd better ask him to stay on here. We might learn something." Dicks confessed amazement that "I could do wrong, but he still loved me." [41]

Affectionate colleagueship extended into the co-authorship of the epochal book, *The Art of Ministering to the Sick.* Cabot and Dicks worked at Cabot's summer home where the physician, who was in his seventies, took dips in the cold sea. Their book was from the first a best seller. It contained Cabot's theory and Dicks's methods. In 1960 Dicks said that *The Art of Ministering to the Sick* sold almost one thousand copies the previous year and had not fallen below five hundred copies in any year since 1936. It has been a spearhead book for the clinical training movement for a third of a century.[42]

In many respects theological education has not caught up with

Cabot even today. His vision has been perpetuated in defining the central purpose of clinical pastoral education as the achievement of pastoral competence in ministry. Looking into the future to the day when clinical learning would not be the business of a Council for Clinical Training but would be integrated into standard theological schools, Cabot saw seminary teachers doing the thing that the students need to learn: "talking with patients, tackling difficult personal problems and often failing." Cabot knew that medical students see their teachers grappling with difficult problems and often making a mess of it, but he also knew that "this is good both for teachers and for students." The students "see their teacher's patience, his courage, his ingenuity, his tact tried, hard pressed, struggling, sometimes splendidly successful, sometimes a flat failure." In coveting the same quality of colleagueship between seminarians and their teachers, Cabot was coveting an increased educative power for the theological professor and a dramatic upgrading of the quality of professional functioning among ministers in society.[43]

Not all segments of the clinical training enterprise have shared Cabot's goals entirely. Some have specialized on ministry in the face of pathological problems, others have pursued research goals. A few have become social engineers in the Keller tradition. The mainstream of clinical pastoral education has been more fully congruent with Cabot's vision of the goals and methods of the field than with either Keller or Boisen, however.[44]

In many ways, Boisen is the most enigmatic of the fathers in spite of the fact that he is the most written about and the only one of the three who left an autobiography. I had hoped originally to incorporate Boisen into the same chapter with Keller and Cabot, but the material is to voluminous. Ironically, therefore, Boisen must stand in the history of clinical pastoral education in a chapter by himself. In a sense this is symbolic of the way Boisen lived—essentially alone.

3

ANTON T. BOISEN

Anton T. Boisen stands in history, as in life, somewhat apart, a problem to others as well as to himself. As he saw himself, his life story could be told under the label "failure." Yet he has been idealized by some clinical training supervisors. It is not uncommon to find interpreters saying: "The modern clinical pastoral training movement is due almost entirely to the genius of one man: the Reverend Anton T. Boisen." [1]

Boisen was diagnosed in the mental hospital: "schizophrenic reaction, catatonic type." [2] Persons who cope with stress in this way characteristically exhibit unrealistic thinking; excessive religiosity; and an expansive delusional system of omnipotence, genius, or special ability.[3] When symptoms are in remission such persons tend to deny the psychotic aspects of their experience and to expend immense amounts of energy convincing themselves and others that their delusional ideas are valid. We must ask, therefore, whether Boisen's whole system of thought and his whole research enterprise is no more than a grand rationalization of a psychotic way of coping with life. His autobiography contains descriptions of six psychotic episodes, three of them involving hospitalization, during the thirty-seven years from 1898 to 1935. If we accept his ideas as having validity in themselves, on what basis may such a judgment stand secure?

Cynics may say, as some have, that clinical training is a bastard child begotten by a bachelor father (Boisen), but the fact remains that clinical pastoral education has been fully legitimized by theological education as well as by the medical and psychiatric professions. The task of understanding Boisen's place as one of the fathers of a new profession remain.

I am not under the necessity of reviewing Boisen's life story in detail, for he has provided us with an intimate and a profoundly moving account of his entire "case record," under the title *Out of the Depths: An Autobiographical Study of Mental Disorder and Religious Experience.* After giving just a sketch of his career for the reader who does not yet know *Out of the Depths,* I shall proceed to a discussion of the issues involved in finding Boisen's place in the history of clinical pastoral education. Four statements summarize my conclusions and may serve as an outline for our exploration of Boisen's world.

(1) Boisen's place in the genesis of clinical pastoral education is instrumental but not intentional.

(2) Boisen's place in the organizational development of clinical pastoral education is peripheral.

(3) Boisen's place in the dynamics of clinical pastoral education or its internal development and its identity as a profession is significant.

(4) Boisen's place in relation to the future of clinical pastoral education is durable, both as a goad and a lure.

Anton T. Boisen (October 29, 1876–October 1, 1965) suffered the death of his father at age seven and the loss of his grandfather (and only other object of male identification) at age twenty. His younger sister was all that he was not. She was outgoing, he was shy; she was "rushed" by the sororities and voted "best-liked" girl in college, he was ignored; she was happily married, he was tragically single, feeling himself an inadequate male and finding relief only in his idealized romance with Alice, of whom he writes in great detail.

Boisen was vocationally confused and at best mediocre in his functioning for the first forty-five years of his life. Upon graduation from college, he floundered for a year before accepting employment as a high school teacher of German and French. His first psychotic symptoms occurred in this period, when he was twenty-two. Invited to become a language tutor in Indiana University, he accepted. Offered opportunity to study in Europe and become a professor, he switched fields to forestry. On the eve of leaving forestry for Union Theological Seminary in New York City to study for the ministry, he suffered psychotic symptoms a second time. He was then thirty-one. For the next ten years, Boisen was employed successively in rural church survey work, in rural pastorates of two years each in Kansas and in Maine, and for two years in YMCA work with the American Expeditionary Force in Europe. On his return from the war at age forty-one, he again had psychotic symptoms in relation to a vocational decision. He accepted an offer to join the Interchurch World Movement, moved to North Dakota to begin the task, and experienced remission of his symptoms.

The Interchurch World Movement folded up in 1920 when Boisen was forty-three. Again he was vocationally adrift, and again he became psychotic. This time he was hospitalized by his sister and his mother. The panic phase lasted three weeks and subsided. Then in March, 1921, faced with a move to White Plains, New York, where he was to have received Freudian psychoanalytic treatment, he became acutely psychotic again and remained so for ten weeks. Convalescence extended into January, 1922, when Boisen was discharged.

As a bachelor minister, aged forty-five, with a mediocre record of professional functioning behind him, Boisen might well have given up. Instead he plunged into graduate study of the psychology of religion and related fields at Andover Newton and Harvard Divinity School. The account of his becoming chaplain of Worcester State Hospital has already been told in the section on Cabot. In the spring of 1925, just as plans for his first summer program of clinical training were taking shape, Boisen was selected Lecturer and Research Associate in the Social Ethics Department of Chicago Theological Seminary. His friend of Kansas rural church days, Arthur E. Holt, had accepted the head professorship in the department on the condition that Boisen be employed for three months each year as Associate. Beginning in 1925 and continuing to 1930, Boisen spent the fall quarter each year in residence in Chicago. To Professor Holt, Boisen says he owes more than to anyone else in getting a new start.[4]

Boisen functioned well as a mental hospital chaplain, researcher, and organizer of clinical training for theological students. In June, 1930, his mother died, and in November Boisen was again hospitalized. As indicated previously, this ended his effectiveness in the orbit of Richard C. Cabot.

In 1932 Boisen became chaplain of Elgin State Hospital near Chicago. He was motivated mainly by his desire to be near Alice, who was employed in Chicago, but he realized also that he would be closer to Chicago Theological Seminary and free again to function as a clinical pastoral educator in an area that had ten first-class theological schools. He immediately organized a Chicago Council for the Clinical Training of Theological Students and again functioned well.

On August 24, 1935, Alice wrote Boisen that she had cancer and the prognosis was poor. On November 11, Boisen's students recognized the old symptoms and spirited him away to a hospital in Baltimore where Boisen remained until two weeks after Alice died on December 2, 1935. Boisen remained symptom free from age fifty-nine until his death, at age eighty-eight, on October 1, 1965.

During the last three decades of his life, Boisen published his major works, including *The Exploration of the Inner World* (1936), *Religion in Crisis and Custom* (1945 and 1955), and *Out of the Depths* (1960). A complete list of his journal publications is to be found in small type covering six pages at the back of *Out of the Depths*. Nearly two-thirds of these were published after he was sixty years of age.[5]

Boisen's Place in the Genesis of Clinical Pastoral Education

The training program that Boisen conceived for the summer of 1925 was not designed to develop competence in pastoral ministries. It was a program in "cooperative inquiry" into the psychology of religious experience. He wanted to study in particular the religious ideation and the meaning of the behavior classified as schizophrenic reactions. He regarded social engineering as important work, but as the work of others, not himself. Unlike Keller, whose concern was social betterment, and Cabot, who wanted ministers to be professionally competent, Boisen wanted colleagues in research. A seminary affiliation was important to Boisen as it was to both Keller and Cabot, but for different reasons. Boisen was intent upon the construction of a clinical theology by the use of empirical methods. For this, he believed there was no better laboratory than the mental hospital and no better library than "living human documents."

Boisen was aware of the gap between his own notions of what clinical training for theological students should be and what actually developed. Looking back on "the movement for the clinical training of students for the ministry" thirty-five years after his first program at Worcester, Boisen wrote, "It has gone forward under its own power, developing a philosophy which differs not a little from mine. For this I can be thankful, so long as it concerns itself with the living human documents of persons in trouble." [6] It was a passion to read the "living human documents" that Boisen bequeathed to a younger generation of churchmen and theological educators. Boisen brought seminarians into direct interaction with mentally ill persons and the professional people who cared for them, and that was all that was required. Students like Donald Beatty, Aleck Dodd, Philip Guiles, Carroll Wise, Wayne Hunter, and Fred Kuether did the rest. They discovered that the living human documents not only spoke of the psychology of religion, but also of one's own development and identity; they spoke not only about ecstatic religious experience, but also about professional functioning in ministry.

The fire that burned in Boisen in 1925 was to explore the next "little-known country" on the map of his experience. He explained his decision of 1902 to study forestry as a decision for adventure, exploration, "cutting loose from the beaten path and starting forth into unknown territory." His plunge into psychosis he described as "the exploration of the inner world" and as a "little-known country." In 1925 he saw the neglect of mental health by the church and the neglect of religious experience by psychologists, sociologists, and psychiatrists as "a great no-man's land which needed to be explored." Boisen and Holt reasoned that "the strategic point of attack lay in the theological schools." Not only did the schools need to be overhauled, but the disciplines of social ethics, religious education, and psychology of religion needed to make use of "scientific method in the study of present-day religious experience." [7] Boisen's momentum for the construction of clinical theology came, then, from prior commitments of long standing to the psychology of William James and of his teacher at Union in New York, George Albert Coe; to the sociological methods of Arthur E. Holt; and to the case method of teaching learned from Richard Cabot.

Boisen felt most comfortable professionally in the field of social ethics in the twenties and thirties. Had he accepted the offer to become the full-time Assistant Professor of Social Ethics at Chicago Theological Seminary in 1925, the sociological orientation of the new movement just possibly might have become dominant, or at least the Keller orientation might have gained more support. Acceptance from sociologists was sought at the outset. The first report of Boisen's work in clinical training before a learned society was given to the American Sociological Society in 1928. Boisen rejected the on-campus post in social ethics, however, in order to maintain his hospital base. After all, a full professorship in any field would have taken Boisen too far from his "little-known country." It would have been too thickly settled, too little like the frontiers he always sought.[8]

Boisen is better known for his research in the psychology of religion than in the sociology of religion, though he devoted himself in large measure to both. He lamented the demise of the psychology of religion as an academic discipline and repeatedly, in the journals, complained that workers in clinical pastoral education were neglecting the task of undergirding their efforts with a program of inquiry.[9] Regardless of what others might do, Boisen pursued relentlessly his own search for the meaning of religious experiences—driven obviously by the need to understand his own.

This is the place to ask again whether Boisen's thought is any more than a rationalization of his own psychotic experiences. I share the opinion of many that we must take Boisen seriously as a scientist and a clinical theologian. In the first place, he was preoccupied with a valid problem in both psychology and theology, the problem of religious ideas, feelings, and behavior. The problem was first defined and explored by William James in his *Varieties of Religious Experience* (1902). Boisen made substantial additions to the work of James. He utilized both psychiatric and sociological methods and perspectives for the study of living cases. In this he took a long step beyond James, who was bound primarily to literary sources for case material.

In the second place, Boisen integrated many strands of inquiry that remained isolated in the hands of his peers. Some psychologists of religion were focused narrowly on certain problems in religious education, others on the philosophy of religion, and still others on social sources of religious experience. Paul Pruyser's study of Boisen as a psychologist of religion claims likewise that Boisen "did much to integrate these various strands." [10]

Pruyser comments on a third contribution of Boisen to the psychology of religion: his organizational work or recruitment of a host of new researchers for the field. Largely because of Boisen's work as a teacher offering "theological education via the clinic," the laboratory for the study of the psychology of religion shifted "from the university campus, with students as the typical subjects, to the hospital, with patients as the sources of observation." Despite differences between Boisen and his successors in the clinical training movement, Pruyser notes that "his work as an organizer enriched the cadre of psychologists of religion with men of different professional qualifications: hospital chaplains, pastoral counselors and other clinically trained clergymen who have added important works" to the field.[11]

Fourth and finally, Pruyser credits Boisen with substantial methodological contributions to the discipline. "Participant observation in therapeutic face-to-face encounters" replaced the paper and pencil tests of other researchers. Boisen "turned James' brilliant vignettes into full-fledged case studies, with a longitudinal perspective." Most significant of all the case studies that Boisen has recorded, however, was his own. It is the incontrovertible evidence that Boisen did emerge from personal failure and radical disorganization into personal integration and socialization within the "fellowship of the best" that dissolves the cynics' suspicion concerning his work. Pruyser says of Boisen's own experience:

Of all the case studies he assembled, this is the richest and the most purposive: to show the dynamics of faith at work in the nooks and crannies of one lonely man's productive existence. I am sure he would want us to see *Out of the Depths* as one of the varieties of religious experience, and as an exploration of the inner world, and to study it until we can understand the roots of his hope and courage.[12]

In summary, Boisen's venture into the clinical training of theological students was not intended to be or to become what we know today as clinical pastoral education. He was intent on recruiting colleagues for cooperative inquiry into the psychology of religious experience. As he struck the future with the force of previous commitments to empirical theology, he and the experience he made available to young theologues struck a fire he did not intend. Philip Guiles and others caught the spark, fed it and built the house that the new fire was to warm. In this sense Boisen was instrumental in the genesis of clinical pastoral education, though his intentions were otherwise.

Boisen's Place in the Organizational Development of Clinical Pastoral Education

Philip Guiles and not Boisen came center stage when the curtain went up on the organization of the Council for the Clinical Training of Theological Students. Guiles stayed on at Worcester after his initial summer's training. During the year 1928-29, he saw that Boisen needed the support of an organization that would help finance students and enlist the cooperation of both seminaries and hospitals. He secured the needed funds from his father-in-law, who "agreed to make a substantial contribution provided those who had been foremost among Boisen's helpers and advisers would form a corporate body to finance and otherwise promote the work." [13]

On January 21, 1930, a group met in the study of Dr. Samuel A. Eliot of the Arlington Street Unitarian Church of Boston to adopt a constitution and bylaws and to sign the incorporation papers. Among those present, in addition to Guiles and Boisen, were Cabot and Dr. William A. Bryan of the Worcester State Hospital.[14] Their aim in founding the Council was to bring students face to face with human misery so that by competent supervision three things might be accomplished:

1. To open his eyes to the real problems of men and women and to develop in him methods of observation which will make him competent as an instigator of the forces with which religion has to do and of the laws which govern these forces;
2. To train him in the art of helping people out of trouble and enabling them to find spiritual health;
3. To bring about a greater degree of mutual understanding among the professional groups which are concerned with the personal problems of men.[15]

From the founding of the Council for the Clinical Training of Theological Students, Inc., Boisen's influence in the organizational life of the new movement began to diminish. This trend was accelerated in the fall of the same year by his second hospitalization and Cabot's firm decision, mentioned previously, that Boisen must not be allowed to function any longer as an educator.

At Elgin State Hospital, to which Boisen moved in 1932, he became an organizer again. He formed the Chicago Council for the Clinical Training of Theological Students "as an autonomous local organization" but "in accordance with the general plan" of clinical training begun in the East.[16] Initially, four seminaries were affiliated with Boisen at Elgin.[17] In 1935 Donald Beatty, one of Boisen's early students, joined his staff, helping him organize support for the Chicago

Council and helping in chaplaincy and supervisory work.[18] The Chicago Council remained closely allied with the national body until 1939. Boisen then separated himself from the central office. The discrepancies between Boisen's goals and those of the national Council for Clinical Training had become more and more apparent, so Boisen registered his protest in this way.

Beatty left for military duty in 1942 just as Boisen turned 65. Wartime conditions made it possible for Boisen to be reemployed at Elgin, and his breach with the Council for Clinical Training came to a head. In 1945 he was effectively removed from the supervision of students by leaders of the national body. He was designated "educational consultant" and given assignment on the road—visiting other supervisors. William Andrew was sent to Elgin State Hospital as chaplain supervisor just prior to the arrival of the 1945 summer class.[19] Andrew soon left Elgin, and Boisen again sought to establish a clinical training program under his own supervision. On December 15, 1947, the Executive Committee of the Board of Governors of the Council for Clinical Training approved Boisen's proposal to conduct a research project with two student assistants. They did not approve Elgin as a training program since a supervisor who met their standards was not available. On May 16, 1949, Boisen was appointed research consultant to the Board of Governors of the Council for Clinical Training, Inc.[20]

When in a personal interview I asked Boisen the reasons for his split with the Council for Clinical Training, he spontaneously told two stories about Pentecostal Holiness churches he had studied in Alabama. In one instance a church split over the issue of men wearing ties vs. not wearing ties. In the other, a church split over the question of whether to use one or two communion cups. He observed that people always have to have issues, but really "it is just that we don't get along." [21]

Whatever the factors, personal or policy or both, Boisen remained on the periphery of the Council for Clinical Training from 1930 until his death. He was honored by the Council in 1950 on the occasion of the Silver Anniversary of the Council's founding. The paper he read on that occasion is a treasure of personal and historical recollections on clinical pastoral education. In it Boisen reiterated his own sense of purpose related to clinical training:

Let me also emphasize the fact that our movement, as I have conceived of it, has no new gospel to proclaim. We are not even seeking to introduce anything new into the theological curriculum beyond a new approach to some ancient problems. We are trying, rather, to call attention back to the central task of the church, that of "saving souls," and to the central problem of theology, that of sin and salvation. *What is new is the attempt to begin with the study of living human documents rather than with books and to focus attention upon those who are grappling desperately with the issues of spiritual life and death.*[22]

Boisen's Place in the Dynamics of Clinical Pastoral Education as a Profession

Boisen's significance inheres in the authenticity of his own person. He was lost and is found. He was disorganized by psychosis in attempting to cope with massive and repeated interpersonal failures. He became reorganized around a sense of divine purpose in his breakdown. A malignant personality malfunction was transformed into creative living. Boisen drew hope from his heritage of faith and from what he called "the fellowship of the best." He found courage in his memories, his commitments, his purposes, and, ultimately, in his relationship with God. Boisen presented himself, as it were, to Christianity and asked what the church had to offer to the mentally ill. He asked what theological education was doing to equip ministers to fulfill their calling as physicians of the soul. He embodied a new authority based on firsthand discovery in the realm of the spiritual life. He stimulated ministers to covet this new authority for themselves, to explore the inner world for themselves, to know their own inner world, and to become sensitive companions for others struggling with the issues of spiritual life and death.

Boisen provided a model for the movement that grew up around him. I shall identify three areas in which his influence is conspicuous. In each of these areas Boisen unified polarities of thought or functioning.

First, Boisen linked traditional, revealed Christianity with modern, empirical theology. Hiltner commented on Boisen's "unusual diversity of theological views and interests," saying that they have "thrown many otherwise able theologians off the track in trying to place him theologically." [23] Boisen's roots were nourished in the soil of nineteenth-century liberalism. He wrote, "The faith of my fathers was, for me, at one with the authority of science." [24] At Union Theological Seminary in New York City, Boisen studied under William Adams Brown, an outstanding liberal theologian of his day. From George Coe, of the same faculty, Boisen cultivated his lifelong taste for empirical methods of study in the psychology of religion. Embracing pragmatism as the principle underlying his theological method, he assumed with all liberal theologians that revelation cannot contradict reason and experience. Identifying himself as a "liberal minister" in 1955, he said

It remains to be seen what will happen when the servants of the church begin to apply the methods of co-operative inquiry to the problems of living men, seeking not only to help but also to understand. It seems not too much to hope that as they learn to ask the significant questions and to verify and reverify the answers there may come a surer understanding of the end and meaning of life and the way to individual and social salvation.[25]

Boisen qualified the picture of himself as a liberal by insisting that he was not trying to introduce anything new into the theological curriculum except a new approach to ancient problems. He affirmed repeatedly that he was calling the church back to its central task of "saving souls" and to its central problem, "that of sin and salvation." [26] Boisen identified himself with the mystics in religion and said, "The mystic is likely to be conservative in his theology. . . . The very strangeness of the experience may cause him to lean more heavily upon the support of tradition." Nevertheless, he added, "many mystics have been pathfinders." Boisen affirmed the possibility of revelation, refusing to rely exclusively upon reason and experience for religious authority.[27]

In relation to the Scopes' trial of 1925, Boisen published an article in defense of William Jennings Bryan and subtitled "A Personal Confession by a Liberal Clergyman." In it, Boisen rejected Bryan's appeal to traditional authority but not his traditional concerns with the human problems of sin and salvation. Boisen concluded that the authority the church needs is "not in a return to the tradition and the written record, but in a return to the experience and the central interest of Him who came to seek and to save the lost." [28]

Kenneth Cauthen's the *Impact of American Religious Liberalism* provides the label that fits Boisen if one wishes to label him. He is an "evangelical liberal," according to Cauthen's classification, and is in the distinguished company of William Adams Brown, Harry Emerson Fosdick, Walter Rauschenbusch, A. C. Knudson, and Eugene W. Lyman.[29]

During my interview with Boisen in 1959 he said with strong feeling that he was surprised to see that the conservative churches have taken up clinical training more enthusiastically than the liberal ones. In reflecting on this, I have been impressed with the benefits of Boisen's boundary-line position theologically. Those who enter clinical pastoral education from a conservative heritage are able to test their understandings experientially without losing touch with their heritage. Those who come from a liberal background recover the urgency of the traditional questions without being forced to choose between science and religion.

Boisen's influence tended toward the unification of polarities also in linking psychological and sociological perspectives. His two major works illustrate the point precisely. *The Exploration of the Inner World* (1936) was a study of the fragmented and alienated individual. *Religion in Crisis and Custom* (1945, 1955) studied the fragmentation and alienation of religious groups. Both studies were built on the presupposition that pathological manifestations accompany severe stress, whether it is in an individual suffering from inner conflict, or a group suffering from economic and social deprivation. Both studies took for their hypothesis the view that the successful resolution of conflict is akin to creative religious experience, whereas unsuccessful resolution of the conflict is labeled mental illness in the individual and destructiveness in groups. In both studies, Boisen presented empirical data to establish the fact that a successful, religious outcome of conflict is one that moves toward unification and socialization of the person or group; unsuccessful outcomes are those which move toward progressive fragmentation and social alienation.

Since both studies affirm the creative possibilities of conflict and suffering, they say that the contrast between the pathological and the normal is a spurious one. As Boisen put it, "The correct contrast is not between the pathological and the normal in religious experience, but between spiritual defeat and spiritual victory." The crucial question for an individual or a group in conflict is not what label to fix—whether sickness or health—but what direction one takes in response to the conflict, whether retreat and withdrawal, or growth toward new insight and a radical reorganization of one's style of life. In questioning the validity of basic psychiatric nomenclature, namely the term "mental illness" or "sickness," Boisen was well ahead of his time as we shall see subsequently.

With regard to the linking of psychological and sociological perspectives and methods, Boisen had the gift, as Pruyser put it, "for a simultaneous vision of the trees as well as the forest. As a clinical worker and while focusing on the individual, he placed great emphasis on social roles and social learning." In this Boisen felt supported by the works of George Mead and Harry Stack Sullivan, both of whom influenced him greatly. "His aim for the 'better life' of the individual always meant a socially more responsible life, and ethics was for him a corporate phenomenon." [30]

A third and final point of significance in the internal development of clinical pastoral education was the way in which Boisen linked seminary and hospital for "cooperative inquiry" in the clinical training of theological students. Boisen refused a full-time faculty appointment, as we have seen, in order to maintain a hospital base. His decision must have been motivated in part by the unusually high caliber of patient care and research programs going on at Worcester State Hospital under the enlightened administration of Dr. William A. Bryan. All who knew Bryan and the Worcester State Hospital during his administration use superlatives in speaking of him. Carroll A. Wise, who succeeded Boisen as chaplain at Worcester, has said that Bryan ought to be named as one of the founders of the clinical training movement. (He cited Boisen, Cabot, and Bryan, omitting Keller) .[31] Had Bryan lacked the venturesomeness to open his hospital to a full-time chaplain or the vision to support him, clinical training might not have begun for many years—in mental hospitals at least.

Bryan was an innovator in mental hospital administration. He initiated such things as a cafeteria system, radio and public address systems on every ward, music therapy, and an exciting research program that attracted top scientists to his staff. Bryan supported Boisen in other innovations, such as founding a hospital newspaper; outdoor celebrations on holidays; and granting access to both Boisen and his students to staff meetings, case records, and consultations.[32]

While maintaining a hospital base, Boisen cultivated his part-time affiliation with Chicago Theological Seminary. The door to Boston University School of Theology was partially opened in 1928. A link was formed between Worcester State Hospital and the Boston seminary when Francis L. Strickland, Professor of History and Psychology of Religion, spent his sabbatical with Boisen and then invited Boisen and Lewis B. Hill, M.D., of the same hospital, to co-teach a seminar with him in psychopathology in 1928.[33]

Chicago Theological Seminary was the first seminary to embrace clinical training. Andover Newton Theological School was the first to employ a professor on a full-time basis in the clinical field. Andover Newton achieved this first in 1931 with the addition of A. Philip Guiles to its faculty. Some speculation is inevitable as to why Boston University School of Theology did not take the lead in developing empirical theology via Boisen's clinic. The question is heightened by the fact that Wise completed his doctoral work under Strickland and succeeded Boisen at Worcester in 1931. Boston University School of Theology eventually embraced clinical training through the influence of Paul E. Johnson in the mid-forties, but only after passing up both Boisen and Wise. One factor may have been the dominance of personalism and the philosophy of religion under Dean Knudsen. Knudsen's preference for abstraction and his suspicion of concrete studies of individuals was marked.[34]

Boisen set a pattern that has been copied by many of the chaplain supervisors who came after him. It involves striking a balance between the autonomy of a local chaplaincy program and seminary affiliations. The teaching chaplain becomes affiliated with one or more seminaries either directly or through the vehicle of a training agency such as the Council for Clinical Training, Inc. He remains answerable to his hospital administrator and to the certifying agency primarily, and to seminaries only secondarily and in many instances quite remotely. This pattern fostered the independence of clinical training from seminary influence, particularly within the Council for Clinical Training. It accelerated the move within the Council toward a heavy dependence upon psychiatry for both the theory and practice of ministry. The problems resulting from this development constitute part of the story of the next chapter. Much to Boisen's surprise and dismay, the relative autonomy of the supervisors from seminary control did not stimulate empirical theology as he defined the term. Perhaps this was because of the scarcity of hospital administrators of the caliber of William A. Bryan as much as to the personal needs of the supervisors.

Boisen's Place in Relation to the Future of Clinical Pastoral Education

We have seen that in certain respects both Keller and Cabot continue to be ahead of the times. The same may be said of Boisen. Boisen was ahead of his own day in seeing mental illness as the attempted readaptation of a person who is under severe stress. In this sense Boisen saw functional mental illnesses as manifestations of "the healing forces of nature." Hiltner picked up this aspect of Boisen's thought and noted: "This very thesis has been most ably documented and asserted by Karl Menninger and associates in *The Vital Balance*" (1963).[35]

Boisen said, in effect, that the word "illness" was not a valid symbol in many instances. When the symptoms being described by the term "illness" lead one toward integration and increased socialization, the word "illness" becomes a misnomer. In such cases the experience that was psychiatrically labeled "mental illness" must be admitted to be "mystical religious experience." At the same time Boisen went on to say that religious experience may be a cover for malingering or social irresponsibility when it has disintegrative and isolating effects. Boisen found the criteria for defining illness and health in the personal and social values enacted by the person's behavior.

To claim that some behavior classified by psychiatry as sickness is in reality religious experience; to insist, further, that it should be so named and treated, and that an adequate therapy of persons with schizophrenic reactions must include a theological understanding is to launch a massive assault upon the bastions of psychiatric medicine. I, for one, did not feel the full force of Boisen's critique and challenge of psychiatry until hearing the same message stated psychiatrically and in far more explicit terms by Szasz and to some extent by Mowrer as well. Judging by the vogue that psychoanalytic theory has enjoyed in some segments of the clinical training movement, especially during the early phases of the movement, one may suppose that Boisen's critique was dismissed as a symptom of his own personal struggles by many who followed him into "the wilderness of the lost."

The revolution in psychiatry today arises from the use of Dewey more than of Freud to understand malfunctioning behavior.[36] We cannot support the claim that Boisen anticipated such a reevaluation of psychiatry. We must recognize, however, a point of similarity. To see psychiatric problems in ethical as well as in medical perspective is to put them in the province of behavioral science as well as medical science. To do this is to claim that psychotherapy is a proper territory for philosophy and ethics—and churchmen would add theology as well. Though traveling different roads, social psychiatrists such as Szasz and the clinical theologian Boisen, arrived at the same point.[37] Boisen impelled his colleagues in theology into dialogue with psychiatrists on the issue of the proper role and territory of each. In the same way the rebels Szasz and Mowrer are challenging psychiatrists and psychologists to enter into dialogue with ethicists, philosophers, theologians, and anyone else concerned with the place of value in human behavior and social organization.

Boisen continues to goad the religious community into examination of unusual experiences and into scrutiny of the philosophical presuppositions and value systems of the psychiatric community. One wishes that he had pressed the exploration of his own experience more rigorously, however. He was aware that some of his psychotic experience was nonproductive. Had he extracted the implications of his nonproductive psychoses he might have discovered the extent to which all psychotic behavior is learned. Ernest Becker's analysis of Boisen's autobiography shows clearly that in Boisen's case psychotic behavior was learned in the absence of more appropriate social learning.[38]

Boisen stands in the future as well as the past with respect to theology, too. In the Preface to *Religion in Crisis and Custom*, Hiltner said that Boisen's methodology applied "rigorous but imaginative methods of science" to religious phenomena with no holds barred, believing that "truth of this order can be far more revealing than we have yet recognized." [39] Boisen beckons clinical pastoral educators to move forward steadily, remaining open to humanistic claims and refining empirical methods of inquiry without losing faith in the power of religious symbols to unite the separated both in personal and in political experience. To be sure, the liberalism of the twenties is dead, whether "evangelical liberalism" or any other kind. The problem of relating science and religion is still very much alive, however, as are the ancient problems of theology—the problems of sin and salvation. These were the bipolar focuses in Boisen's field of vision. The "living human documents" have not all been read, nor have they been read in depth from the perspective of Boisen's dual concerns.[40]

We have met the fathers of clinical pastoral education and felt

70

something of the force of their vision for the education of ministers. Next we shall meet the elders of the profession—those men and women who were caught up in the momentum initiated by Keller, Cabot, and Boisen. We shall see the initial thrust of the fathers becoming a movement and the movement growing into a new profession. To ask what has happened since the period of beginnings is to ask how those who were taught by the fathers heard them. It is to ask how the elders built. Over what did they quarrel and why. It is to inquire about the growing pains of a movement on its way toward becoming a profession. As the subsequent chapters show, the answers define an era of separatism followed by an era of unification.

Part II

The Era of Separatism, 1930-1946

4

THE COUNCIL'S STORY

The period from 1930 to 1946 was a time of sibling rivalries, of preadolescent style chumship, of adolescent rebellion against Mother Church, and of responsible young adulthood all mixed together. The story of these years is the story of strong personalities laying claim to a new territory in the realm of education and ministry. It is enlivened by the activities of a few mavericks, but in the main it is the story of inner-directed men and women whose sense of group consciousness formed around their common commitment to pursue an exciting experiment.

They were, as Helen Flanders Dunbar said in 1934, a group of people who got together to carry out an experiment in a radically new form of education and ministry and to try to sell what they were developing to the seminaries and to the medical world at the same time.[1] They quickly became self-conscious as a "movement." A few commonly accepted procedures and skills were expanded and reflected upon until a theory emerged and the foundations were laid for a new profession. This shift of identity from "movement" to "profession" was accompanied by a subtle change in the titles by which the leaders referred to their field. Early in the period the term clinical training was used exclusively. By the end of the period the term most often applied was clinical pastoral training.

At another level the whole period was characterized by separatist attitudes and behavior. I have chosen to define the period as the era of separatism. After recounting the original schism between Guiles and Dunbar, I shall concentrate in this chapter on the story of the Council for Clinical Training and reserve for Chapter 5 the story of the New England group and a summary evaluation of the whole period.

Schism: Guiles vs. Dunbar

The movement split apart almost as soon as it took organizational form. The Council for the Clinical Training of Theological Students was incorporated on January 21, 1930, in Boston. Philip Guiles was field secretary and interim director until the fall of 1930. He then welcomed to the post of director a woman, Helen Flanders Dunbar. Her selection as Director of the Council was a fateful decision. Cooperation turned quickly into conflict. The relationship between Guiles and Dunbar became so bitter by 1932 that Dunbar simply declared the headquarters to be New York City rather than Boston. Guiles responded by launching a clinical training program in Boston. Support came from the Earhart Foundation, a family Foundation headed by Guiles' father-in-law, Mr. H. B. Earhart.

Who were these two personalities who reacted against each other so explosively? A. Philip Guiles was a tall, handsome, vivacious, outgoing, and thoroughly disorganized man. He had a striking personality. He married Louise Earhart of Detroit, a woman of wealth. They met on a trip to Alaska while he was a student at Union Theological Seminary and she was at Vassar. Guiles was seen by some of his early associates as an empire builder. His lack of organization limited him, however. He is said to have written three books, none of which were seen by publishers.[2]

Guiles's strength in the clinical training movement derived not only from his personality and his financial resources but also from his seminary relationship. When the two theological schools, Andover and Newton, joined hands in the fall of 1931, Guiles became a member of the Andover Newton faculty, with the title, Director of Clinical Training. President Everett C. Herrick initiated conversations between Guiles and a faculty committee during the summer of 1931, so that when the appointment came, it represented substantial endorsement by the faculty as well as the president. Guiles remained at Andover Newton for twenty-three years until his death in 1953. By 1932 he was clearly committed to the proposition that clinical training should become "an inherent and accepted part of theological school education." By this he meant its "inclusion in the seminary budget" and seminary affiliation "with nearby hospitals or institutions as clinical training centers." [3] Andover Newton was the first seminary to offer a full-time faculty appointment in the field of clinical pastoral education. It is doubtful whether Guiles could have led the new movement to achieve the scope and excellence that marked the New England group had he not enjoyed the acceptance of a secure seminary home.

Helen Flanders Dunbar, B.D., Ph.D., M.D., was an intellectual amazon, as her academic pedigree suggests. She was educated at Bryn Mawr College, Columbia University, Union Theological Seminary, and Yale Medical School. As a middler at Union, she learned about Boisen's experiment and joined his group at Worcester during the summer of 1925. She was working on her Ph.D at Columbia concurrent with theological studies. Since her dissertation was on "Medieval Symbolism and Its Consummation in the Divine Comedy," she was curious about the symbolism of mental patients as well.[4] She gained the favor of leading New York City physicians and clergy and in 1929 was selected by the Joint Committee on Religion and Medicine of the New York Academy of Medicine to study psychosomatic medicine from the perspective of both psychiatry and religion. On the basis of precocious professional achievements and the very special regard of Anton Boisen, she was offered the leadership of the newly formed Council for the Clinical Training of Theological Students, Inc. in 1930.

Dunbar was petite, less than five feet tall, quite beautiful, vital, and charming. She had a preference for tailored garments that were at the same time dignified and feminine. Those who worked with her during the thirties experienced her as also ambitious, cold and calculating, noncommunicative, and basically rather shy. Her administration of the Council for Clinical Training was authoritarian. All the young ministers who worked with her found it necessary to struggle against her manipulativeness. They were fascinated, nevertheless, by her political adroitness, her somewhat cynical view of established values and important people. They were loyal to her because of her intense commitment to the cause of relating the clergy to physicians in a constructive way and because of her genuine religious interest.[5]

Dunbar knew that it was important to get people of means interested in the new venture. She took the Social Register seriously, and early in the life of the Council for Clinical Training gained substantial financial support from the William C. Whitney Foundation. Modest sums were contributed during 1933, 1934, and 1935. During 1936 and 1937 support from the Whitney Foundation increased to $2,000 per year. In 1938 it doubled and in 1939 increased again to $4,500.[6] The termination in 1940 of all Whitney Foundation support without prior notification created a major crisis for the Council threatening its very survival, but this is the story of a subsequent section. By the forties Dunbar's influence in the Council for Clinical Training had diminished greatly. Several Council supervisors had become professionally mature enough to question her point of view. Her interest in the training of the clergy was diluted during the financial crisis of 1940-41, and personal pre-occupation may have contributed also to her gradual withdrawal from Council activities.[7]

Clinical training grew in two rival camps following the rupture of relationship between Guiles and Dunbar. During the years 1933-38, Guiles built his program around Andover Newton and other New England seminaries with major assistance from the Earhart Foundation. Dunbar built her program with a New York City headquarters, supported increasingly by the Whitney Foundation. She used the mental hygiene movement as an organizational model and spoke often of the Council for the Clinical Training of Theological Students as a standard-setting body by analogy with the American Medical Association. Cabot exerted a mediating influence for several years. As the first president of the Council for the Clinical Training of Theological Students, Inc., Cabot said in a letter to President Herrick of Andover Newton Theological School in 1933: "I think there is plenty of room for both ventures and that they can help each other by exchanging experiences. I am heartily interested in both." [8]

Initially the schism between Boston and New York City was a conflict of personalities. Russell Dicks believed that the Guiles-Dunbar relationship remained "the mystery" in the history of clinical pastoral education.[9] Both Guiles and Dunbar were ambitious people dedicated to high causes. Other factors, if there were any, remain obscure. The Guiles-Dunbar conflict broke into the open during a meeting of the Council's Board of Governors. Guiles attacked Dunbar, focusing on her psychoanalytic influence in the Council for Clinical Training. The Board supported Dunbar, however, and Guiles resigned.[10] Everyone connected with the events of the time whom I have consulted insists, nevertheless, that the issue of psychoanalytic orientation was not the real basis for the split.

Though issues had nothing to do with the schism initially, an ideological polarization gradually took place. The appropriateness of mental hospitals as training centers emerged as one ideological factor. Cabot terminated his support of Boisen's program at Worcester State Hospital after Boisen's second hospitalization in November, 1930. Even though Cabot was the first president of the Council and Worcester remained a Council center, Cabot did not resume his financial or moral support of the program even after Carroll Wise became the supervisor. In fact Cabot told Wise at a private dinner meeting that his continued support of the Worcester program was conditional upon a decision by Wise to renounce the views of Boisen, particularly psychogenic theories about mental illness. Wise was unable to do so in good conscience. Cabot turned away from Worcester State Hospital and invested his support thereafter in the program at Massachusetts General Hospital.[11]

The first few years of clinical training at Massachusetts General Hospital were stormy ones. As indicated in the previous chapter, Guiles was excluded from the hospital and Russell Dicks was sent to Boston to succeed him. Dunbar appointed Dicks to Massachusetts General Hospital with instructions "to hold it for the Council." By this she meant to carry her fued with Guiles into Guiles's own territory of Boston. Dunbar was unable to follow through with the promised salary for Dicks, however. Dicks turned to Cabot for support. Cabot offered to support Dicks at Massachusetts General Hospital on the condition that Dicks cooperate with Guiles as well as with Dunbar. Dicks moved steadily away from Dunbar and the Council for the Clinical Training of Theological Students, and by 1935 he was fully identified with Guiles as part of the New England group. Dunbar lost the first round of her contest with Guiles as a result. Simultaneously she lost the support of Cabot.[12]

On April 28, 1934, Cabot wrote Guiles indicating his availability to teach at Andover Newton Theological School since he was facing retirement at Harvard. Guiles moved fast. In September, 1934, Cabot joined the Andover Newton faculty.[13]

Conflict erupted between Dunbar and Cabot in 1935. Dunbar confronted Cabot in the course of a dinner at the home of John W. Suter, an Episcopal clergyman in New York City. Other guests were Robert E. Brinkman, who was to become the next Director of the Council for Clinical Training, and Robert A. Preston, who was in training with Brinkman and who succeeded Brinkman later as supervisor in Greystone Park, New Jersey. Cabot and Dicks had completed the manuscript of *The Art of Ministering to the Sick* and had made comments about the Council for the Clinical Training of Theological Students, Inc. without submitting these to Dunbar for clearance. Dunbar confronted Cabot about this, raising questions about his point of view regarding mental hospital training. She asked Preston to testify to the value of mental hospital training as a student. When Preston finished, Dunbar turned to Cabot and said, "What do you think of this?" "Just plain bosh!" Cabot snorted. Dunbar then countered: "Do you consider that your point of view has so changed that you are no longer part of the Council so long as it has mental hospital training?" "Absolutely!" Cabot said. "Psychiatry is all on the wrong track and I have no interest at all in mental hospital programs. And if this means I have withdrawn from the Council, that's the way it will have to be." [14]

The conflict came rapidly to a head. The dinner at Suter's took place in the early fall of 1935. By the time of the annual meeting of the Council for Clinical Training in the late fall, the separation was completed. Cabot was removed as president of the Board of Governors of the Council. In the conference of supervisors which followed the Board meeting, Russell Dicks took the same point of view as Cabot and withdrew from the Council. Within three years of the original breach between Guiles and Dunbar, then, Guiles succeeded in bringing Cabot into his orbit completely and through Cabot gaining the full cooperation of Dicks. Reviewing these events a decade later, Guiles wrote:

By the spring of 1936 . . . he [Cabot] concentrated his attention on Andover Newton Project in Clinical Experience for Students of New England Theological Schools. Thereafter, until the establishment of the Institute of Pastoral Care . . . the training center at Massachusetts General Hospital became the facility of Andover Newton and cooperating theological schools in Boston and vicinity.[15]

Ideological polarization accelerated in the wake of these personality clashes. In 1938 both groups changed the names under which they were functioning. This provided an occasion for the articulation of distinctive goals. The Council for the Clinical Training of Theological Students, Inc. became simply the Council for Clinical Training, Inc. Dunbar and a neurologist on the Board of Governors, Dr. Edwin G. Zabriski, persuaded the Board to change the name in order to extend the Council's services to all the professions rather than just the clergy. Dunbar was particularly interested in making clinical training available to law students. The purposes of the Council were redefined, therefore, as an educational venture seeking to prepare "the future professional man to perform more adequately his functions with reference to community health and to know when and how to seek specialized assistance." To see the Council as a bridge between religion and medicine was called a "misapprehension" in a 1941 statement reflecting the views of Dunbar and a majority of the Board.[16]

In 1938 Guiles and Cabot reorganized their work under the title, the New England Theological Schools Committee on Clinical Training. The new name symbolized clearly the dominant role of the seminaries—a role the seminaries had been playing from the beginning of the Earhart Foundation project. Guiles and Cabot continued to provide most of the funding and to be prominent in leadership, but authority was vested unambiguously in the deans and presidents of the affiliated seminaries. Ideological distinctions associated with the change of name in the Boston area were articulated by David R. Hunter, one of the leading supervisors associated with Guiles. "Since 1938," Hunter said, "there has been a strong emphasis on making clinical training a means of preparing men for the general pastoral ministry, not alone nor even primarily for work with the sick." Hunter concluded his discussion of this change of focus by saying it was "highly stimulating and one of the most fruitful changes in our total program." [17]

The myth persisted well into the fifties that the split between the Council for Clinical Training and the New England group was rooted in the exclusive use of mental and general hospitals respectively. This issue did not arise until the forties. In 1935 the New England group offered training in the Rhode Island State Hospital, the Foxborough State Hospital, and the State Prison Colony at Norfolk in addition to general hospitals.[18] State Hospitals continued to be under the Earhart Foundation and the New England Theological Schools Committee. In New York City, meanwhile, Dunbar and her new Executive

Secretary, Seward Hiltner, were busy during 1935-36 opening a training center in the Pennsylvania Hospital of Philadelphia, and during 1936-37, developing another general hospital program at the University of Michigan Hospital in Ann Arbor, Michigan. By this move, Dunbar effectively recovered from the loss of Massachusetts General Hospital to the New England group.[19]

Typical of the manner in which Guiles opened new training centers and simultaneously enlisted seminary support for clinical training is the work at Bangor, Maine. In September, 1937, Guiles underwrote the expenses of Dr. Alexander D. Dodd as teaching chaplain offering clinical training for Bangor Theological Seminary in the Bangor State Hospital and the Eastern Maine General Hospital concurrently. Dodd was one of Boisen's early students who had served with Guiles as chaplain at Boston City Hospital before moving to Bangor. Seminary support increased as Earhart Foundation funds decreased. Bangor Seminary continued the program until 1945 when Dodd retired.[20]

The separation of the two groups was maintained during the forties on the grounds that the New England group represented a pastoral orientation whereas the Council for Clinical Training was predominantly psychoanalytic. The New England group was incorporated in 1944 as the Institute of Pastoral Care. During discussions in 1947 and 1948 of a possible merger of the Institute of Pastoral Care and the Council for Clinical Training no little anxiety was expressed by Board members of the Institute lest the proposed "new organization . . . continue the psychoanalytic orientation of the Council rather than the pastoral focus of the Institute." [21]

Competition between the Boston and New York City groups continued into the sixties, but not without a number of constructive results. They stimulated each other to diversify the types of centers in which training was offered as we have just seen. Competition was a spur to growth in the number and in the quality of supervisors. Each group started its own professional journal in the late forties, and in the process of merging the two journals they were forced to face the advantage of an eventual merger of their respective organizations.

I shall now narrow the focus and tell the Council's story from 1930 to 1946 and then that of the New England group. The first National Conference on Clinical Training in Theological Education occurred in 1944. With this the separatism of the movement was weighed and found wanting. Momentum developed then toward the unification of the field—a goal that was not to be finally reached until 1967.

The Council's Story: Hiltner and Brinkman Traditions

Council supervisors whom I interviewed during the late fifties were unanimous in identifying two wings or two traditions within the organization. Some spoke of "the right wing" and "the left wing," others of contrasting trends toward conformity and individuality, of the needs for security and freedom. Frequently the theme of churchly concerns was set over against existential concern. These are value laden categories in the main. Supervisors communicated regularly a nostalgic longing for the previous decades when the left wing and the themes of freedom and individuality were dominant within the Council. Historical investigation supports in part these memories of how it was in the Council for Clinical Training. The left wing was indeed dominant from 1938 to 1946. This was the period during which Brinkman was Director of the Council. Change came rapidly after Keuther became Director in 1947. Few supervisors recalled that the so-called churchly concerns prevailed in the first period of the Council's history, 1930-37, the period culminating in Hiltner's executive leadership.

Rather than employ evaluative categories, I shall present the Council's story under the names of its executive leadership. I shall set the stage initially with some further information about Dunbar as Director, 1930-35; then proceed to the Hiltner tradition, 1935-37; and the Brinkman tradition, 1938-46. Finally the comparisons and contrasts will be put as clearly as possible.

Dunbar functioned administratively with absolute authority. Until the mid-thirties she was what her title said, the director. Following an administrative reorganization, which she planned in 1935, she ruled no less surely, but less obviously. After her split with Guiles, Dunbar made Russell Dicks her Field Secretary. When it was clear that Dicks was going into the Guiles camp, she found Seward Hiltner to replace him. Hiltner became Executive Secretary in 1935. But Hiltner exercised too much initiative and assumed too much authority to suit Dunbar. By early spring of 1936 she began to cultivate Robert Brinkman to replace Hiltner. In the summer of 1936 Brinkman became Dunbar's unofficial assistant and in the fall Board meeting, Administrative Assistant with salary. All this was done without consulting

Hiltner. Hiltner found the situation increasingly distasteful. Early in 1938, Hiltner moved to the Federal Council of Churches to head the Commission on Religion and Health. Dunbar then set Brinkman in the forefront of the Council's administration. For a few years her influence was conspicuous, but by 1941 Brinkman and the supervisors emerged in control of the Council for Clinical Training. The Council remained in the hands of the supervisors from 1941 to 1967.[22]

Dunbar's first achievement was to win the confidence of the medical profession and to establish new centers. She interpreted clinical training in pragmatic terms, telling physicians that through the Council for the Clinical Training of Theological Students they were helping the clergy to do better what they must do anyway; they were preventing the clergy from doing what they ought not. The Council grew in all respects as the accompanying chart shows.[23]

year	centers	supervisors	students trained	supervisors trained	seminary affiliates	receipts (office)	estimated total receipts
1930	3 (3M)	3	16	0	2	none	$6,450
1933	8 (4M; 1G; 1JD; 1GC; 1OS)	7	38	1	23	$4,000	$14,325
1935	9 (5M; 1G; 1GC; 2OS)	10	50	4	31	$7,500	$24,744
1938	14 (5M; 2G; 6P; 1GC)	18	60	7	58	$8,400	$45,609
1940	20 (6M; 3G; 8P; 1GC; 2JD)	19	78	6	63	$8,059	$48,959

Code for types of centers:
M, Mental Hospital
G, General Hospital
P, Penal and Correctional Inst.

GC, Guidance Centers
JD, Inst. for Juvenile Delinquents
OS, Other Schools

A quick look at the chart shows that Dunbar tripled the number of centers from three to nine by 1935; and from nine to twenty by 1940. Other increases were proportionate. Most remarkable is the increase in seminary affiliations from two to thirty-one by 1935. During Hiltner's term of office, seminary affiliations almost doubled, going from thirty-one to fifty-eight. Prime growth during Brinkman's term up to 1940 occurred in the number of centers. The diversity of centers is remarkable, also. In 1930 training was offered only in three mental hospitals. A decade later the Council administered programs in mental hospitals, general hospitals, penal and correctional institutions, institutions for juvenile delinquents, and a child guidance center.

On the strength of Dunbar's name and the resourcefulness of her executive assistants, the Council for the Clinical Training of Theological Students consistently found itself during the thirties with more medical institutions seeking to sponsor training programs than it could staff. Similarly, more students sought training than could be accepted.[24] Dunbar deserves credit for resisting the temptation to grow rapidly at the expense of high standards. She held up to the Council supervisors the model of the American Medical Association and issued warnings to the public and to the seminaries against substandard programs.[25]

The standards that the Council held to be minimal in 1934 were three: (1) to develop a program that would guarantee a student's discovering his distinctive role as minister in relation to the physician, the psychiatrist, and representatives of social agencies in the community; (2) to avoid the introduction of psychoanalytic technique into a student's clinical training; (3) to provide in every training center dual supervision by "a graduate in theology on the one hand, and on the other, a staff adviser qualified to give the point of view of his institution, be he physician, psychiatrist, prison superintendent, social worker, or other specialist." The ultimate objective of these standards is to give the student "a basis on which to bring this new knowledge and experience into harmony with his professional tradition, in such a way as to make it possible for him to assimilate the new knowledge and to make his own unique contribution." [26]

The Council was clearly in agreement with the New England group with respect to objectives and standards at this stage. Hiltner was urging the addition of the term "pastoral" to clinical training as early as 1935.[27] The New England group described its task as the work of "clinical theology" in the early thirties. It was Hiltner, reflecting the concerns of the New England supervisors, who chose the phrase, clinical pastoral training, as the title of the first volume to be published on the educational goals and methods of the profession. Only one real difference distinguished the Council's methods under Dunbar and Hiltner from the Boston group under Guiles. The Council insisted on a minimum training period of twelve weeks of full-time work. Guiles developed part-time training of a few hours a week during the academic year and six-week periods of summer training.

One of the most exciting developments for the supervisors during Hiltner's term was the contract with the Federal Bureau of Prisons and the Federal Council of Churches to provide prison chaplains trained under the auspices of the Council for Clinical Training. In 1936 Sanford Bates was Director of the Federal Bureau of Prisons and F. Lovell Bixby was his assistant. They met Dunbar in her New York City apartment to ask how they could obtain better trained, more dependable Protestant chaplains for the Federal Prisons. Dunbar and Hiltner worked out a plan with the Federal Council of Churches to nominate Protestant Chaplains through a new Commission on Prison Chaplains (incorporated into the Commission on Religion and Health in 1938). The understanding was that the Council for Clinical Training would provide the training that would constitute the basis for the nominations. The development proved a real stimulus to Council supervisors because the salaries were better than in mental hospitals. Robert Preston reported that a certain cohesiveness arose among prison chaplains within the Council for Clinical Training, and this "had some influence on the general workings of the Council." [28]

Wayne Hunter laid the foundation for a chaplaincy program at the U. S. Industrial Reformatory in Chillicothe, Ohio, serving as chaplain without salary in 1936. He offered training to a group of three students. Eight vacancies were waiting to be filled in the Federal Bureau of Prisons, however. The pressure was on the Council for Clinical Training to fill them promptly. In September, 1937, Fred Kuether, one of Boisen's students at Elgin State Hospital, became chaplain supervisor on salary from the Chillicothe Reformatory. From January, 1938, until 1952, Chillicothe was designated by the Bureau of Prisons as *the* training center for all their chaplains. Kuether left Chillicothe in 1942, but the field of prison chaplaincy was well served during the next three decades by such clinically trained men as Henry Cassler, Robert Preston, Mark Shedron, and others.[29]

By 1936, the Council offered clinical training in four types of institutions—mental hospitals, child guidance clinics and special schools, general hospitals, and penal institutions. The dream of offering a clinical year with a quarter in each of four different settings as a part of one's theological education had become a reality. Supervisors and a few seminary educators found this a tremendously exciting possibility.

The cornerstone of the Council's edifice of standards was and is the competence of the chaplain supervisor. Almost everyone who wrote or spoke about standards in the mid-thirties stressed this point. Unhappily, the Council failed to enforce high standards for the training of supervisors in its first decade. The only "rule on the books," according to Hiltner, was that a prospective supervisor "shall have had training in at least two centers" before becoming eligible. The matter of standards for the training of supervisors was discussed at the 1936 Fall Conference, but the minutes record that "it was agreed that no further actual rules should be put into effect than that of training in two institutions." [30] The selection of new supervisors was controlled by group pressures from within the Council itself. In neglecting to raise minimum standards for supervisors, however, the Council became vulnerable to numerous professional ills.

Brinkman reported to the National Conference in 1944 that standards for supervisors had risen substantially. The supervisor must be "an ordained clergyman, graduated from a recognized theological school. He must be a well-adjusted person himself, emotionally and spiritually stable, with ability to face trying situations calmly and objectively." Poise was discriminated from "passivity," and the supervisor was to be "sufficiently alive to be capable of enthusiasm, and yet not compulsive, effusive or overly enthusiastic." Ecumenicity was the style. The supervisor must hold religious convictions "without dogmatism." He was expected to be "interested primarily in the ministry" and have "a sustained interest in the bearing of the training experience and theological and pastoral problems upon each other." He was required to have had at least one year of training in two or more types of centers and "a period of service and training as Assistant Supervisor." As an Assistant he was expected to demonstrate "the ability to enable others to observe for themselves, to evolve their own conclusions and applications, and above all to grow." [31]

The excitement of opening new centers was matched for Hiltner and the Council's Board of Governors by dramatic success in securing new seminary affiliations. Dunbar's role in winning the approval of theological educators was conspicuous and dramatic. Hiltner tells the story succinctly:

What might be called our Billy Graham experience occurred in 1934. Helen Flanders Dunbar . . . attended the biennial meeting of the American

Association of Theological Schools, and made an address about clinical training. . . . She took the Association by storm. Although she did not issue a clinical training altar call, she did note those schools which expressed a positive interest; so that there was something to follow up which had not existed before. Dr. Dunbar did many positive things for the clinical training movement in those early days; but none was so spectacular as her conversion of the professors.[32]

Dunbar presented the Council for Clinical Training program as an internship in the ministry of healing marked by three results: (1) increased effectiveness in the detection and prevention of ill health—both physical and mental; (2) the wisdom to avoid pseudo-professional functioning; and (3) the enrichment of one's understanding of the pastoral role—both in preaching and in prayer. She charged untrained ministers with being a public health menace because of their ignorance about mental illness and mental hygiene. She concluded by calling for a wedding of medicine and the ministry to meet the crisis of the times.[33]

The response of the American Association of Theological Schools was registered officially two years later. President A. W. Beaven was chairman of a Committee on Supervised Training from 1934-36. He reported for his committee:

> With regard to the high value of clinical training your committee feels no slightest doubt. . . .
> We believe, moreover, that the seminaries should voice very deep appreciation to both organizations sponsoring clinical training, and especially to those who have pioneered its development in the early years. They have initiated a work which was really the responsibility of the seminaries themselves, have guided it through the critical stages of experimentation, and have borne the major share of expense throughout.[34]

The committee further recommended that every student take a curriculum course in personal counseling, social work, or rural sociology; then take a summer of clinical training; then return to the seminary and take a practicum course to help him "review, analyze and summarize the values of the summer experience." They observed that "the Seminaries should have a voice (though not necessarily a controlling voice) in the determination of clinical training policy." They recommended an advisory committee of the seminaries to counsel both organizations. Such a committee was formed subsequently but was seldom consulted by either clinical training group.

The approval of clinical training by the Committee on Supervised Training was not unconditional, however. The burden of the committee's report had to do not with clinical training but with fieldwork. No clear discriminations were made at this time between the two kinds of experience. The impression of the whole report is that the committee saw clinical training as a novel but worthwhile variety of fieldwork.[35]

Interest aroused among theological educators by Dunbar was followed up by Hiltner from 1935 to 1938. Hiltner recruited students from twenty-seven schools that had not participated in the Council's program before. The significance of Hiltner's efforts comes clear when we study the Council's growth chart. Only eight new seminary affiliations were secured in the three years prior to Hiltner's term and only five in the three years following. Hiltner enlisted more than twice as many seminaries during his three-year term than were added during the six years on either side of him. The most original and far-reaching seminary program of the period was that of Philadelphia Divinity School, from 1937 to 1944. Dunbar and Hiltner both served as consultants to Reuel Howe and others in developing a New Plan of Theological Education in which three quarters of clinical training were required of all students as an integral part of their course of study. No more will be said about the New Plan at this point. It was so imaginative that I am featuring it as a case study in Chapter 9.

Developments from 1930 to 1938 are presented under the heading, "the Hiltner tradition." It is in order to ask who Hiltner is, and how the Hiltner tradition may be defined. Seward Hiltner graduated from Lafayette College in Eastern Pennsylvania in 1931. He was awakened to the empirical study of religion by a college professor, Henry E. Allen, who became Hiltner's instructor when he was fresh from Ph.D. studies in the History of Religions at the University of Chicago Divinity School. A course in psychology included a field trip to Allentown State Hospital, and a senior seminar introduced Hiltner to psychoanalysis. Hiltner enrolled in Chicago Theological Seminary, and he responded positively to Anton Boisen when Boisen came to Chicago recruiting students in the spring of 1932. Hiltner's baptism in clinical work occurred in the Pittsburgh City Home and Hospitals under the supervision of Donald C. Beatty (who was one of Boisen's first students). In 1933 Hiltner returned to Pittsburgh to work a second summer with Beatty. He followed this in 1934 as an Assistant Supervisor under Carroll Wise at Worcester State Hospital. Dunbar invited Hiltner to New York City in December, 1934, to discuss a staff position with the Council for the Clinical Training of Theological Students. After qualifying for the Ph.D. in theology, Hiltner bypassed the B.D. degree, was ordained in the spring of 1935, and then entered his first full-time position working for Helen Flanders Dunbar, M.D. The former maid's room of her apartment at 730 Park Avenue became his office. Hiltner left the Council in 1938 to become the Executive Secretary of the Commission on Religion and Health of the Federal Council of the Churches of Christ in America. In 1948 he took a leave of absence to complete his Ph.D. at the University of Chicago while Paul Maves substituted for him. He joined the Federated Theological Faculty of the University of Chicago in 1950 and the faculty of Princeton Theological Seminary in 1961.[36]

The Hiltner tradition within the Council for Clinical Training had two marks: (1) a basic commitment to a professional model for theological education—a model that equips seminarians for effective pastoral work and creates a research community dedicated to empirical inquiry into the religious dimension of life, and (2) a commitment to relate science and religion by the mode of correlation—moving dialogically between theological presuppositions and cases; between behavioral science and theology.

The Council under Dunbar and Hiltner lived a life of dialogue with medicine and psychiatry. A cardinal principle in Council for Clinical Training standards was that the theological student receive dual supervision from the scientific and theological perspectives, and that he devote sufficient time to his clinical training experience to assimilate the experience into his theological tradition. Clinical training was described by both Dunbar and Hiltner as "a new opportunity in theological education." Both Dunbar and Hiltner worked vigorously to move clinical training closer to theological education and to stimulate creative dialogue. Hiltner, in particular, hoped for the day that clinical training would become integral to the theological curriculum.

Paradoxical as it may seem, the goals of the Earhart Foundation coincided with the Hiltner tradition of the Council. The Boston group was equally committed to theological education and in the same terms as the Council for Clinical Training. The two groups extended the intentions of Cabot and were compatible with the purposes of Boisen. They both developed consistently from "movement" to "profession"—that is, toward a new professional identity as clinical pastoral educators. Discontinuity appeared in the life of the Council for Clinical Training with the Brinkman tradition, 1938-46.

The use of the phrases Hiltner tradition and Brinkman tradition raises a question about the role of Helen Flanders Dunbar in affecting the basic policy changes that occurred as Brinkman became Director of the Council for Clinical Training in 1938. Hiltner did not enter the scene nationally until 1935. By this time Dunbar had already set the goals that Hiltner implemented. Dunbar was associated as fully with the early Brinkman years as with Hiltner. By the late thirties, however, Dunbar's influence in the Board began to diminish. Edwin Zabriski, M.D., Earl Bond, M.D., and later, Augustus Knight, M.D., became dominant. Dunbar's understanding of the aims toward which the Council for Clinical Training should move did change in the late thirties, but Dunbar's influence was negligible in the forties.

Robert E. Brinkman stands six feet tall, moves with an easygoing style and the benefit of keen intelligence. He left Ohio Wesleyan College with an athletic record and a lively interest in psychoanalytic theory—an interest awakened during his freshman year in college. He chose Boston University School of Theology in the hope of further exposure to psychiatric personality theory. He discovered clinical training when Carroll Wise taught a course at the Seminary. In the summer of 1932 Brinkman was in training with Wise at Worcester State Hospital. He served as Assistant Supervisor in the same hospital in the summer of 1933.

Brinkman's most significant learning did not occur in the Boston Seminary itself but in affiliated programs. Dr. William Healy of the Judge Baker Foundation and Dr. Macfie Campbell at Boston Psychopathic Hospital were profoundly stimulating for Brinkman as they had been for Boisen a decade earlier. Though interested in theology, Brinkman found the methods of instruction deadening. He recalled getting into a bit of trouble with Dean Knudson because he persisted in asking what Knudson's theology meant for people in trouble.[37]

Brinkman was ordained a Methodist minister, but fellow supervisors saw him as one who had difficulty feeling comfortable in the role of minister. His students recall that he tended to psychologize religious beliefs, interpreting them in Freudian terms and considering that this summed up most of their meaning.

He became chaplain supervisor at Greystone Park, a State Hospital in New Jersey, in the summer of 1934. He was supported initially by the Council for Clinical Training, but was subsequently paid out of the hospital's "Patient Amusement Fund"—a fund derived from the concession stand at the hospital. Brinkman was well liked as a supervisor. He was discreet concerning his private life, but sensitive toward others and careful not to offend them. He had an emancipated attitude toward conventional standards, but he was never dogmatic about his liberated views, nor did he impose his own values on others.

During the later phase of his term as Director of the Council for Clinical Training, Brinkman became a serious student and something of a devotee of Reichian psychoanalysis. Several of his fellow supervisors shared his appreciation for the Reichian viewpoint and methodology of treatment. At no time did Brinkman allow the Council to become explicitly identified with any psychoanalytic or theological school of thought, however. Theodore Wolf, who married Helen Flanders Dunbar in the late thirties influenced Brinkman's development as a psychotherapist. Wolf encouraged Brinkman to consider private practice as a phychotherapist. Upon resignation as Director of the Council, Brinkman did, in fact, become a full-time psychotherapist in New York City where he has remained.[38]

Brinkman's contribution to the Council for Clinical Training was two-fold: he gave leadership toward a radical transformation of the meaning of ministry, and he accepted responsibility for keeping the Council alive and autonomous during its most critical period, the financial crisis of 1940-41.

When I asked Brinkman what clinical pastoral training meant to him in the thirties and what had been his central purpose as a supervisor, he replied, "clinical observation." He said that the basis of ministry is the observation and understanding of human personality. "Before ministering too much to the needs of others, one should know who and what it is that one is ministering to." Brinkman's concern was for diagnosis prior to treatment, for awareness of the depth dimensions of personality, and for the re-formation of ministry in ways congruent with new understandings of the needs of man and of the processes by which change occurs. He had little concern to maintain a traditional, churchly image for the minister, and in this he embodied a conviction shared by most of his fellow supervisors during the forties.[39]

He interpreted the purposes of the Council for Clinical Training during the forties in a twofold way: (1) to assist seminarians and clergymen to better understand people and (2) to equip them to cooperate with other professional groups "in the maintenance of the health of the community.[40] Brinkman subordinated other goals to the end of community health, and in so doing he stood in bold contrast to those in the Hiltner tradition who saw pastoral ministry and theological thinking about human experiences as the chief ends.

Supervisors of the Brinkman era shared a common hostility against seminaries, seminary faculties and seminary educational policies—in fact, against everything that the conventional religious establishment stood for. Annual Conferences of the Council for Clinical Training were sometimes the occasions for acting out these feelings. Within their defiant behavior was a real earnestness and a searching to find their way toward a style of ministry that would be personally authentic and relevant to the needs of people even though unconventional.[41]

Reuel Howe was deeply involved in the struggle of supervisors to find their way toward a constructive relationship with theological education. As a professor at Virginia Theological Seminary (Episcopal), Howe was liaison between the Council for Clinical Training and his own seminary. A quarter of clinical training was required for graduation at Virginia Theological Seminary. Howe's students numbered, at one time in the late forties, almost 90 percent of all the students receiving summer training under Council auspices. Out of this kind of involvement, and with a profound appreciation of the Council's supervisors, Howe reflected on the problems both he and the supervisors shared—problems of how maturely to carry out the role of pioneer. He said,

We were all the products of a theological education that was highly irrelevant. Many of our teachers were most hostile to any attempts to make theological education relevant. Many of the supervisors were from puritanical churches, and when they discovered some of the insights of modern psychotherapy, they experienced a great sense of liberation from the taboos and moral imperatives under which they had grown up. They broke free into a freedom that became sometimes libertine in character. It took them a while to achieve a balance. Gradually, the sense of license disappeared and we began to see a sense of moral responsibility for the things which they represented.[42]

Just as many clergymen of the sixties abandoned the familiar clerical role to become involved in the social and political revolution of the times, so supervisors in the Brinkman tradition of the Council for Clinical Training abandoned familiar stereotypes in search of deeper involvement with people caught up in psychic distress. They gained for their pains more effective methods of psychotherapy and more authentic modes of interpersonal relationships generally.

The decision of many Brinkman era supervisors to move outside the framework of the organized religious community is an index of the character of the times as much as of the religious attitudes of the men themselves. Less than twenty years after the Brinkman era, clergymen motivated by similar concerns were able to organize the American Association of Pastoral Counselors and function as psychotherapists within their original professional identification as pastors. Interestingly, one of the moving spirits in the formation of the American Association of Pastoral Counselors in 1963 was Fred Kuether, who in 1947 succeeded Brinkman as Director of the Council for Clinical Training. Today's certified pastoral counselor utilizes understandings and methods of ministry fundamentally akin to those hammered out by the supervisors of the Brinkman tradition. Insofar as Reichian principles have been reinterpreted by Gestalt Expressive therapists, pastoral counselors (and other psychotherapists) may function with full legitimacy today in ways that many even within the psychiatric community considered illegitimate only two decades before.

Brinkman lived out his commitment to the clinical training of theological students during the Council's most severe crisis in 1940-41. In 1938 Dunbar and the Board began maneuvering to change the fundamental character of the Council for Clinical Training into a training agency for students of all the professions in the interests of mental health. Boisen and Beatty pulled out their Chicago Council for the Clinical Training of Theological Students in 1939 in protest against what they felt to be Brinkman's leadership away from the training of theological students. When the financial crisis hit, Brinkman and the supervisors who remained showed their true colors. They opposed the redefinition sought by Dunbar and assumed responsibility for the Council when the non-supervisors on the Board of Governors decided to dissolve the Council for Clinical Training.[43]

The financial crisis occurred upon the sudden and unexpected decision by the Whitney Foundation to terminate its financial support of the Council for Clinical Training. Income at the central office dropped instantly from approximately $8,000 to $3,500 in September, 1940. The Board faced 1940-41 with a debt of $3,000 and almost no cash on hand. Dunbar engaged the services of R. S. Rubinow as financial consultant. Supervisors were asked to approve the charging of tuition for clinical training in the amount of fifty dollars per quarter, and plans were made to appeal for emergency aid from the seminaries.[44] Though seeking to raise $6,000, the Council received only $1,175 from the Seminaries.[45] By February, 1941, Rubinow's relationship to the Board of Governors had soured. Instead of helping the Council he was demanding payment of his own fees. Dunbar was pushing hard for the implementation of plans to become a mental health training agency and on this basis to seek new foundation support. Feverish efforts to save the Council proved futile. Charles J. Symington proposed to the Board of Governors in its meeting of February 14, 1941, that the Council for Clinical Training be dissolved.[46]

In March, 1941, Brinkman brought forward a plan to save the Council based on tuition, membership fees, and scholarship grants from church boards and seminaries. On April 24, 1941, in a joint meeting of supervisors and the Board of Governors, matters came to a head. The supervisors stated their conviction "that the chief problems recently, as in the past, lay in the lack of clarity or centralization in the administrative arrangement." By these words they meant that Brinkman's hands had been tied by Dunbar and Rubinow in particular. They forced a showdown with Rubinow, decisively removing him from the decision-making process. They next spoke to the proposed redefinition of the objectives of the Council. As recorded in the minutes of the Administrative Committee:

They expressed conviction that many of the Council's problems were related to the fact that it had tried for so long to please too many groups, and their further conviction that the recently expressed intention to broaden the program so as to include students of all professions and other qualified graduate students in nearly all fields was an added step in the wrong direction. . . . In addition, they made known their personal feelings that as clergymen equipped especially for training other clergymen, it would be out of harmony with both their professional task and their specific training to spend any great portion of their time helping to prepare students of non-religious professions.[47]

Finally the supervisors offered to assume responsibility themselves for the direction and support of the Council should the members of the Board of Governors be unsuccessful in their efforts to keep the organization afloat.

This is precisely what happened. On June 6, 1941, the Board voted to terminate all expenditures. On June 13 the Administrative Committee was dissolved, and all authority was turned over to an Executive Committee composed of supervisors. The new regime was organized by July 10, 1941, with Thomas J. Bigham, Jr., as chairman of the Executive Committee and Brinkman as "Director, with full executive powers." [48] The supervisors inherited a bankrupt organization, but they did so with large reserves of dedication and a readiness to pay the price in dollars as well as in effort to save the Council for Clinical Training.

One of Brinkman's immediate needs was to get free from the domination of Dunbar, who had been appointed Medical Consultant to the Executive Committee. Brinkman enlisted the services of Augustus S. Knight, M.D., a strong and responsible man who had been chairman of the Board of Greystone Park but was then retired. Knight overruled Dunbar regularly and from this point on she lost the dominant position she had long held in Council affairs.[49]

In spite of these adversities, the Council held its own during the years of World War II. The number of its training centers remained approximately twenty, and the number of students trained remained constant at approximately seventy each summer. Supervisors supported the central office with student fees and their own meager funds. Brinkman's popularity waxed and waned. He neglected correspondence with the supervisors. During the intervals between Conferences, the supervisors would build up resentments against Brinkman. At the next spring or fall conference Brinkman would woo them back into friendship and loyalty. Then the cycle of resentment would begin over again for lack of adequate correspondence from the central office.

Brinkman was functioning without a staff, however, and with a steadily increasing amount of unpaid salary on the books.[50]

The Brinkman tradition was, like the Hiltner tradition, committed to a professional model for theological education. In contrast, however, the Brinkman tradition was concerned primarily to build ministry on a foundation of psychiatric personality theory, no matter how radical this seemed to be nor what was lost of the traditional pastoral image. Science and religion were related within the Brinkman tradition by assimilating theology into science. As Bigham put it, in addressing the 1944 National Conference, "the Council is for a contemporary and Christian humanism." [51]

Bingham analyzed the history of the Council for Clinical Training and by analogy the biographical histories of some of the Council's supervisors as follows:

I seem to find, first, a feeling for the need, not met in theological education, for acquaintance with and explanation of the profundities of life; then a period of absorption in the professional concerns of medicine and psychiatry and penology to the exclusion in part of pastoral and parochial concerns; but lastly and at present a quickening interest in the fullness of the pastoral life and office with the inclusion of all the insights gained from the modern study of psychology and sociology—in brief, a true pastor in the modern world.[52]

Perhaps the simplest characterization of the differences between the Hiltner and Brinkman traditions is that the Hiltner tradition emphasized the third stage of the above process so much that the first and second stages were sometimes experienced only superficially, whereas the Brinkman tradition sought immersion in the first and second stages of such a radical and thoroughgoing sort that some ministers were delayed in moving on to the third level of pastoral identification, or were diverted into other professions.

Witness to the educational effectiveness of supervisors during the Brinkman administration of the Council is found in a doctoral dissertation completed at Teachers College, Columbia University in 1947. Studying "Some Clinically Trained Ministers and the Programs of Their Churches," Maria Brick used a sample of six clergymen. Three men, called Group A, received training after 1937; three men in Group B received training between 1933 and 1936. Group B had received only one quarter of training, while Group A had all received some advanced work. Brick concluded that the men in Group A "showed sound diagnostic knowledge, good case work techniques and an assimilation of their knowledge into the total realm of their pastoral activities." Group B, in contrast, "showed diagnostic misconceptions, misuse or avoidance of case work contacts and merely an academic use of psychological knowledge." [53] The differences between Brick's two groups are related to the differences between introductory and advanced training more than to the quality of work done during the Hiltner and Brinkman periods. Her findings constitute, nevertheless, solid evidence of the positive values in the Brinkman tradition of clinical training.

A final qualification is in order before the discussion of the Brinkman tradition is complete. The Brinkman tradition was dominant from 1938 to 1946, but it was never altogether synonymous with the Council for Clinical Training. Hiltner helped establish training at the University of Michigan Hospital in 1936-37, and a Michigan Committee of the Council for Clinical Training, Inc., was founded in 1937. This program, under supervisor John Bell, embodied the features of the Hiltner tradition. Analyzing his program in a doctoral dissertation at Teachers College in 1942, Bell argued against the psychotherapeutic emphases prevailing in the Council for Clinical Training at that time and defined his program as one that was seeking to add a vocational training dimension to theological education.[54] Other Council programs that developed in direct affiliation with seminaries reflected seminary concerns more consistently than centers geographically removed from the schools.[55] In the main, however, it is accurate to characterize the Hiltner and Brinkman traditions as I have done, so long as we realize that each supervisor and training center had its own unique character within larger trends of the Council for Clinical Training as a whole.

When we measure the Council under Brinkman by the criterion of development from "movement" to "profession" and when we use the present form of the profession as a norm, we must say that the Council's growth was delayed during the early forties. The New England group, in contrast, enjoyed a growth spurt during the same period. We go next to Boston and the story of the Guiles wing of the movement.

5

THE NEW ENGLAND GROUP

The New England group centered in Boston and grew on a Guiles-Cabot axis. Guiles and Cabot appear to have been in agreement with regard to clinical pastoral training during the thirties. The New England group was, as I have suggested, congruent with the Hiltner tradition as it developed in the Council for the Clinical Training of Theological Students.

Under the Earhart Foundation from 1932 to 1937, the New England group multiplied centers in general and mental hospitals, in a prison, and a Tuberculosis Sanatorium. Seminary sponsorship increased from Andover Newton in 1931 to include by 1936 Boston University School of Theology, Harvard Divinity School, and the Yale, Bangor, and Tufts schools of theology. Andover Newton, Boston, and Harvard were granting credit toward theological degrees for part-time clinical training conducted during the academic year 1936-37. The training of new supervisors was being done by Russell Dicks primarily in Massachusetts General Hospital with the assistance of Guiles and support from a Cabot Trust. The supervisors offering year-round training, in addition to Dicks, were David Hunter at the State Infirmary at Tewksbury and Alex Dodd at Boston City Hospital during 1936-37. The New England group had seven centers and offered training to thirty students in the summer of 1936. Developments under the Earhart Foundation prior to 1938 parallel those of the Council for Clinical

Training under Hiltner in the multiplication of the number and types of training centers and the establishing of new affiliations.

Guiles was personally responsible for adding a pastoral counseling dimension to the work of the New England Group in the early thirties. In 1931 he opened a pastoral counseling center at the Wellesley Hills Congregational Church and in 1933 another center in the Old South Church, Boston. These centers were operated under the auspices of Andover Newton Theological School and were staffed by Guiles and students whom he selected and supervised.[1]

When the Brinkman era began in the Council for Clinical Training, Guiles and Cabot launched a second phase of the New England program. A new name was chosen—the New England Theological Schools Committee on Clinical Training. With the name change, the role of the seminaries increased and the types of centers being used decreased. Andover Newton, Harvard Divinity, and Episcopal Theological School constituted the Committee initially. Later the Boston University School of Theology was added.[2] General hospitals were used almost exclusively after 1937-38. David Hunter indicated that the move toward concentration on general hospital centers was designed to allay the anxieties of seminary officials who were distrustful of psychiatric environments for theological learning. It was associated with a change of focus in which supervisors attempted to demonstrate the relevance of clinical training to the total range of pastoral functioning rather than simply to the pastor's work with the sick.[3]

The effort to bring clinical training under the control of theological schools and to preserve a distinctly pastoral orientation became the distinguishing mark of the work in New England. By a pastoral orientation is meant: (1) the cultivation of traditional pastoral identity, and (2) relatively less attention to psychiatric personality theory than to methodological innovation in the training of seminarians and clergy.

In 1938 the Cabot Club was organized in Boston. It was a professional organization composed of persons active in clinical pastoral training. The Cabot Club organized with Cabot's blessing upon the use of his name, and of course with Philip Guiles and his associates as its core. Guiles described the Cabot Club as a group of teachers, hospital chaplains, pastors, and students in Boston and Hartford "who have trained under the method originated by Richard C. Cabot, and who meet each fortnight through the fall, winter and spring for

55919.
the reading and discussion of a clinical study presented by some member." [4]

The Cabot Club Method, as it was called in the New England group, was a forerunner of the pastoral case conference familiar in every clinical pastoral education program today. Participants paid close attention to the psychodynamics of the cases reviewed; they debated counseling theories and consistently engaged in the discipline of theological thinking about persons in crisis situations. Detailed minutes were kept by the secretary of the Club containing "verbatim" accounts of the comments of every club member along with the initial presentation on the patient or counseling client.

In the minutes for May 2, 1944, I discovered that Guiles brought to the club a husband and wife with whom he had been engaged in marriage counseling. The club members interviewed the couple during the meeting focusing on their experience as clients and their evaluation of the counseling experience. This is but one of many examples that could be presented of the way in which the Cabot Club nourished the growing edge of its members and led, as well, to a sense of need for a more inclusive and durable professional organization.[5]

The emergence of self-consciousness of the new profession may be traced by examining the papers read before the annual conferences of supervisors from 1936 to 1943. Longing for the maturity of a professional group was more evident in 1936 than were the signs of its achievement. Cabot defined the intellectual task before the group as the task of rebuilding theology out of cases. Dicks called for the development of a literature in pastoral care, and Guiles exhorted his students to be faithful to their newly acquired skills of consultation with other professional people and clinical reading. He encouraged them to rebel against traditional methods of teaching in order to recover the curiosity of the scientist and thus inaugurate a new day for "the profession of religious ministry." [6]

By the conference of 1941, supervisors were calling for the development of a pastor's manual that would incorporate the learnings from clinical training applicable for general pastoral work. Papers were read on the value of clinical training for preaching and for involvement in rural cooperatives. Some were urging that clinical training be developed in parish settings because they did not see Boston hospitals providing learning approprate to ministry in small-town situations. Dodd discussed "Clinical Training and Theology," and Guiles gave "Suggestions from Recorded Experience for a Clinical Psychology of Religion." David Eitzen proposed the incorporation of a "National Association of Teachers and Supervisors in Clinical Ministry." Both Eitzen and Dicks, who returned for this conference, urged the advantages of a professional organization with formal memberships, regular newsletters, and standardized accreditation procedures.[7]

A Second Biennial Conference of Workers in Clinical Religion was held by the New England Group, May 31–June 2, 1943. Seward Hiltner presented a study of "Pastoral Theology in the Schools," which was later published in the proceedings of the first National Conference on Clinical Pastoral Training. Eitzen presented a paper on "Salvation," and Rollin Fairbanks reported some creative innovations in teaching methods that stand in the Dicks tradition. Fairbanks developed "dual calling" in which the supervisor accompanied the student in making pastoral visits upon patients in a general hospital. He also originated what he called "the controlled interview"—familiar today as role playing. So stimulating was this conference, and so fully had the supervisors adopted the image of a new profession, that enthusiasm was high for calling a national conference that would take an initial step toward the unification of the entire field—a field that was being described regularly not as clinical training, but as clinical work or as clinical pastoral training.

On January 28, 1944, the New England group was reorganized again—this time in a legally incorporated body, the Institute of Pastoral Care, Inc.

Two newcomers to Boston were the co-founders of the Institute of Pastoral Care. They were Rollin J. Fairbanks and Paul E. Johnson. Fairbanks was a graduate of Episocal Theological Seminary in Cambridge and received clinical training at Worcester State Hospital and Massachusetts General Hospital. He held pastorates in Michigan where he gained distinction in the field of labor mediation. He returned to Boston to become chaplain of Massachusetts General Hospital, succeeding David Hunter, who had previously succeeded Russell Dicks. Fairbanks and Johnson wrote the first draft of the constitution together as they launched the Institute of Pastoral Care, Inc. Fairbanks served as its Executive Director from 1944 until 1950.[8]

Paul Johnson received his Ph.D. from Boston University in 1928 after serving a term as a missionary educator in China. He remained in college work as a Director of Guidance and as Dean and Professor of Philosophy at Morningside College in Sioux City, Iowa, prior to returning to Boston University School of Theology in 1941. He was deeply involved in clinical pastoral training and related concerns by 1943 as we shall see.[9] Both Fairbanks and Johnson enjoyed the resources of Cabot and Guiles as they began their work. Fairbanks was supported by funds from two Cabot Trusts plus a small subsidy from a seminary affiliation.[10] Johnson received financial support from Guiles to establish clinical training at Boston University School of Theology.[11]

The plan that was under discussion in the fall of 1943 called for an expansion of the New England Theological Schools Committee on Clinical Training to include annual meetings, more centers, approval by the American Association of Theological Schools, the publication of a journal, the establishment of archives, and a research library of case material. The name for the expanded organization was suggested by the Right Reverend Norman B. Nash, then Episcopal Bishop of Massachusetts. Bishop Nash was a patient at Massachusetts General Hospital. Chaplain Fairbanks took the occasion to discuss these matters, and Bishop Nash suggested the phrase "pastoral care." The word "Institute" was added subsequently.[12]

The wish to publish a professional journal was a large factor in motivating the plans for an enlarged and formalized organization.[13] Hiltner offered to implement the idea of establishing a journal through the Commission on Religion and Health of the Federal Council of Churches, of which he was Executive Secretary. Johnson favored Hiltner's plan, but Guiles leaned toward publishing under the auspices of the New England group.[14] The journal became a kind of status symbol both to the New England group and to the Council for Clinical Training. It was an obvious indication of having passed beyond the stage of "movement" to that of "profession." Within a few months of each other in 1947 the Council for Clinical Training launched the *Journal of Clinical Pastoral Work,* and the Institute of Pastoral Care published its first issue of the *Journal of Pastoral Care.* Competition between the New York City and Boston centers was clearly motivating these publication ventures.

Guiles' home was the scene of the final decision to form an Institute of Pastoral Care. Johnson's notes of the meeting, under the date of January 13, 1944, reflect some of the motives operative in making the decision: (1) a sense of competitiveness with the Council for

Clinical Training, Inc.; (2) pride in the distinctiveness of the New England group; (3) hope for the eventual establishment of a national organization including all groups engaged in clinical pastoral training; and (4) the wish to publish a journal in Boston rather than to allow Hiltner to do so in New York City.[15]

When incorporation papers were signed on January 28, 1944, creating the Institute of Pastoral Care, a Board of Governors was formed, "made up of representatives of the four participating theological schools, the two Foundations, the Earhart Foundation and the Ella Lyman Cabot Trust, the Massachusetts General Hospital, the Massachusetts Council of Churches and the Federal Council of Churches." Its purpose: "To organize, develop and support a comprehensive educational and research program in the field of pastoral care, with special reference to the sick, using the opportunities offered by clinical training as a primary means to this end." [16] Standards for clinical training contained four requirements: the work shall be of a *pastoral* nature; it shall be done *under supervision*. It shall be *recorded* and the notes *submitted for criticism*. Preference for general hospital centers was stated explicitly. The supervisor was termed a Director of Clinical Training and required to be "an ordained clergyman with parish experience who will have had a minimum of two periods of clinical training under qualified direction." [17] No stipulations were made concerning the length or location of the two required periods of training. This gave rise to serious reservations by supervisors in other groups about the qualifications of Institute of Pastoral Care "directors." The pastoral orientation and the preference for general hospital settings were stressed to such an extent that these items also remained issues between the Institute of Pastoral Care and the Council for Clinical Training in succeeding years.

Fairbanks became the first Executive Director of the Institute of Pastoral Care, Inc. He launched a Summer School at Massachusetts General with thirty-four students enrolled in two six-week terms. During the academic year 1944-45, he conducted an inter-seminary seminar on psychiatry at his hospital with fifteen students representing four schools.[18] On March 6, 1945, Fairbanks announced to the Board of Governors that the Cabot Trust had established a "Clinical Fellowship in Pastoral Care." The following November it was awarded to James Burns.

Burns is mentioned in this connection because he was to become the next Executive Director of the Institute of Pastoral Care. In 1945, he was engaged in graduate work under Paul Johnson and was serving as Fairbank's assistant chaplain at Massachusetts General Hospital. Two months after the award was made to Burns, Fairbanks wrote Johnson expressing his concern that Burns was engaged in nonpastoral care studies at the seminary. Fairbanks saw the fellowship in terms of chaplaincy service. Johnson maintained that the fellowship was degree-oriented. Language studies and other nonpastoral subjects were appropriate, therefore. The resolution of the matter in favor of Johnson helped to set the pattern that has prevailed in most seminary-related centers.[19] Three centers of leadership initiative were emerging within the Institute by 1946—one in Fairbanks-Burns, another in Johnson, and the third in Guiles-Billinsky. These alignments remained relatively stable for about a decade.

Early in 1946 Fairbanks organized the Board of Governors into committees. Johnson was chairman of the Committee on Graduate Study along with Guiles and Fletcher. These men launched vigorous plans to encourage qualified men to seek advanced degrees in research-oriented programs. Fairbanks presented plans designed to make the Institute of Pastoral Care financially independent of the Cabot Trust. New self-supporting training centers were projected, along with a full-time salary for the Executive Director and the perennial dream: the publication of a journal.

In the summer of 1946, Fairbanks expanded his work at Massachusetts General Hospital to include seven course assistants. Guiles told the Institute's supervisors in the fall of 1946 that his own concerns were shifting toward "clinical theology," and he called for major attention to be paid to problems of *quality* rather than of quantity in clinical pastoral training.[20] As the year 1946 came to a close, the Institute established a pastoral counseling center at St. Paul's Cathedral in Boston. In all these matters, the Institute of Pastoral Care clearly identified itself as a group that had turned the corner from "movement" to "profession."

As World War II came to an end, clinical pastoral educators felt the stimulus of new demands for clinical training and for competence in more specialized forms of pastoral counseling. Whereas some Council for Clinical Training supervisors, including Brinkman, responded to these new needs by going into psychotherapy on a full-time, private practice basis, the Institute of Pastoral Care responded by establishing a pastoral counseling center in connection with an inner-city Episcopal church. The relationships between the Institute's Board and their counseling center and between Council supervisors and programs like the American Foundation of Religion and Psychiatry are curious and may be studied as the history unfolds. Many of the issues that are very much alive between clinical training and pastoral counseling groups in the sixties were present in the history from 1946.

Before leaving the era of separatism for that of unification, we must take note of an event that symbolized more adequately than any other single happening the transition between the two historical periods. This event was the first National Conference on Clinical Training in Theological Education, June 6-7, 1944.

The First National Conference on Clinical Training, 1944

Interaction between the New England group and Seward Hiltner of the Federal Council of Churches produced the first National Conference on Clinical Training. The Conference reflected a growing identification as a profession of educators who had something significant to contribute to church and seminary. Hiltner engineered the Conference at a most propitious time. It met in juxtaposition with the American Association of Theological Schools at Western Theological Seminary in Pittsburgh, June 6-7, 1944. All the major groups and traditions within the several groups were represented. Joseph Fletcher spoke for the Graduate School of Applied Religion; the Council for Clinical Training and the newly formed Institute of Pastoral Care were well represented, and so were the theological educators. Almost as many seminary deans and professors attended as chaplain supervisors.

Hiltner evaluated the Conference as "another sign that the training is coming of age." [21] Clinical training was coming of age as a new thrust in theological education—a thrust toward pastoral training on a professional model of education. The proceedings were published under the title *Clinical Pastoral Training,* and the definitions accepted by the conference stressed the goals of achieving pastoral identity in doing pastoral work.[22] As the Conference unfolded, continuity with Keller, Cabot, and Boissen became apparent. The professional training goals of Cabot were more in evidence than the social engineering or research goals of Keller and Boisen, but continuity with all three of the founders was affirmed and demonstrated.

106

Another sign of the "coming of age" was the way the participants took responsibility for understanding their own fragmentation and their identity as an emerging profession of educators. Hiltner commented on this in his conclusion to the published proceedings, saying,

it is the first conference on clinical training . . . which has brought honest disagreements into the open and yet has avoided acrimony . . . there has been no attempt . . . to suggest that complete uniformity or organic union be achieved now or in any foreseeable future within the clinical training movement. Yet there has been agreement that cooperative relationships must be maintained now that they have been established, and that there needs to be a representative group conferring together on additional specific points at which cooperation is possible.[23]

The Conference became, then, the pivot point for clinical pastoral education in turning from separatism to unification. Many battles remained to be fought before a conscious intention to unify the field would gain widespread acceptance. But in the 1944 Conference the vision of unification was seen, and it could not again be forgotten. The direction for the next two decades was set, as the next chapters will show.

A Summary Evaluation

Before looking forward, however, a backward look and a summary evaluation is indicated. The whole period from 1930 through 1946 was an era of separatism. Keller and Fletcher developed their program in Cincinnati without regard to what was happening on the Eastern seaboard. Guiles and Dunbar split, and clinical training developed autonomously and competitively with centers in Boston and New York City. Within the Council for Clinical Training, Boisen pulled out altogether with his Chicago Council for the Clinical Training of Theological Students, Inc. Subregional Councils formed in Michigan and Philadelphia, too. While they remained more closely related to New York City than the Chicago group, they, too, were somewhat autonomous and had discernible philosophical differences during the early forties. Separatism is perhaps inevitable in the "movement" stage of any new venture. Strong leaders provide needed integration and objects for identification. The intimacy of an ingroup that lives on a face-to-face basis provides needed emotional nurture. The resulting competitiveness with outgroups stimulates creative innovation and bestirs a group to expand its sphere of influence.

I am struck also by the success of the entire movement. Clinical training centers increased from four in 1930 to nearly thirty by 1944. The number of students trained in all these programs is unknown, but a conservative estimate would be two thousand students. Seminary participation increased from two to sixty-five within the Council for Clinical Training alone. Counting New England and Cincinnati, the number would be closer to seventy-five schools affiliated to some degree with clinical pastoral training by 1946,[24] In addition to statistical evidences of success, the movement developed multiple types of centers enabling men to train in general, mental, and specialized hospitals, and in penal and correctional institutions. Training periods grew from summer terms to year-round internships in several centers, with generous scholarship support available in a few instances.

Several traditions have become clear as personality clashes were wrapped in issues. Ideological polarization occurred initially within the Council for Clinical Training, but by 1944 differences were associated with the Council and the Institute of Pastoral Care respectively. What I called the Hiltner tradition in the Council characterized the New England group as well. Both stood over against the Brinkman tradition. The shibboleths of competition were pastoral vs. psychoanlytic orientations; the valuing of general hospital vs. psychiatric and penology settings; training for general pastoral ministry vs. specialized functioning as chaplains and psychotherapists. The contrasts were between pastoral care and pastoral counseling, between a shepherding and a healing perspective on the minister's work. To a degree the so-called pastoral group were more lax in their diagnostic thinking than the psychiatric group. In the literature of the period, Cabot and Dicks wrote for the general hospital and the pastoral care orientation, Boisen and Wise for the mental hospital and the psychodynamically oriented supervisors. The Hiltner tradition was more articulate about the educational theory underlying clinical training and its relation to theological education than was the Brinkman tradition. Yet Brinkman opened the Greystone Park center to scrutiny by University educators, resulting in at least two doctoral dissertations and five studies by social work students engaged in degree programs.[25] Under the rubric of "clinical theology," the Cabot-Guiles team did their homework in pastoral theology with more relish and hence with more impressive results than any other group in the movement. Looking at all the groups together, the intellectual achievement of the period was substantial and well balanced.

Ecumenicity colored the movement from the first. The Episcopalians were prominent in the Keller program and in offering Cabot the setting in which he developed his idea for a clinical year in theological education. Rollin Fairbanks, the first Executive Director of the Institute of Pastoral Care, was an Episcopal priest as was Reuel Howe. Just as much in evidence were Congregational and Baptist leaders and seminaries. Boisen and the Chicago Theological Seminary, Guiles and Andover Newton were in the vanguard of the movement. Methodists became active in the persons of Dicks, Wise, and Brinkman among the pioneers. Paul Johnson brought the Boston University School of Theology clearly into the picture in the early forties. Cabot was Unitarian, Hiltner Presbyterian, Kuether Evangelical and Reformed, and Cassler Lutheran. Ecumenicity was pan-Protestant but not yet interfaith.

While passing out leadership credits, I want to single out certain farsighted medical and theological statesmen. In addition to Keller, Cabot, and Dunbar, who have been amply discussed, mention should be made again of William A. Byran, M.D., who opened the doors of Worcester State Hospital to Anton Boisen. Lewis B. Hill, M.D., Bryan's assistant administrator, served a vital role on the Council for Clinical Training Board of Governors. Earl D. Bond, M.D. was president of the Council, succeeding Cabot, and Augustus S. Knight, M.D. served with distinction a few years later. Most of the medical men who have contributed substantially to the clinical training movement remain nameless, known to those with whom they worked in local centers, but not to the movement nationally.

Dean Mercer of Bexley Hall, President Herrick of Andover Newton Theological School, President Palmer of Chicago Theological School, and Dean Evans of Philadelphia Divinity School were first among the many seminary deans and presidents who risked supporting actively the bold idea of theological education via the clinic. Arthur Holt and Fred Eastman have become known through Boisen's testimony. They are representative of scores of faculty members who helped to open the doors of the seminaries to clinical pastoral education.

Blue ribbons for the leadership of ministers within the movement go to A. Philip Guiles, who was the most creative spirit in the New England group, and to Hiltner and Brinkman for their leadership of the Council for Clinical Training. Dicks and Wise made substantial contributions both to the literature and to the training of supervisors in the thirties. Reuel Howe deserves to be ranked along with these elder brothers because of the imagination and courage demonstrated in the New Plan of Theological Education, which will be discussed thoroughly in a later chapter. Joseph Fletcher pioneered the first graduate school exclusively devoted to clinical training and developed more highly than any program since that time the social work dimensions of the movement. Beatty, Kuether, Hunter, and Dodd played important roles in the early days. Appearing in significant positions as the period came to an end were Johnson, Fairbanks, Bigham, and Otis Rice (who was chairman of the first National Conference in 1944).

Turning from review and roll call to preview, three trends were clearly in motion as World War II came to an end and a new historical era began. First was a trend toward unification of the field as a new profession of clinical pastoral educators. Second was a trend toward increased impact upon the curricula of theological seminaries. Third was the trend toward specialization, not only as supervisors but also as clinicians in the pastoral care and counseling of persons in crisis experience. Each of these trends was expressly articulated in the papers and discussion of the 1944 Conference. They will be much in evidence as the succeeding chapters unfold.

Part III

The Era of Unification, 1947-1967

6

A BEACHHEAD ON STANDARDS, 1947-1953

The postwar forties were years of consolidation and merger everywhere. The momentum for mergers had been building for a decade. Diverse groups were unified into a national political party under the New Deal, and the labor movement had exchanged the weakness of separatism for the strength of federation in the thirties. World War II pulled up millions of people and forced them out of parochial modes of thought. With the big war over, educators and religionists set about the business of consolidating schools and multiplying the services of universities, transforming a federal into a National Council of Churches, and unifying all manner of charitable services in nearly every city of the land under a United Fund appeal.

Progressivism remained in vogue in education until Sputnik I, and theological educators began to soften in their insistence upon a traditional, classical approach to education for ministry. Neo-orthodoxy had already buried the liberalism of the twenties. Neo-orthodox realism about sin proved to be a belated discovery for many thelogians of the irrationality of unconscious mental processes on which Freud built his understanding of man. Existentialism was the new thing in postwar theology. The language of psychology became the language of theology, too. Even systematic theologians began to struggle with the correlations between sin and neurosis, temptation and anxiety, sanctification and maturation, vocation and individuation. The identity crisis of the times was matched by subjectivism in theology as well as in clinical pastoral education. As rational barriers between the several theologies collapsed, a new level of unity was disclosed.

Clinical pastoral educators found the seminary climate changing rapidly with respect to themselves in the postwar years. The Brinkman-type stance was less and less appropriate. Suspicion and hostility on the part of theological faculties toward clinical supervisors gave way to appreciation. A number of clinically trained men became seminary professors in the forties and early fifties. Fletcher moved from the Graduate School of Applied Religion to the Episcopal Theological School in Cambridge in 1944; Guiles and Johnson were already established at Andover Newton and Boston University School of Theology respectively. Oates became an instructor in the psychology of religion at Southern Baptist Theological Seminary in 1945; Dicks, Hiltner, Mahnke, and Wise joined the faculties of Duke, Chicago, Concordia, and Garrett respectively in 1948. Fairbanks went full-time at the Episcopal Theological School in 1951; Westberg received faculty appointment at Chicago in 1952; Billinsky succeeded Guiles at Andover Newton in 1953.

The fullness of the time had surely come in the postwar years for clinical pastoral education to emerge from a movement into full professional identity. Pastoral counseling skills were becoming increasingly salable in churches as in society generally. Both the Council for Clinical Training and the Institute of Pastoral Care established professional journals in 1947 and merged them in 1950 under the title *Journal of Pastoral Care. Pastoral Psychology* was launched by Doniger with Hiltner as consultant in 1950. Dicks edited *Religion and Health* for a few years in the early fifties. The literature of the field began to grow rapidly with Dicks, Hiltner, Johnson, Oates, and Wise publishing basic textbooks in pastoral care and counseling. Roy Burkhart stirred excitement in the Protestant world by his "full guidance" concept of church programming at First Community in Columbus, Ohio. The alliance of Peale and Blanton issued in the formation of the American Foundation of Religion and Psychiatry in New York City. Kuether, who was Director of the Council, became consultant to the American Foundation's clergy training and pastoral counseling services in 1950. In 1952 the Danielson Pastoral Counseling Center was established in the Boston University School of Theology.

Medical recognition of the value of clinical training for institutional chaplains was symbolized in the formation of the Chaplain's Section of the American Protestant Hospital Association in 1946 and the Association of Mental Hospital Chaplains, meeting concurrently with the American Psychiatric Association, in 1948. Billinsky and Dicks were the founding fathers of the former, and Bruder of the latter group. Both groups moved rapidly into the mainstream of their respective professional communities, winning recognition for their own standards not only in guiding ecclesiastical groups in the proper recognition of chaplains but also influencing hospitals in their establishment of employment policies.

In a new climate of acceptance and with merger and consolidation in the American air, what happened to the Council for Clinical Training and the Institute of Pastoral Care? What was the character of the postwar leadership in clinical pastoral education? Brinkman went into the private practice of psychotherapy, and by 1953 Guiles was gone, the victim of an untimely death. Postwar leaders were Kuether, Rice, Bigham, Bruder, and Plack in the Council, and Fairbanks, Billinsky, Johnson, Burns, and Leslie in the Institute. These two groups and others appearing for the first time in the fifties were impelled into dialogue. For what purpose did they come together? Were they seeking full organic unity or merely control of the fast-breaking developments in the field?

By 1957 it was generally conceded that "Clinical Pastoral Education is a field of theological endeavor which no longer needs to prove itself, but must now struggle to consolidate the many and rich gains achieved over the years." [1] In order to tell this story of the "struggle to consolidate" we must turn from generalities to specifics. In addition to a colorful kaleidoscopic scene, we shall be looking for the organizational processes and the personal factors that constituted the dynamics of change from separatism to unification in the life of an emerging profession. The experience of clinical pastoral education may add something, thereby, to the social psychology of all professions and be instructive for other movements facing the same stage in their own development.

The Committee of Twelve

The search for standards that would unify the field of clinical pastoral education began in October, 1951, at the Second National Con-

115

ference on Clinical Pastoral Training and culminated in the adoption of national standards on October 13, 1953, at the Fourth National Conference on Clinical Pastoral Education. Members of the Lutheran Advisory Council on Pastoral Care called together leaders of the Council for Clinical Training and the Institute of Pastoral Care during the 1951 Conference in Boston. Those who met at that time were: Charles Bachmann, Frederic Norstad, and Carl Plack of the Lutherans; John Billinsky, James Burns, Paul Johnson, and Joseph Fletcher of the Institute; Fred Kuether, Otis Rice, and Ernest Bruder of the Council; and David Roberts, professor of theology from Union in New York, as a concerned spokesman for theological education. In writing a historical note on the Committee of Twelve, Bruder said:

This gathering was representative of the trend of the times. Though expressed overtly in the Lutheran councils, it was a sign of the growing interest on the part of many communions equally concerned about the preparation of men for the pastoral ministry. Hence, the men who gathered in Boston that night in October, 1951, represented those who were "actively concerned" about clinical pastoral education. . . . There is seldom given to men an opportunity as stimulating as the assignments we have undertaken in the Committee, which have covered much of our basic area of involvement—and in the company of men who, though from extremely diverse religious orientations, could work together harmoniously for the common good.[2]

The Committee of Twelve was composed of three persons from each of four participating groups: the Council for Clinical Training, Inc.; the Institute of Pastoral Care, Inc.; the Lutheran Advisory Council; and the Association of Seminary Professors in the Practical Fields. Since two representatives of clinical training groups also wore hats as representatives of the Association of Seminary Professors in the Practical Fields, the actual membership was ten. The Committee met eight times from 1951 to 1957 with the following goals in view: the formulation of standards that would be acceptable to all groups in the field; the sponsorship of national conferences; and the search for ways and means of enforcing standards through a national accrediting agency of some kind.[3]

The Lutheran Advisory Council on Pastoral Care

Lutherans were awakened to the clinical training movement because their investments in two areas were at stake. They had long-term investments in general hospital chaplaincies which were challenged by clinical training standards, and they had deep investments in a theology that was being questioned radically by many clinical training supervisors.[4]

The way in which Lutheran activity in clinical training was stimulated is illustrated by events in St. Louis. The St. Louis Federation of Churches installed a Council for Clinical Training chaplain supervisor in the City Hospital in 1945, replacing a Missouri Synod Lutheran chaplain. The change resulted from the initiative of Kuether, Associate Director of the Council for Clinical Training. Kuether won the support of Eden Theological Seminary for a Council program. Through the influence of the Evangelical and Reformed ministers, the City Hospital accepted the clinical training program. The Lutherans had held this position for decades prior to 1945. The change called into question their work in the entire hospital field.[5]

Dr. Louis J. Sieck, President of Concordia Theological Seminary, added Edward J. Mahnke to the payroll of the Seminary and sent him off for a year of training under superviors of the Council for Clinical Training. Mahnke received his supervision from Ernest Bruder, William Andrew, and Henry Cassler during the year 1947-48. He returned to Concordia to teach in the fall of 1948. He began giving clinical training in 1949 to institutional chaplains who were already employed in the St. Louis area. These men completed their training with Fredric Norstad in the Twin Cities.[6]

With the organization of the Chaplain's Section of the American Protestant Hospital Association (1946), clinical training standards gained wider acceptance in the general hospital field. By 1949 Lutheran seminary leaders were concerned about increasing evidence that some supervisors in the Council were anti-seminary. Dr. Henry Wind, Executive Secretary of the Board of Social Welfare of the Missouri Synod, began to plan the creation of a clinical training program under Lutheran control for Lutheran chaplains and seminarians. As early as 1945, Dr. Wind corresponded with Dr. Clarence Krumbholz, who was head of the National Lutheran Council. Ultimately, a meeting was planned for those most directly involved. It coincided with the American Protestant Hospital Association's meeting in Cleveland, September 23-25, 1949. The group decided to hold subsequent meetings in order to draw up clinical training standards and clarify policies with the deans and presidents of Lutheran seminaries.[7]

117

Out of this sequence of meetings came the Lutheran Advisory Council on Pastoral Care. The Council was an unofficial group appointed by the National Lutheran Council and the Missouri Synod. It had a threefold objective: (1) to promote interest in clinical training, which is a part of theological education, (2) to assist the Lutheran seminaries in establishing training centers and securing clinical instructors, and (3) to establish standards for clinical training programs while remaining within the limits of a consultative committee for Lutheran theological seminaries.[8]

The Lutheran supervisors who triggered the formation of the Committee of Twelve in Boston (1951) were acting on their own initiative. They were moved to call the meeting by "their knowledge of the developing interest in the Lutheran Church, and the increasing demand that all seminarians and future clergy obtain some clinical training."[9] The Lutheran Advisory Council and its successor, the Department of Institutional Chaplaincy and Clinical Pastoral Education, Lutheran Council in the U.S.A., stimulated so much support for clinical pastoral education that by the sixties Lutheran seminarians were among the most numerous in programs of basic clinical pastoral education. The full impact of this change of attitude toward pastoral training among Lutherans may not be sensed apart from historical perspective. Charles Bachmann wrote a doctoral dissertation in 1949 demonstrating that Lutheran pastoral care in America varied little in goal or method from the time of Luther to the midpoint of the twentieth century. The changes of the past two decades are revolutionary when seen from the perspective of more than four centuries of Lutheranism.[10]

Leaders of the Council for Clinical Training and the Institute of Pastoral Care welcomed the Lutherans' interest in clinical pastoral education and responded positively to their pressure for articulation of national standards. Some were alarmed by the prospect of a new clinical training organization having a denominational rather than an interdenominational identity, but the Lutheran request for consultation and eventual recognition could not be ignored. Leaders of the Lutheran group had been trained in Council and Institute programs. They sought consultation for the development of programs that would measure up to the standards of the older groups. The Lutherans, then, more than any other single group, triggered the formation of the Committee of Twelve and so initiated conversations that were to prove highly beneficial for the field as a whole.

The Association of Seminary Professors in the Practical Field

A second group represented on the Committee of Twelve was the Association of Seminary Professors in the Practical Fields. Hiltner made the first overtures toward professors in the practical fields during the year 1947-48. As Executive Secretary of the Department of Pastoral Services of the Federal Council of Churches, Hiltner initiated a conference of seminary administrators to consider "the practical field in theological education with special reference to pastoral care and counseling." [11]

A crucial decision affecting the relationship of clinical training to the seminaries became explicit during the conference. Lewis Sherrill, who was unable to attend, wrote a letter expressing his opinion that the conference should focus attention on the need for integration of the whole course of theological training and not alone within the practical fields. Hiltner read Sherrill's letter to the conference, agreed with the importance of Sherrill's point of view, but stated that the conference had been called to deal with the smaller question of the integration of the practical fields rather than the larger question of the whole curriculum. Hiltner further stated that those who planned the conference believed that integration of the practical fields was a necessary step toward integration of the entire curriculum.[12]

Hiltner's decision to woo the practical fields as the academic mate of the clinical training movement led quickly to the wedding of the two groups in the Committee of Twelve. By June, 1950, the Association of Seminary Professors in the Practical Fields became a reality and held its first biennial conference. It was only a year later that the Committee of Twelve invited the new Association to be the official voice for theological education in its deliberations.

Clinical training married into an old family when it allied itself with the Association of Seminary Professors in the Practical Fields. It came into the family of theological education. It entered into old rivalries as well as new relationships. It became explicitly involved in the struggle between the classical and the practical fields. It took sides in a debate that dates back to the Kelley study of theological education in 1924. Both possibilities and necessities were realized by this union.

Affiliation with the Association of professors in the practical fields actualized the professional identity of the clinical training enterprise. It fulfilled the promise implicit in Boisen's becoming a lecturer in the department of Social Ethics of Chicago Theological Seminary (1925) and in the department of Religious Education of Boston University School of Theology (1928). Clinical training leaders continued to identify with and find encouragement from the professors in the practical fields more than from those in the classical fields, at least until the sixties. Alliance with the professors in the practical fields eased the pain of feeling separated from the theological community, and it expanded the horizons of clinical training to include the ministry of the church as a whole to persons in every phase of their life and growth.

Formal identification with the practical fields limited clinical pastoral education to affiliation with only one segment of the whole theological community and made more difficult the task of demonstrating the relevance of clinical methods of theological inquiry to classical disciplines. Cabot's original call for a clinical year in theological education was not in support of the special interests of the practical fields. Cabot called for the participation of theological professors from every department of the curriculum in the theological supervision of students in clinical settings. By analogy with clinical professors in medicine, Cabot dreamed of clinical professors of theology and clinical professors of biblical interpretation. As the case studies will show in later chapters, the realization of this goal was attempted in the late thirties at Philadelphia Divinity School but proved to be an acceptable educational method only in a few seminaries seeking deliberately to be in the vanguard of curricular development.

The ultimate outcome of the relationship between clinical pastoral education and theological education as a whole depends in part upon the quality of communication and mutual appreciation between leaders of the practical and the classical fields. Innovative programs excite hope that the strengthening of the practical fields will prove to have been but a single step toward integration of the entire curriculum as Hiltner predicted would be the case when the Association of Seminary Professors in the Practical Fields was formed.

With a vigorous third force—the Lutherans—knocking at the door of the Council and the Institute, and with new seminary allies ready to sponsor clinical pastoral training in seminary curricula, we must ask how the Council for Clinical Training and the Institute of Pastoral Care responded. Where were they in their own internal development in the fall of 1951? Were they ready for cooperation with other groups? For acceptance by theological education? The question is especially apropos for the Council. How could a group largely identified with the Brinkman tradition be seriously involved as allies of seminary professors for example? To answer these questions, I shall review the development of the Council and the Institute in turn from 1947 to the final approval of national standards in 1953.

The Council for Clinical Training, Inc., 1947-53

Frederick C. Kuether succeeded Brinkman as Director of the Council in 1947. The son of a German-speaking minister of the Evangelische Synod von Nordamerika (merged in successive stages into the United Church of Christ), Kuether graduated from Eden Theological Seminary in St. Louis, took clinical training with Boisen at Elgin State Hospital in 1934 and with Dicks at Massachusetts General Hospital in 1935. After a pastorate in Ohio, Kuether joined the vanguard of Council supervisors who entered federal prison chaplaincies. He became in 1937 the first supervisor with benefit of salary at the Federal Reformatory in Chillicothe, Ohio. In 1942 he moved to the St. Charles School for Boys in order to continue graduate studies at the University of Chicago. President Palmer prevailed upon him to become lecturer at Chicago Theological Seminary succeeding Boisen who retired in 1942, and thus Kuether's plan for gradute work was postponed.

Kuether became secretary of the Chicago Council for Clinical Training, Inc., exercising a mediating role between Boisen and the New York office. Brinkman made Kuether his Associate Director during the early forties, and it was in this capacity that Kuether was instrumental in opening positions for Council supervisors in the City Hospital of St. Louis and eventually becoming chaplain, himself, of Cook County Hospital in Chicago (1945-46) under the auspices of the Church Federation of Greater Chicago. In January, 1947, he moved to New York City to become Director of the Council for Clinical Training, Inc.[13]

As Director of the Council for Clinical Training Kuether faced staggering problems. His analysis of the problems included: (1) an ineffective structure. For example, a quorum of the Board of Governors was not present to ratify actions of the Executive Committee for six consecutive meetings, from November, 1946, to early 1948. (2) Chronic financial deficits in an organization that depended upon the fees of students almost entirely. (3) Inadequate selection and training of supervisors. A series of crises involving personality problems of supervisors plagued Kuether's administration in its first few years as we shall see. (4) Poor relationships with seminaries. Kuether described the standing of the Council with seminaries as "very weak." (5) Poor communication from the central office to the supervisors and chronic tardiness in publication of catalogues.[14]

Kuether's attack on these problems consisted initially of a plan "to change the Council from a one-man show, as it was under Brinkman, into a democratic organization." To democratize the Council's administration, he appointed committees and invested a large measure of both authority and responsibility in his fellow supervisors. Kuether then set out to function as a supervisor for the supervisors. He quickly won a place in the affections of most of his colleagues by visiting their training centers regularly and by being particularly sensitive to the needs of the newer men.[15] The inner circle of leadership included Thomas Bigham, Ernest Bruder, Ralph Bonacker, Robert Morris, Carl Plack, Otis Rice, Maurice Riseling, and Hal Wells.

Bigham assumed leadership in financial planning. His success in securing seminary support for the Council from General Theological Seminary in which he was a professor provided an early model for subsequent fund-raising plans.[16] Plans for foundation proposals and an enlarged base of individual support were also formulated for the first time since the financial crisis of 1940-41.[17] Aside from Bigham, the Council's new leadership did not come to the fore until after a critical incident in the fall of 1948.

The incident was created by a supervisor who was also chairman of the accreditation committee. The supervisor was in trouble with his hospital administrator, who asked him to resign in December, 1947. The administrator charged him with incompetence both as a chaplain and as a supervisor. The supervisor maintained his position until September, 1948, by threatening to expose the hospital to Grand Jury investigation. But on September 26, 1948, he called Kuether in New York City stating that he was leaving the hospital the following day and had made no provision for the training of students who were to arrive on the same day.[18]

The issue was joined at Perkiomen, Pennsylvania, during the Fall Conference of 1948. Kuether appointed an Advisory Committee to hear grievances. The offending supervisor was present and was heard at length by his fellow supervisors. Out of an agonizing process, the supervisors who composed the Advisory Committee took responsibility upon themselves and ejected the one in question from the Council. Their decision was based largely on an evaluation of the man personally, but since he was an outspoken advocate of Reichian analysis, the vote to remove him from the Council had the effect of dissociating the Council from this school of analysis more decisively than had been true before.[19]

Supervisors active during the forties recall the conference at Perkioment as the high-water mark of rebellious acting out. No program was planned, and no formal sessions were held. The leadership was preoccupied with the internal struggle caused by their own ambivalence as well as by the behavior of the offending supervisor. The Council had been a fraternity of rebels. The issue at Perkiomen in 1948 was whether or not to become a professional organization.[20]

The decision for professional responsibility was made behaviorally in dealing with the chairman of the accreditation committee. Leadership in standards and accreditation passed to Ernest Bruder in October, 1948. In December, 1948, Otis Rice was asked to become chairman of a committee to study the function, structure, and future of the Council. With Bigham, Bruder, and Rice at the helm of the key committees, Kuether was on the way toward revitalizing the administration of the Council and launching a massive attack on its basic problems.[21]

Rice and his committee brought in a preliminary report on January 21, 1949. The report began with the affirmation that "the institutional training center and the Supervisor are the *sine qua non* of clinical pastoral training. Standards for their selection and certification are, therefore, of greatest importance." The problems facing the Council were found to root in the lack of "close working relationships between individual Supervisors and the theological seminaries." On this matter the report said:

Many Supervisors have felt out of the mainstream of theological education, either because of distance from the seminary or because of lack of understanding between them and the seminaries. For example, many seminaries have sent students for training because they thought clinical training "would straighten them out." Supervisors who could well be used for teaching in seminaries have been passed over for men with little or no clinical experience, but with academic degrees.[22]

Finally the committee faced the issue of relying on student fees for financial support. The solution that was proposed was based on the premise that "the Council cannot properly charge the student a tuition fee, since it does not actually do the training." A schedule was projected on the basis of deriving funds from those who received services. Students were to be charged a five-dollar registration fee and a twenty-dollar certification fee; seminaries were to be charged seventy-five dollars per student, and denominational sources were to be tapped for an additional twenty-five dollars per student.[23] Such a scheme required Council leaders to look beyond themselves and their students for support and necessarily to become answerable to the seminaries and to ecclesiastical leaders from whom the support was to come. The committee's report provided a blueprint for the future, an agenda that occupied the major committees of the Council for the next three to four years.

During 1949 Kuether cut back his functioning as Director of the Council to half time and began doctoral studies at Columbia University. The move was necessitated by the financial limitations of the Council as well as by his educational aspirations. Supervisors continued to function responsibly within the committee structure, however. The Board approved the beginning of negotiations for the merger of their *Journal of Clinical Pastoral Work* (which had been launched soon after Kuether became Director of the Council) with the Institute's *Journal of Pastoral Care*. Affiliations were strengthened with the William Allenson White Institute in New York City and with a group of psychiatrists under the leadership of Lewis Wolberg, M.D. Both groups established the requirement of one quarter of clinical pastoral training for all clergy candidates seeking certificates in applied psychiatry. Ten new seminaries sought membership in the Council; standards were under careful scrutiny by Bruder and his committee; and negotiations were continued with the Institute of Pastoral Care looking for areas of mutually useful collaboration.[24]

Negotiations with the Institute began in 1948. Kuether and Fairbanks presented their respective Boards with a plan for the union of the Council and the Institute under the name "American Institute of Clinical Pastoral Training." [25] Three levels of training were identified. Supervisors would be required to have had a clinical year, plus experience in parish ministry, plus a term as an assistant supervisor, plus an advanced degree in the field of human relations and religion. The proposal was vigorously discussed but finally shelved. Robert Morris expressed the majority view in an Executive Committee meeting on December 13, 1948, saying that the Council should concern itself with its own internal reorganization rather than to attempt to solve its problems externally by affiliating with the Institute of Pastoral Care.[26]

The following year the Council and Institute scheduled their Fall Conferences together at Schwenksville, Pennsylvania. Their purpose was to facilitate the work of a joint committee seeking ways and means of cooperation short of merger. The supervisors brought to the Council's Board a recommendation from the Schwenksville Conference, which the Board adopted on October 24, 1949:

That the Board accept the recommendation of the Conference of Supervisors of the Council and appoint members to a joint committee on clinical pastoral training in cooperation with the Institute of Pastoral Care, with the understanding that this committee is charged to do four things: (1) to plan for ultimate combined catalogue of the two organizations; (2) to plan for a combined journal for the two organizations; (3) to plan for a national conference on clinical pastoral training, inviting all people who can subscribe to the four goals as outlined; and (4) to arrange for another meeting between the Council supervisors and the Institute instructors.[27]

Kuether, Rice, and Bruder were the Council's respresentatives to the joint committee. The goals of the committee were systematically achieved during the succeeding two years, at which time the Committee of Twelve was born.

The period from 1948 to 1953 saw two major accomplishments in addition to those already discussed. The first was the raising of standards, and the second, improvements in seminary relationships. Discussing these in reverse order, we find the first move toward bridging the gap between seminaries and Council for Clinical Training supervisors to be a decision by the Board on March 27, 1950, to hold a meeting in New York City with representatives of six or seven nearby seminaries. The deans and heads of departments of practical theology were to sit down with Council supervisors to seek "the development of strategy for a closer relationship between clinical pastoral training and the theological curriculum and between the Council and the seminaries." [28]

The next move was initiated by Reuel Howe, who set up a series of conferences between the faculty of Virginia Theological Seminary and the Eastern supervisors of the Council. The occasion for this is seen statistically in the fact that by 1949 Episcopal students engaged in summer programs accounted for 64 percent of all students receiving training under the Council. Reuel Howe sent 80 seminarians from Virginia Theological Seminary into Council centers in the summer of 1950. Reports of Perkiomen-type behavior on the part of supervisors, combined with the inevitable increase of student autonomy and sponteneity as a result of clinical training, activated the anxiety of the most loyal among the Council's friends at Virginia Theological Seminary.[29]

Intensive conversation began in Alexandria, Virginia, April 27-28, 1953, and continued during a Thanksgiving conference the following fall and for two more conferences early in 1954. Both supervisors and professors discovered that they did not have to be as afraid of each other as they had supposed. The supervisors began to perceive themselves as participants in theological education. They began to think in terms of the correlation of behavioral science and theology rather than in terms of the assimilation of theology to science. The professors, on the other hand, grew in their trust of the supervisors. This stabilized the seminary's new requirement that all students take a quarter of clinical pastoral training as part of their seminary course.[30] Kuether said that these conferences completed the change from a rebel movement to a profession integral to seminary education for ministry. The supervisors who could not see themselves as a part of theological education moved out into other fields; those who could, stayed in the Council.[31]

Finally, the period from 1948 to 1953 saw substantial progress in raising standards. Bruder became chairman of the standards and accreditation committee in October, 1948, and by November he was proposing, as we have seen, that each supervisor receive a full clinical year and a quarter of training as an assistant supervisor, in addition to meeting stringent requirements for parish experience and for graduate academic degrees.

The gap between the ideal and the real took a few years to close, however. On October 10-11, 1949, the acting supervisors, themselves, proposed that the Board adopt a policy that would merely "encourage everyone to have experience as an assistant supervisor." They further suggested setting the optimum ratio of supervisor to students at one to four. They called for a new item to be added to the confidential report on students, i.e., a report on student-supervisor relationships. They urged as policy that supervisers discuss the reports to the seminaries with the students "before the final draft is written and forwarded to the seminary." [32]

It was April, 1952, before Bruder succeeded in winning approval for a standards document that effectively upgraded supervisory training and functioning. In a sixteen-page document (prepared by the Standards Committee in the spring of 1951) a set of standards was articulated that served as both a goal and a goad for the Committee of Twelve and the respective training groups. The standards hammered out by Bruder and his committee in 1951 provided the structure and much of the substance for standards committees right down to the unification of the field of 1967.

Supervisors-in-training were required by the 1952 standards to be seminary graduates, to be ordained, and to have completed a period of successful parish ministry. Not less than four quarters of clinical pastoral training were required in at least two different types of institutions with at least two supervisors. Personal qualifications were stressed including "skill in close interpersonal relationships" and "a mature and deepening religious philosophy." Emotional and spiritual stability was interpreted to include "a capacity for enthusiasm, a degree of objectivity and personal insight, and . . . the ability to be reasoning and to have convictions without dogmatism." The achievement of such qualities "can in some instances only be attained if the candidate himself undertake psychotherapy." Standards also specified many areas of functional competence. They required the candidate for certification to be evaluated in a personal interview with the accreditation committee. Prior to the interview he must submit "one complete set of notes . . . on conferences with one of the students he has supervised during each quarter that he has been in training as an assistant supervisor." He shall have supervised not less than three nor more than five students at a time.[33]

The 1952 standards remained in force until revised in November, 1957. The 1957 revision differed from the 1952 document in a few details. The requirement of successful parish ministry for certification of a supervisor was omitted. It made possible the revocation of supervisory status by action of the Board of Governors but without a two-thirds vote by the conference of supervisors as stipulated in 1952. The 1957 document did not presume to stipulate how a seminary should evaluate clinical pastoral training for credit. It did not say that the qualities desired in a supervisor "can in some instances only be attained if the candidate himself undertake psychotherapy." The concern voiced in 1952 for emotional maturation by means of psychotherapy has remained strong even though the language of the standards is less specific in subsequent documents.[34]

The Council's adoption of the 1952 standards was significant not only because it strengthened the position of the Council for Clinical Training in the Committee of Twelve but also because it required of Council supervisors that they assume the posture of professional men. They left behind in the limbo of oral traditions and unqualified permissiveness the image of "rebel." In adopting comprehensive standards, the Council entered responsible communication with other clinical training groups, with seminaries, and with the institutions in which training was offered. The Council became committed. It took a position publicly in a way that it had not done since the days of Dunbar and Hiltner.

The Committee of Twelve completed its work on national standards in the fall of 1952. The Board of Governors of the Council for Clinical Training approved the national standards in the fall of 1953 in spite of the fact that many regarded it as a compromise document. In the fall of 1953, the Council enjoyed an advantage over the Institute in the development of standards. The Council was not ready, however, to move from national standards to the formation of a national accrediting agency that would enforce standards. Many supervisors feared that their distinctive emphases would be compromised too much. The recommendation from Kuether, Bruder, and Don Shaw to the Board of Governors of the Council was, therefore, that the Board indicate a desire for "an eventual National accrediting body" and an intention to "work cooperatively to achieve such a body," but that the Board not favor such a body then on the grounds "that the time is not ripe at present." [35]

Bruder continued to quarterback the Council in the Committee of Twelve. He prepared a detailed summary of "questions and concerns" about the projected national accrediting body and prepared for the negotiations that were to continue from 1953 to 1960 before they fell apart on the shoals of frustration and failure.

Before leaving the subject of standards for that of accreditation, we must review developments within the Institute of Pastoral Care leading up to their adoption of national standards. Finally the great debate on standards that occurred in the Committee of Twelve in April of 1952 will be reviewed and analyzed.

The Institute of Pastoral Care, Inc., 1947-53

The late forties saw a burst of growth in the Institute of Pastoral Care. The Summer School enrollment increased from 51 in 1947 to 84 in 1950. Memberships in the Institute soared from 237 in early 1948 to 530 by the end of 1950.[36] Rollin J. Fairbanks, who became Executive Director of the Institute upon its incorporation in 1944, provided leadership that was in the main consistent with the patterns established by Cabot and Guiles in the preceding decade.

As the Era of Unification began for the Institute of Pastoral Care, Fairbanks and the Institute's Board of Governors were struggling with the demand for specialized pastoral counseling services as well as for increased training opportunities in pastoral care. The Board established its first counseling center in cooperation with St. Paul's Cathedral (Episcopal) in downtown Boston. The center opened January 1, 1947, with Henry H. Wiesbauer as chief counselor. Wiesbauer and Burns had become Associate Directors of the Institute on December 3, 1946. They were to work under Fairbanks in the counseling center and at Massachusetts General Hospital respectively. After only ten months, Wiesbauer reported having seen 200 people, plus spending many hours in consultation with ministers and other professional persons. He offered public seminars to which 1,575 persons came, and supervised 35 theological students who did interviewing in the center and made written reports.[37]

Policy differences between Wiesbauer and Fairbanks came into view in the Board in June, 1948. Wiesbauer saw pastoral counseling as a part of general "social services." He wished to build the program of the center on a social work model.[38] Almost immediately thereafter Wiesbauer resigned, and within six months St. Paul's Cathedral had established its own counseling program with a social worker in charge.[39] The Institute's pastoral counseling program found a new home in the Emmanuel Church in Boston and secured financial support from the Episcopal City Mission and the Cabot Trust jointly. A psychiatric model was in evidence, and fees were established on a sliding scale within a year of the move.[40]

Fairbanks attempted next to develop the training dimensions of the counseling center by assigning three seminarians to the staff for periods of three months each. After nearly two years on this basis, a reorganization was clearly in order. Late in 1951 Emmanuel Church offered to take over the service as a part of its own Healing Services, but the Church was not interested in having students on its staff. On December 31, 1951, the Institute of Pastoral Care terminated its venture in the training of pastoral counselors in church-related counseling centers.[41] The following year the need for training pastoral counselors was addressed in the founding of the Danielson Pastoral Counseling Center under the auspices of the Boston University School of Theology.

The Institute of Pastoral Care was in an expansive mood in the late forties. It was thrusting out in many experimental programs in addition to clinical pastoral training in general hospitals. In March, 1948, the Institute co-sponsored a Conference on Religion and Psychiatry at the College of Preachers in Washington, D.C. Other sponsors were the National Committee for Mental Hygiene, the Council for Clinical Training, and the Commission on Religion and Health of the Federal Council of Churches. [42] In April, 1948, the Institute participated officially in an Inter-Professions Conference at Buckhill Falls, Pennsylvania, under a grant from the Carnegie Foundation. Ninety-five persons from five fields participated: law, medicine, engineering, business, and divinity. They centered upon the use of clinical or casework procedures and on the place of values in professional education. In June, 1948, the Institute sponsored clinical pastoral training in a mental hospital center for the first time since 1938 (and for the first time ever since the founding of the Institute of Pastoral Care). Worcester State Hospital re-entered the orbit of the New England group with Al Greene and John Smith as chaplains. In December, 1948, as noted already, the Institute re-established its counseling center on a psychotherapeutic rather than a social work model.

The spirit of the Institute's leaders was both experimental and inclusive of other professional groups. Activities in the postwar years sought a broad base of appeal and tended toward the unification of different but related fields. The "professional" character of the Institute of Pastoral Care continued to be actualized without equivocation. An exclusive spirit and separatist attitudes did not appear in the Institute until there was talk of merger with the Council for Clinical Training, and this came as a by-product of launching a professional journal.

Seward Hiltner was added to the Board of Governors late in 1946 and was assigned immediately to the Editorial Board of the Institute's proposed *Journal of Pastoral Care*. Hiltner, Guiles, and Fairbanks engineered the publication of the first issue late in 1947. Concurrent with its appearance Fairbanks, with Guiles's full support, initiated discussions with the Council for Clinical Training about merging the Institute's *Journal of Pastoral Care* with the Council's *Journal of Clinical Pastoral Work*.[43] The idea of merging journals grew quickly into a consideration of merging the two organizations. Fairbanks and Kuether came up with a plan for organic union in a new organization which they presented to their respective Boards in the fall of 1948. Their hope was to create a new organization that would accept the distinctive emphases of both groups "as equally important." [44]

The fate of merger plans was the same in the Institute of Pastoral Care as we have seen in the Council for Clinical Training. The enthusiasm of the Directors and a few supervisors was dampened by the counsel of other supervisors. In the Council for Clinical Training, Robert Morris based his advice to table proposals for merger on the need to solve internal problems first. In the Institute of Pastoral Care, James Burns became the primary spokesman opposed to merger. His appeal was to protect the distinctive pastoral emphases of the Institute against the psychiatric bias of the Council.

A running debate may be traced in the minutes of the Institute's Board of Governors from December, 1947, to November, 1949. Protagonists were Fairbanks and Burns initially. By 1949 Robert Leslie became an Associate Director along with Burns. Leslie took up Fairbanks' case for openness to the Council for Clinical Training in opposition to Burns.

Fairbanks stressed the need to eliminate overlapping of activities and "the impression of rivalry." He wanted to establish a National Conference on Clinical Training in which the training centers would be semi-independent. Minimum standards would be set by a board of the National Conference. Ample breathing room would be made for the distinctive emphases of both the Council for Clinical Training and the Institute of Pastoral Care in such a plan.[45] Burns expressed concern about the Council's encouragement of supervisors to enter psychoanalysis. He saw this contradicting the pastoral approach of the Institute.[46]

The joint Fall Conference of Council for Clinical Training and Institute of Pastoral Care supervisors at Schwenksville, Pennsylvania, October 10-11, 1949, brought the differences between Burns and Leslie into focus. Burns was offended by the Council supervisors' lackadaisical and disorganized style. He complained that they viewed the conference "as a kind of vacation whereas the Institute representatives went prepared to work." Leslie urged the Institue's Board of Governors to take a positive attitude toward the joint conference in spite of these frustrations. He observed that it was healthy for an organization to have an outside evaluation, and he noted the tendency in the Institute to become complacent with its own ideas and methods. He said that "the Institute would be well-advised to profit by what it learned from the Council's techniques and to increase its own emphasis on working with the students." He favored, therefore, "continuing negotiations with the Council and commented that although the differences were highlighted at the conference, there is probably more agreement than was uncovered there." [47]

The Schwenksville conference resulted in agreement on minimal forms of cooperation, as I have shown in discussing the Council's role in the conference. It deepened distrust of the Council in some Institute supervisors on the basis of the Council's style, standards, and commitments within the field. For other Institute supervisors it proved to be a challenge to explore new methods and to take psychiatric theory more seriously than was then popular in many Institute of Pastoral Care training programs.

The years 1950 and 1951 were a time of troubles for the Institute of Pastoral Care. Contrary to what we might expect from the earlier history, the Institute did not move into the Committee of Twelve without difficulty.

Fairbanks began to withdraw from full-time leadership of the Institute of Pastoral Care in 1948. His teaching commitments at the Episcopal Theological School and the Harvard Divinity School increased during 1948 and 1949. As they increased, he turned over more and more responsibility for the Institute's business to Burns. Fairbanks resigned from his chaplaincy at Massachusetts General Hospital at the end of 1949 and announced his intention of resigning as Executive Director of the Institute as soon as a successor could be chosen during 1950. An interim plan was devised with Leslie and Burns as Associate Directors until November 30, 1950, when Burns was elected Executive Director. Fairbanks became Field Secretary and continued as Managing Editor of the *Journal of Pastoral Care*.[48]

Guiles underwent major surgery in the fall of 1949 and withdrew steadily from Institute leadership from then until his untimely death in the fall of 1953. Friends gave him a testimonial dinner in 1951, and on November 18, 1953, Andover Newton Theological School instituted the Austin Philip Guiles Chair of Psychology and Clinical Training.[49]

The first occupant of the Austin Philip Guiles Chair was John M. Billinsky. Billinsky was active in the New England group from the late thirties. He rose to prominence in the life of the Institute of Pastoral Care in response to the financial crisis of 1950-51. On May 4, 1950, the Board received the unwelcome news that the Cabot Trust would terminate support in the near future. Billinsky stepped into the breach as Treasurer of the Institute and began to wrestle with the problems created by a legacy of incomplete records and poor financial management, as well as the immediate problem of dwindling revenue. He stimulated an administrative reorganization leading to revisions in the Constitution and Bylaws of the Institute. He put the Institute on an austerity budget and initiated a drive for new members. On February 6, 1951, for the first time in four years, the Board received a budget that showed no deficit.[50]

The Board of the Institute of Pastoral Care found some encouragement during this period in the opening of two new centers: Augustana Hospital in Chicago, under Granger Westberg, and Emmanuel Hospital in Portland, Oregon, under George Randolph.[51] Leslie, as chairman of a Committee on Promotion, engaged in long-range planning and brought in an optimistic report early in 1951.[52] In spite of these efforts, however, the fear of organizational extinction was real. The counsel of the timorous was to dissolve the Institute, to turn over their principal activity—the Summer Schools of Pastoral Care—to a seminary such as the Boston University School of Theology, and to rely on the Institutional Committee of the Massachusetts Council of Churches as an advisory board.[53]

The Policy Committee, under the chairmanship of Walter E. Barton, M.D., had other ideas. They challenged the Institute of Pastoral Care to take the offensive. They recommended expanding the functions of the Institute from summer schools to specialized training for institutional chaplains. They proposed the establishment of one-year clinical internships for clergymen who were a few years post-seminary, and graduate degree programs under seminary auspices that would incorporate advanced clinical pastoral education in their curricula. They proposed, furthermore, an aggressive membership campaign with a goal of one thousand members. After a vigorous discussion the report of the Policy Committee was accepted and the membership committee was instructed to get to work on plans for its campaign.[54]

By the time of the Second National Conference on Clinical Pastoral Training, which met in Boston, October 11-12, 1951, the Institute was on its feet again. Billinsky reported a cash balance of over one thousand dollars in the treasury, and the membership drive was taking form. The mood of the Board was optimistic. Before the year was out the Board received an overture from the General Service Foundation concerning a grant to establish a Clinical Fellowship for Pastoral Counselors. A number of promising new supervisors were being introduced to the Board, including Malcolm Ballinger, Granger Westberg, David Belgum, and John Smith.[55]

The Institute of Pastoral Care entered the Committee of Twelve with a positive attitude toward the search for unified standards. At the Annual Meeting in February, 1952, the Institute's delegation was formed. Burns was chairman with Albers, Billinsky, Fletcher, and Johnson as members. The Institute found itself on the eve of the Committee of Twelve discussions in an unenviable position, however. Nothing had been done to upgrade Institute standards since December, 1949. At that time the clinical requirements for a supervisor (called in the Institute a "Director of Clinical Pastoral Training") were merely two quarters of full-time training "including supervised teaching experience." In addition the Director of Training was required to have a graduate theological degree, ordination, denominational approval, and a minimum of three years' parish experience. A Course Assistant needed only one quarter of clinical training or six weeks of training "plus significant professional experience."[56] The contrast between this statement and Bruder's sixteen-page document with which the Council for Clinical Training entered the Committee of Twelve accounts for some of the anxiety that characterized the debate at Buckhill Falls, Pennsylvania, in April, 1952.

The Institute of Pastoral Care endorsed the work of the Committee of Twelve as preliminary reports were made to the Board. The proposed standards were found generally acceptable but were seen as "goals that lie far ahead." The Minutes of the Board reflect a flurry of activity "regularizing supervision" in affiliated centers. A ratio of one supervisor to five or six students was set; tuition fees were made uniform; and approval was given to Ballinger for the first forty-eight-week internship under Institute of Pastoral Care sponsorship at University Hospital, Ann Arbor, Michigan.[57]

Once standards were drafted, attention focused on the question of a national accrediting agency. Immediately concern arose in the Board for a "major enlargement" of the Institute's program. Billinsky activated the concern through the Finance Committee, and Leslie helped to give it form through the work of an *ad hoc* committee on long range problems.[58] The Institute of Pastoral Care, like the Council for Clinical Training, accepted national standards in the fall of 1953, but rejected the idea of organic union for purposes of accreditation.

The response to talk of a national accrediting body within the Institute of Pastoral Care was divided. Burns, speaking as Executive Secretary, offered a basic policy statement on September 16, 1953. He favored organic union with the Council for Clinical Training provided both groups would accept assimilation into the National Council of Churches, Division of Christian Education. He saw theological schools taking over the training of chaplains within the context of master's degree work and stated, therefore, that the Institute's proper work was "training for the parish ministry." Involvement in training beyond the first unit level could be done under Institute auspices "whenever it is possible," provided it is clear to everyone that the goal of training is "to provide a ministry for the church, rather than being primarily concerned with saving the soul of the theologue." Burns's case was based admittedly on the assumption "that the theological student or clergyman who presents himself for training *already* has a vocation and is dedicated to it." [59]

Leslie brought a minority report to the Board on October 6, 1953, urging quite a different type of basic policy for the Institute of Pastoral Care.[60] Supported by Billinsky and an *ad hoc* committee, Leslie pressed for "regional expansion" of the Institute. He envisioned "the emergence of a Federation of Institutes on a national level" with a strong central organization in Boston. Expansion of this type would place the Institute of Pastoral Care in a favorable position for receiving foundation grants. It would foster closer seminary relationships with centers outside the Boston area, and it would, thereby, "preserve the gains" of the Institute over the past several decades.[61] December 1, 1953, the Board of Governors accepted the report of the *ad hoc* committee. In so doing, the Institute of Pastoral Care launched upon a development program that had the effect of strengthening their position in subsequent struggles with the problem of national accreditation.

To summarize the factors precipitating the Committee of Twelve, we have seen the Council for Clinical Training changing from a fellowship of rebels to professionals and the Institute of Pastoral Care emerging from a time of troubles to discover that they were substantially behind the Council in standards development. Neither group was ready for more than limited contact in 1953 because of their preoccupation with internal problems. They were encouraged by the successful merger of their two journals, however, to believe that some kind of merger might be possible eventually. Both clinical pastoral education agencies were under growing pressure from seminary professors generally and from Lutheran supervisors and theological educators in particular to reach a concensus on standards and accreditation. The result was the formation of the Committee of Twelve, a series of meetings and debates, and on October 13, 1953, the final ratification of national standards. This date became, therefore, a milestone marking off the first leg of the journey toward the unification of the field of clinical pastoral education.

The Great Debate About Standards, April 25-26, 1952

The first full discussion of the Committee of Twelve occurred at Buckhill Falls, Pennsylvania, on April 25-26, 1952. The discussion turned into a two-day debate and proved to be such a memorable event in the history of the emerging profession that it merits retelling.

Discussion began at the point of educational philosophy. Participants identified their own viewpoints on clinical pastoral training, and each appealed to his own training program for illustration and for proof. Quickly the group polarized between Council for Clinical Training supervisors, whose identity was in the hospital chaplaincy, and all the others on the Committee, whose most articulate spokesmen were seminary professors of pastoral care. One professor, for example, urged the substitution of the phrase "clinical pastoral education" for the phrase most often on the supervisors' lips, "clinical pastoral training." The word "education" triggered the anxiety of some of the chaplains lest their work be mis-identified with traditional theological education. They felt that the word "training" offered more protection for the distinctive quality of their goals and methods.

Agreement appeared on the point that the crux of clinical pastoral education is supervision, that the setting is less significant than the quality of the supervision. But here the ways parted again. Council for Clinical Training supervisors insisted that quality control required evaluation of the personality structure, the interpersonal competence, and the overall emotional and spiritual health of the candidate for supervision. Others agreed in principle, but insisted that criteria pertaining to subjective factors could not be used in national standards. Only objective criteria were admissible. The objectivists, as I shall call them, kept hammering on the theme that subjective criteria would not be acceptable to the seminaries because theological educators are accustomed to evaluate students and curricula on objective criteria alone. So the battle raged between the objectivists and the subjectivists.

Debate became most intense when two perspectives on pastoral ministry were set over against each other by representatives of the Council for Clinical Training and the Institute of Pastoral Care. The Institute spokesman argued for the shepherding perspective as normative, while the Council spokesman argued for the healing perspective. Their terms were "shepherd of souls" vs. "physician of souls." Arguing for at least one year of clinical training as a minimum, the Council representative warned that psychiatrists were pushing clergymen out of their proper field as "physicians of souls." His antagonist relegated the healing ministry of the clergyman to a specialty interest and asserted that the proper concern of clinical training is educating men to be "shepherds of souls." Then the professors and the Lutheran representatives closed ranks with the Institute of Pastoral Care group. They equated "training" with the healing perspective and "education" with the shepherding perspective. They opted for education and for exclusively objective criteria in any statement of minimum standards.

As passions subsided, mediators in the group appealed for a united front in order to control the ground swell of activity in the clinical training field. To do so required agreement on some kind of minimum standards. Compromise solutions were proposed such as defining the first quarter of clinical pastoral education as fieldwork with advanced units appropriate for those who would specialize in institutional chaplaincy or pastoral counseling. The majority on the Committee of Twelve tended to relegate the education of healers, that is of pastoral psychotherapists, to a peripheral place. They defended the view that only the shepherding perspective is appropriate for the majority of seminarians. As defensiveness dissipated, a professor speaking in the Boisen tradition criticized the entire clinical training movement for not having standards that required graduate professional degrees in pastoral theology and in related disciplines.

The reference to graduate degrees heated up the debate again. Professors urged the recognition of degrees as equivalent to quarters of clinical pastoral training, while the subjectivists protested. Anxieties were heightened by the assumption that the enforcement of standards would be in the hands of a national accrediting agency that probably would be dominated, as the Committee of Twelve was, by the professioral point of view. The fear of an enforcing agency was never faced squarely, however. By common consent the subject of an accrediting body had been postponed in the interest of standards.

Paul Johnson formulated the compromise document that eventually won unanimous approval. In the standards as approved in 1953 objective criteria predominated. As a concession to the subjectivists on the Committee, the standards required "personal qualifications to be appraised by the accrediting committee in a face-to-face interview." Council supervisors won the requirement of "at least one year full-time clinical pastoral education, and in addition, three months of supervised clinical teaching." Institute precedent appeared in the addition of "an adequate period of pastoral experience" to the requirement for ordination and denominational approval. The professors and supervisors alike settled for an equation whereby "six months' credit toward clinical pastoral education may be given for an appropriate Doctor's degree. Three months' credit may be given for an appropriate Master's degree." [62]

Issues in the debate on standards were intensely felt not only at Buckhill Falls. They surfaced wherever chaplain supervisors and pastoral care professors gathered for the next decade. The polarities of hospital-seminary, supervisor-professor, subjective-objective, therapy-education, and healing-shepherding appeared in kaleidoscopic combinations. Subsequently the shepherding and healing perspectives were seen to be only two of many possible perspectives on pastoral work. It became clear that they were not mutually exclusive. The case for pastoral psychotherapy has been made and has won widespread acceptance through the work of the American Association of Pastoral Counselors in the sixties. Both chaplain supervisors and professors of pastoral theology enjoy increased acceptance in the seminaries and find common cause in coping with the challenge to their standards for supervision from educational traditionalists on the right and advocates of action training on the left.

In 1952 the Committee of Twelve failed to find an overarching, unifying understanding of ministry. The field had not become theoretically sophisticated enough in either pastoral theology or educational philosophy. Participants were still too near to the traditional modes of theological education from which they had broken and too unsure of their own distinctiveness as educators to risk claiming boldy that they were educating for the personal maturation as well as the professional competence of seminarians. History has vindicated both the supervisors who argued for frank recognition of the subjective dimensions of learning and the professors who noted the failure of the movement to stress graduate degrees, research, and writing. History has vindicated, also, the compromise document of 1953. It served well for the next fourteen years to set a minimum standard that assured orderly and professionally responsible growth of the field. It established a beachhead for the unification of the field and thereby inspired hope for an eventual unification of the accrediting function —the core function of any professional association.

Accreditation remained to plague, puzzle, and tease the field of clinical pastoral education for the next fourteen years. It is to the frustrating fifties that we turn in the next chapter to understand why proposals of 1956 and of 1960 both failed to find the formula for full and final unification.

7

THE FAILURE OF FEDERATION, 1953-1960

Eight meetings of the Committee of Twelve produced agreement on standards, but eight years of negotiation produced nothing but two stillborn proposals for the enforcement of standards. To understand the failure of initial efforts toward unification, one must understand the feelings associated with accreditation. A high level of anxiety was attached to the word. For clinical pastoral educators the word accreditation referred to the procedures and criteria for the certification of supervisors and the accreditation of centers for clinical pastoral education. Accreditation was the very essence of the new profession.

What was distinctive about the education offered in clinical settings was not the setting itself or the novelty of the experience the student received; not even the teaching methods employed. The essential service of the new profession of clinical pastoral educators was believed to be the nurture of authentic persons free to invest themselves caringly and wisely in the lives of others. The goal could not be achieved unless the supervisor were himself in process toward authenticity. To utilize the supervisory methods of the field effectively, the supervisor must be the recipient of the disciplines he employed. He must understand human behavior and the teaching-learning process to be sure. The best guarantee of a student's becoming free for effective functioning in ministry, however, was the supervisor's own maturity and interpersonal competence.

Accreditation procedures in the fifties carried the hope of the emerging profession that authenticity could be guaranteed for supervisors, at least in part. Not infrequently supervisors referred to the accreditation process by analogy with ordination. Some spokesmen for the field suggested that the accreditation process effected a quasi-mystical change in the candidate. The majority found no need for appeal to mystical meanings in the process. They understood accreditation as a stiff, existentially focused evaluation of the candidate's identity as a ministering person, his interpersonal sensitivity, emotional freedom, and competence as a clinical educator. Lack of precision about what it meant to facilitate psychological growth in one's students may have contributed to the tendency of some to appeal to mystical interpretations.

Many supervisors depended upon clinical training organizations to meet basic emotional and religious needs. Some needed to rebel against tradition and the status quo while engaged in religiously meaningful work. Another need was to grow in self-understanding while mastering the tasks necessary to possession of marketable skills. For others there was the need to belong to a group where each man was known, hazed, and pledged while belonging as well to a larger community of faith and of learning. These were some of the needs the clinical training organizations met for their supervisors.

Whether a group of supervisors saw themselves as a fraternity of rebels or as a religious order of missioners, they uniformly made large emotional investments in their respective groups. The security of these investments was believed to inhere in the accreditation committees of the respective groups. Great importance was attached to the purity of the accreditation committee. It must be composed only of fully accredited members of one's own group, preferably members whose commitment to the organization, whose personal authenticity and demonstrated professional competence was unquestioned. Secrecy was as important as purity. For several years accreditation committees functioned under a heavy veil of secrecy as to both their procedures and their criteria. Efforts to unify the field in the fifties tore open the veil of secrecy but failed to penetrate the barrier of purity. It remained for the sixties to mix the membership of accreditation committes by crossing agency lines. Not until such mixing was mutually and freely done did the profession find the key that unlocked the door to unification of the field.

Another factor contributed to the failure of efforts toward unification in the fifties. This was the factor of leadership. No one clearly

141

commanded the loyalty of supervisors and seminary professors all across the field. In 1953 Guiles died an untimely death. Boisen was in the geriatric stage of life and had never been interested in the organizational problems of the movement, anyway. Hiltner, Wise, and Dicks had achieved professioral stature. Dicks had withdrawn from the Council for Clinical Training in 1935 and from the New England group in 1938. He re-entered the picture during the Fifth National Conference (1956) and was given a chance to reassert his leadership by the Southeastern Region. Again in 1957 Dicks withdrew from clinical pastoral education. Hiltner was suspect among many Council for Clinical Training supervisors in the fifties because of his academic leanings, whereas Wise was so fully identified with the Council that he could not command leadership of the entire field. Many new leaders arose during the late forties and fifties, but all were identified primarily with one of the separate and competing organizations. Leadership from the seminary and ecclesiastical world was disqualified from the outset because of clinical training's radical departure from conventional forms of church, ministry, and theological education.

Only one option remained: to grow up together as siblings under the same roof; to work through vestigial needs for separatism and to move slowly and painfully toward professional maturity; and only then to symbolize that maturity by formal organizational unification of the profession. This growing-up process is the underlying dynamic in the search for unification by means of a federation of accrediting agencies.

A Chronicle of the Search for Federation

The Committee of Twelve was sufficiently encouraged by the adoption of national standards on October 13, 1953, to schedule a spring meeting in March, 1954. The goal was to do for accreditation what had just been done for standards, namely, to discover a concensus that would unify the field at a national level.

The initial effort faltered. Bruder, Kuether, and Plack were designated a subcommittee "to be the recipients of statements from all groups and interested individuals as to their experience with accrediting problems and concerns." Only one statement was received, and that was the work that Bruder and the Council for Clinical Training had done the previous fall of 1953. In retrospect Bruder reported:

"Internal concerns of sponsoring organizations" were sufficient to warrant allowing matters to lie dormant until the spring of 1956.[1]

Early in 1956 the Committee of Twelve met again to plan the Fifth National Conference on Clinical Pastoral Education for the following October in Atlantic City. A Committee on Procedures was authorized to prepare a proposal for a national organization. Thomas W. Klink, who was chairman of the committee, brought to the National Conference a proposal "that an Association for Clinical Pastoral Education be formed." A sixth National Conference on Clinical Pastoral Education was proposed for the following year (1957), and regional meetings of all groups represented in the National Conference were to be held in the spring of 1957. Five regions were designated, matching the geographical divisions currently in use by the Council for Clinical Training.[2]

The conferees exploded with anxiety when first presented with the proposal for an Association for Clinical Pastoral Education. Leaders from within the Committee of Twelve made another try on the following day. They reviewed the history and purposes of the Committee of Twelve and set the proposed Association in the context of "an organization in process of formation." [3] They were able finally to gain acceptance of the plan for regional meetings but nothing more.

In March, 1957, the Committee of Twelve met again and reconstituted itself an Advisory Committee on Clinical Pastoral Education. Membership was enlarged, and a Steering Committee composed of Paul Johnson, Chairman, Carl Plack, and Ernest Bruder was chosen and charged with responsibility for "keeping things moving." The enlarged committee included, in addition to the original Committee of Twelve, one representative from each of the five regions, one from the American Association of Theological Schools, and the Executive Director of the Department of Pastoral Services of the National Council of Churches.[4]

A critical incident occurred in the October meeting of 1957. The Advisory Committee was faced with a request for recognition by the newly formed Southern Baptist Association for Clinical Pastoral Education. Samuel Southard presented the request initially to the Committee on Procedures. Southard was a member of the Advisory Committee by virtue of being the representative from the Southwest Region. He had been active in founding the Southern Baptist Association only a few weeks prior to the October session of the Advisory

Committee. The Committee on Procedures recommended acceptance of the Southern Baptist Association, but when their report came to the entire Advisory Committee, a sharp division arose over the question of recognition. Lutherans found common cause with the Southern Baptist representative because they, too, had a denominational identity. A few Council and Institute representatives were vehemently opposed. The motion to welcome the new group into membership finally passed with a substantial majority.[5] As subsequent sections of this chapter will show, the arrival of the Southern Baptist Association for Clinical Pastoral Education upon the national scene had far-reaching consequences for the Advisory Committee and its program of national unification.

Bruder succeeded Johnson as chairman of the Advisory Committee at the February meeting, 1958. Much of the confusion associated with events of the previous year was dispelled by the report of the Committee on Procedures, under Klink's continuing and able leadership Klink's report cut the Gordian knot that had bound previous efforts. In a word he defined the alternative of a federation of accrediting agencies. He removed, thereby, the threatened loss of identity and autonomy within the existing groups. The Advisory Committee would thereafter concern itself primarily with meeting the conferential needs of the field.[6]

Unbeknown to the Advisory Committee, its effort to achieve a federation of agencies was effectively nullified in June, 1958. The presidents of the Council for Clinical Training and the Institute of Pastoral Care were Carroll Wise and Paul Johnson, neither of whom was then a member of the Advisory Committee. In connection with the Sixth National Conference at Plymouth, Massachusetts, in June, 1958, Wise and Johnson initiated unilateral negotiations reviving the possibility of a merger of the Council and the Institute. From the perspective of a decade later, this appears to have been one of the felicitous events in the history of the young profession. For the next few years, however, it set the stage for a considerable degree of frustration within the field as a whole.

The Advisory Committee met in Louisville in February, 1959, and its members were encouraged to believe that federation was just around the corner. The contrast between this discussion and the debate of 1952 was a measure of the rate of maturation of the profession during the seven years that intervened. Many of the old issues were raised, such as the merits of education vs. training and of professors vs. chaplain supervisors. The committee as a whole refused to become embroiled in arguments, however. Members commented on the invalidity of any such either/or classification. The interpenetration of functions and the reciprocal needs of professors and supervisors for one another were affirmed. Serious groundwork was done toward upgrading the existing national standards. The value of cross-fertilization among the several organizations was cause for congratulation within the committee.[7]

By February 15 and 16, 1960, the Advisory Committee had received a green light from its constituent groups to proceed toward formation of a constitution and bylaws for the incorporation of a national association. Full and formal unification of the profession was expected to coincide with the Seventh National Conference on Clinical Pastoral Education, October 27-29, 1960, in Washington, D. C.[8] As the Conference opened, the Advisory Committee was informed that the Institute of Pastoral Care had reversed its decision of April to favor incorporation. Just two days prior to the beginning of the National Conference, the Institute's Board decided "to vote against incorporation as long as there are denominational groups involved." [9] The Council for Clinical Training representatives came with instructions to postpone incorporation, too. They supported the Institute, therefore, and the game was over.[10]

Prospects for unification of the entire field were more bleak after the Seventh National Conference (1960) than at any time since the formation of the Committee of Twelve in 1951. Within seven years, however, organic union of all groups actively involved in clinical pastoral education had been achieved. What factors frustrated the efforts of the fifties to achieve unification? What factors motivated persistence in the search for unity despite repeated frustration and failure? To these questions the rest of this chapter is addressed.

A Lack of Understanding and Trust at the Grass Roots

The irruption of opposition to the 1956 plan for an Association for Clinical Pastoral Education revealed an immense gap between the attitudes of Committee of Twelve members and the supervisors at the grass roots of the respective groups. Regional meetings were only partially successful in closing the gap during the next four years.

Part of the problem was structural, and part was a failure of leadership. The five regions were based on divisions currently in use within the Council for Clinical Training, and they did not take sufficiently into account the distribution of members in the other groups. The Central and Pacific regions were almost completely inactive. The Central Region extended from Ohio to Montana and from Kentucky to Wisconsin. The Pacific Region stretched from Idaho and Washington down to Arizona. In the Central Region Hiltner and Carl Wennerstrom used mail polls to foster communication among members and to gather data for reporting to the Advisory Committee. The Pacific Region remained unrepresented in meetings of the Advisory Committee. It is noteworthy that a question was raised about the organization of the Central Region during the business session at the Fifth National Conference (1956), but the question was answered defensively and then ignored by the Committee of Twelve.[11]

In both the Southeast and the Southwest, leadership problems blocked the goals envisioned by regional organization. Dicks was Chosen representative of the Southeastern Region to the Advisory Committee. The region had a highly successful meeting in January, 1957. Differences between various groups were aired and a beginning made toward mutual appreciation. But Dicks vacated his post in relation to his leaving Duke Divinity School, and no one took the iniative to select a successor. The region did not meet again in spite of the fact that two members of the Steering Committee of the Advisory Committee were from the Southeastern Region.[12]

In the Southwest an active and well-organized region developed. At the conferential level it functioned well, meeting annually from 1957 to 1967. Creative developments in the region were stimulated by the founding of the Institute of Religion in the Texas Medical Center of Houston and the formation of the Council of Southwestern Theological Schools, Inc. Some of these developments will be described in a later section. So far as accreditation was concerned, the region was deadlocked by a struggle between interests associated with the Institute of Religion and the Council for Clinical Training respectively. A 1957 proposal to establish "a Regional Committee on the Accreditation of Pastoral Supervisors" died, and no headway was made priod to 1960 to transcend the old loyalties to the separate groups. Protagonists initially were Dawson Bryan, Director of the Institute of Religion, and Armen Jorjorian, a Council for Clinical Training supervisor

146

functioning in St. Luke's Hospital. The two centers were located in the Texas Medical Center of Houston within a few steps of each other. They were established virtually simultaneously in 1954. Their leaders were unable to develop cooperative working relationships for many years, however, and local struggles were often projected into regional concerns.[13]

Another factor limiting the effectiveness of regional organization from 1956 to 1960 was a lack of the necessary imagination or perhaps the boldness to bring competitive groups together with the intensity and duration of interaction needed for unification. The Northeastern Region was the only one of the five to display the kind of imagination that might have made a decisive difference by 1960 had it been duplicated everywhere. The Northeastern Region was well organized and met regularly. In the initial meeting in March, 1957, substantial headway was made toward the definition of terms and clarification of the model by which unification might be achieved. The model of a federation of accrediting agencies was described first in this regional meeting. In February, 1958, the first step was taken toward joint accreditation. In effect, a group of Council for Clinical Training supervisors staged a role play of an accreditation session. The general principles by which the Council's Accreditation Committee functioned were stated, and then the progress reports on a candidate were read. The candidate, himself, presented his own report as to his experiences in training, and the floor was opened for discussion.[14] The program met with an enthusiastic response from other supervisors and from denominational representatives in attendance. It pointed the way to the eventual creation of joint accreditation committees—committees that moved beyond role-playing to actually doing the job together as one group. But this is anticipating the story of the next chapter.

In spite of the progress toward unification made in the Northeastern Region from 1956 through 1960, it was the Boston-based Institute of Pastoral Care that struck the death blow to the 1960 plan for a national association. Some observers felt, however, that plans for federation were put to sleep partly because of the success of regional meetings in the Northeast. The vision of organic union came clear enough through these regional meetings and through Council-Institute merger talks begun in 1958 that the work of the Advisory Committee had to be sacrificed in order to prepare the way for an organic union of the accrediting agencies.

The Proliferation of Clinical Pastoral Education
Independent of the National Conference

The fifties saw the proliferation of programs engaged in clinical pastoral education but choosing to remain unrelated to any of the established groups in the field. As new centers gained monies, built buildings, and expanded their programs without benefit of accreditation, the pressure for unification of the old-line agencies increased.

In an editorial in 1956, Carroll Wise described eight new programs.[15] First in the list was the Institute of Religion in the Texas Medical Center of Houston, Texas. The Institute of Religion was as ambitious as Texas is big. It brought together the five Protestant seminaries of Texas in a graduate program of pastoral care and counseling. Clinical pastoral education was its primary business. Within five years of its origin, the Institute of Religion broke ground for a three-quarter-of-a-million-dollar building located at the hub of the Texas Medical Center. Professors of pastoral care shared supervisory responsibilities with six chaplain supervisors. They directed and supervised the pastoral counseling center located in the Institute of Religion building. They taught courses in religion and medicine in Baylor University School of Medicine, the Texas Women's University College of Nursing, and they participated extensively in interdisciplinary conversation. During its first five years the Institute of Religion enrolled 276 ministers in various levels of training, 165 medical students, and 605 nursing students.[16]

Dawson C. Bryan, the Director of the Institute of Religion, visited the centers and interviewed leaders of established clinical training agencies in 1954 and 1955. He decided to affiliate educationally only with the seminaries of Texas. Professors were chosen with certification from the Council for Clinical Training and the Southern Baptist Association for Clinical Pastoral Education. Supervisors trained in the Institute of Religion, itself, were certified by an organization of seminary deans and professors of pastoral care, the Council of Southwestern Theological Schools, Inc. The appearance of a growing number of supervisors who were answerable only to seminaries and not to a recognized accrediting agency proved deeply disturbing to the clinical training status quo.

Another deviation from familiar patterns of clinical pastoral education was the development of the Pastoral Training Service of the American Foundation of Religion and Psychiatry in New York City. Kuether became consultant to the program in its initial stage (1951), and following his resignation as Director of the Council for Clinical Training (1954), he became responsible for the clergy training program of the Foundation. Training in pastoral counseling was soon being offered on several levels ranging from short-term summer courses to three-year residencies. In 1959 students in the counseling service carried from four to five hours of counseling a week initially. They spent two days a week in seminars and supervision. The experience was more explicitly oriented to the goals of a mental health clinic than to those of a parish. In fact the American Foundation was already licensed as a mental health clinic in the State of New York. It supported a professional staff of thirty-five people and served over one thousand clients during the year, a fourth of them in group therapy.[17]

When Kuether sought accreditation of the program as advanced clinical pastoral training, the Board of the Council for Clinical Training found itself in a quandary. The Accreditation Committee reported to the Board on November 11, 1955, that "the institution meets all the requirements as set forth in the Standards except that there is no full-time chaplaincy service." Board members felt that "such a specialized training experience belongs in the category of advanced training," but they were unable to act favorably on Kuether's request for accreditation. The chief obstacle was that Council standards were focused exclusively on health and welfare institutions and so did not apply specifically to a pastoral counseling center as such.[18] The question was referred by the Board to a subcommittee, and indecision on the matter persisted for some time before the program was accredited in a special category.

Speaking before the Council's 1959 Fall Conference of Supervisors, Kuether described his program at the American Foundation as "a triple deviant." Clergymen deviated from their traditional role functions; psychiatrists and other mental health professionals deviated from their expected roles by working under the auspices of a church; and the Council for Clinical Training deviated from its traditional position in accrediting the center for an advanced clinical year.[19]

Speculation has persisted as to what a different response by the Council for Clinical Training in 1955 might have produced. Had the

Council found a way to include Kuether's program under its auspices in a more wholehearted way and with more room to develop as a related but distinctive form of pastoral ministry and education, the necessity might not have arisen to found the American Association of Pastoral Counselors in 1963. Neither the Institute of Pastoral Care nor the Council were able in the fifties to include specialized training in pastoral counseling within their framework for long. Anxiety about pastors becoming full-time psychotherapists was strong. Perhaps this contributed to the separation in the sixties of clinical pastoral education and pastoral counseling as distinct fields of professional specialization. In any event, the American Foundation of Religion and Psychiatry in New York City disturbed the clinical training status quo in the late fifties, as did the Institute of Religion in Texas.

Clinical training leaders occasionally found themselves in the embarassing position of having to run to catch up with those they were supposedly leading—particularly in relation to graduate theological education. The Program in Psychiatry and Religion at Union Theological Seminary was one instance. Earl Loomis, a psychiatrist, joined the Union faculty in 1956. By 1958, Loomis and his associate, Charles R. Stinnette, Jr., offered a graded curriculum in which introductory courses in human development, psychopathology, and pastoral care were followed by a summer quarter of clinical pastoral training. Advanced courses, such as psychodynamics of groups, theology and psychiatry, and research seminars were built on clinical prerequisites.[20]

The Menninger Foundation became active in studying interrelations of religion and psychiatry in 1953.[21] Late in 1959 the Foundation announced "Fellowships in Psychiatric Theory for Clergymen and Theological Scholars." Doctoral candidates from theological schools of all faiths were invited to apply for one-year scholarships. The clinical experience at Menninger was integrated with doctoral degree curricula of the related schools. Two concepts shaped the program: (1) the relationship between psychiatry and religion requires mutual exploration of basic issues on a "post-graduate scholarly level"; (2) the educational methodology must require participant observation by clergymen in an interdisciplinary, psychiatric setting, and it must require "scholarly study and systematic exploration of the issues discovered." Educationally, this represents " 'a third position' in contrast to the methods of clinical pastoral education on the one hand and the methods of graduate academic study on the other." [22]

The Menninger Foundation program drew its leadership from the Council for Clinical Training in the person of Thomas W. Klink. No recognition was given by the Council to advanced clinical work at the Menninger Foundation, however. It was not surprising that Klink called upon the Council to re-evaluate its standards for advanced training during the Fall Conference of 1959.[23]

At no point were clinical pastoral educators more deeply disturbed by new developments than by the announcement in 1956 of a one-half million dollar grant by the National Institute of Mental Health to study the communication of mental health concepts to seminarians. The project was planned and staffed as if clinical pastoral education did not exist. The goal of the grant was to create a curriculum that would integrate the teaching of mental health principles with the special functions and educational needs of the clergy. Clinical pastoral educators saw this as one of their central concerns. Hans Hoffman, the Protestant participant in the project, saw clinical pastoral education as specialty training for hospital chaplaincy only. He advocated that mental health resources be acquired by seminarians *"through ways and methods which are indigenous to their role."* His challenge was not met adequately within clinical pastoral education for nearly a decade.[24]

Clinical pastoral educators were being excluded from the big money grants and from many educationally prestigious developments in theological education. They were doubly bound, however, in being unable to speak with a single voice in their own behalf. No one in the fifties could represent the entire field of clinical pastoral education. Neither could any group honestly sponsor programs of an interfaith character, for each agency was at best pan-Protestant. As if to compound an already serious problem of fragmentation, the Southern Baptist Association for Clinical Pastoral Education was formed in 1957 and presented itself on the national scene. It is little wonder that some of those who had invested much in the cause of unification prior to 1957 met the arrival of the Baptist group with groans of dismay.

Formation of the Southern Baptist Association for Clinical Pastoral Education, 1957

The third force in clinical pastoral education, which appeared in 1951 in the form of the Lutheran Advisory Council, was substantially increased in 1957 by the formation of the Southern Baptist Association for Clinical Pastoral Education. Eighteen men met in Nashville, Tennessee, in September, 1957, to organize as a section meeting concurrently with the annual Southern Baptist Counseling and Guidance Conference. The group was about evenly divided between professors of pastoral care or religious education and chaplain supervisors in 1957. By 1959 the Southern Baptist Association numbered thirty certified supervisors, of which twenty were chaplains and ten were seminary professors.[25]

The original eighteen became nearly eighty supervisors by 1967. They were offering clinical pastoral education in general and mental hospitals, in penal institutions, and in schools for the mentally retarded. The Southern Baptist Association was virtually a national accrediting agency in 1967, having supervisors in seven of the nine regions and having nearly a dozen denominations represented among the 25 percent of its supervisors who were not Southern Baptists. The Southern Baptist Association posed a greater threat to the control of the field by established groups than did the Lutheran Advisory Council. The majority of Lutheran supervisors were certified by either the Council for Clinical Training or the Institute of Pastoral Care as well as by the Lutherans. None of the supervisors in the Southern Baptist Association held dual certification. The group was not an extension of the older groups in the sense that was true of the Lutheran Advisory Council.

The proposed incorporation of a national association was rejected in 1960 on the grounds that denominational groups were involved. Since the Lutherans had been assimilated into the National Conference on Clinical Pastoral Education for several years, one must suppose that it was the appearance of the Southern Baptist Association that upset plans for unification. Other factors were involved, but the stereotype that many supervisors had of Southern Baptists and a misperception of the Association as an agent of the Southern Baptist denomination contributed significantly to the negative feelings that were aroused by its appearance.

Where then did the Southern Baptist Association for Clinical Pastoral Education come from? If it was not the creation of denominational leaders to protect their own interests, whose creation was it? And for what reasons did it come to be? Why did so much of clinical pastoral education develop in the South independently of the Council for Clinical Training and the Institute of Pastoral Care? And how may we account for the surprising growth of the Association so that within a decade it was a national, pan-Protestant group numbering nearly one-third of all the clinical pastoral educators in the nation?

The origin of the Southern Baptist Association for Clinical Pastoral Education may be traced to three centers representing three traditions: Louisville, Kentucky; Winston-Salem, North Carolina; and New Orleans, Louisiana. Undoubtedly the central figure in the development of clinical pastoral education in the South was Wayne E. Oates of the Southern Baptist Theological Seminary in Louisville, Kentucky. Interest in clinical training at the Seminary preceded Oates by several years. Seward Hiltner visited the Louisville school in 1937 on the invitation of professors Dobbins and Carver. The seminary was prepared to establish a clinical training program in the Louisville General Hospital as soon as the Council for Clinical Training could provide a supervisor. But no supervisor was available.[26]

In 1943 Professor Gaines S. Dobbins found the man he had been looking for to develop a full-scale program of clinical pastoral education in the seminary. Dobbins recalled the story as follows:

When World War II broke upon us . . . a call of distress came from the superintendent of the Louisville General Hospital. He explained the shortage of orderlies and attendants, due to war conditions, and asked if some arrangement could be made to secure the services of theological students on a part-time basis. A call for volunteers brought hearty response from the class. In the group was a student of unusual maturity and discernment, with a rare combination of insight and practicality. He was assigned supervision of the work of fellow students in the hospital.[27]

This man was Wayne E. Oates.

Oates was born in Greenville, South Carolina, where his earliest memories were of the "company commissary" and of the ten- and twelve-hour days his family spent working in the mills. Later memories "were of industrial riots and social upheavals that came with the organization of labor." At age thirteen, he became a page in the United States Senate. He completed his education at Wake Forest College, Duke University, and Southern Baptist Theological Seminary.[28]

Interest in clinical pastoral training dates from an episode that occurred when Oates was a minister in a rural church. A woman was advised by her doctor to "call the preacher," and she sent her small son to find Dr. Oates. During Oates's visit, she "unburdened an involved story of marital unhappiness, personal guilt and morbid despair. Not knowing what else to do, and overwhelmed by the complexity of the woman's plight, Oates simply listened, without condemnation and without sentimentality." Much to Oates's surprise, the woman who had been confined to her bed was soon able to do her housework, and she moved back into neighborhood relationships. Subsequently the doctor who referred her to Oates gave the country "preacher" a bit of advice. "We are entering upon a whole new understanding of the nature of disease," he said. "I believe this will draw the minister closer to the work of a doctor. You train yourself for this. I don't know where you will get the training but wherever you can find anybody who knows anything about it, listen to him." [29]

The first man Oates found to listen to on the subject was Gaines S. Dobbins of Southern Baptist Seminary. In 1944 he began to learn from Ralph Bonacker, a Council for Clinical Training supervisor who had just become chaplain of the Norton Infirmary in Louisville. Oates took his first quarter of clinical training with Bonacker in 1944. Bonacker and Oates (under Dobbin's sponsorship) taught the first course in clinical pastoral education at Southern Baptist Seminary the following year, 1944-45. In the summer of 1945 Oates was joined by a fellow student Richard K. Young in taking clinical training at Elgin State Hospital under William Andrew and Anton Boisen. The year 1945-46 found Oates developing Kentucky Baptist Hospital as a clinical center with the help of a group of graduate students on a part-time basis.

In the spring of 1946, with two quarters of full-time training behind him and two years of part-time experience as a supervisor of seminarians, Oates was ready, according to the standards then in vogue, to seek accreditation. He arranged an interview with Kuether, who was Associate Director of the Council for Clinical Training. Oates proposed to work in consultation with Bonacker in developing the clinical training program of the Seminary and requested recognition as a supervisor. Kuether rejected Oates's application, however, and offered him no alternatives for developing an indigenous program under adequate supervision.[30]

Oates was thrown back on his own resources at this point. He determined to develop clinical facilities and supervision that would be wholly responsible to seminary educational policies. His first venture was a full-time program in the Kentucky Baptist Hospital in the summer of 1946. The summer of 1947 found Oates and Myron C. Madden opening a training center at the Kentucky State Hospital in Danville, Kentucky. Leaving Madden as chaplain, Oates and Young opened another center the same summer at North Carolina Baptist Hospital in Winston-Salem. Later, Oates moved his Louisville program to Central State Hospital where Aaron L. Rutledge had become chaplain. Rutledge and his successors at Central State provided the primary base for year-round training. Fifteen months after Oates was rejected as a Council for Clinical Training supervisor, he had become the hub of a clinical training program in which four chaplains were participating—two in mental and two in general hospitals.[31]

Oates was the principal actor in the Louisville story, but the Southern Baptist Seminary was the stage. The openness of the Seminary to clinical pastoral education is as remarkable as the energy and ability of Oates and his colleagues. Both missionary motivation and commitment to a professional model for theological education were involved. The Seminary affirmed Oates at both points. Writing under the title, "Our Mission to the Sick," Oates declared that "the central objective of this work is to strengthen and enlarge the missionary ministries of the student." Reacting against the Brinkman tradition in clinical training, Oates said, "The Southern Baptist Theological Seminary is not even remotely interested in training workers for a ministery which ignores or makes incidental the Christian gospel."[32]

Clinical pastoral education became a major part of the curriculum that Oates developed at the Southern Baptist Theological Seminary. Both Th.M. and Th.D. students were required to invest major time in clinical learning. By the time the Southern Baptist Association for Clinical Pastoral Education was formed (1957), Oates had all his clinical facilities concentrated in the Louisville area and staffed by four supervisors.[33] He had succeeded in developing a clinical program that was seminary-controlled, academically respectable within the context of a graduate school of theology, and to a considerable degree integrated into the total curriculum of the Seminary.

North Carolina Baptist Hospital developed its clinical training program rapidly under Young's direction and became a second major source of leadership for the Southern Baptist Association for Clinical Pastoral Education. Young's program was ten years old when the Association was formed. The School of Pastoral Care, as it was later named, had a staff of five full-time chaplain supervisors in 1957. They offered clinical pastoral education in six- and eight-week terms to sixty-six students; in addition there were five chaplain interns for twelve months of training and one supervisor-in-training. An out-patient counseling service gave attention to 718 clients during the year 1957, approximately 10 percent of whom were ministers and their wives.[34]

The third source of initiative in the formation of the Southern Baptist Association was the New Orleans Baptist Theological Seminary and the Southern Baptist Hospital in New Orleans. The seminary representative was John Price, Dean of the School of Religious Education and Professor of Religious Psychology and Counseling. Along with Oates and Samuel Southard (of the Institute of Religion in Houston), Price was a prime mover in organizing the Southern Baptist Association for Clinical Pastoral Education. He served for two years as its first chairman. Soon after the Association came into being, Madden, who began his supervisory work with Oates and Young in 1947, became chaplain supervisor at the Southern Baptist Hospital. Price and Madden have, since 1959, guided the training of a substantial number of clinical pastoral educators.

The roots of the New Orleans program were older than either the Louisville or the Winston-Salem programs. During the thirties and forties, under A. E. Tibbs, who was then head of the Religious Education division, the Seminary followed the model set by Karl Stolz of the Hartford School of Religious Education. Stolz was an early member of the Cabot Club and was a substantial contributor to the clinical training movement. Th.D. candidates majoring with Tibbs in Religious Pyschology and Counseling were given interdisciplinary instruction and placement through on-campus services and related university-agency cooperation in the city. After succeeding Tibbs, Price simply continued this tradition. In 1951, he set up a clinical training program in the Southern Baptist Hospital with Don Corley as the chaplain supervisor.[35]

Three distinct traditions had taken form by the time the Southern Baptist Association appeared. In addition to geographical and leadership differences, each tradition emphasized a different perspective on pastoral work. The Louisville center under Oates stressed the shepherding perspective. The Winston-Salem center under Young emphasized the healing perspective. The New Orleans center under

Price accented the perspective of guiding personal growth in the context of religious education through individual and group counseling.

The grandfather clause of the Southern Baptist Association for Clinical Pastoral Education extended membership to supervisors "who have been chosen by one of the Southern Baptist Seminaries to give courses in which credit has been given for degrees," and to "professors who are actively engaged in supervision of students in Clinical Pastoral Education." [36] By the time the grandfather clause expired in September, 1959, members of the Southern Baptist Association felt that they had some clear distinctions in relation to the Council for Clinical Training and the Institute of Pastoral Care. One was the high proportion of seminary professors in relation to chaplain supervisors and the strong feelings of identification among them as if they were members of the same fraternity.

A second distinction was in standards. From its founding the Association reached beyond the national standards of 1953. When Southard presented the credentials of the Southern Baptist Association to the Advisory Committee on Clinical Pastoral Education for recognition in October, 1957, a major misunderstanding centered on the fact that the Association had "adopted for consideration" the national standards of 1953. Opponents of recognition fixed upon this as proof of substandard functioning. In reality the Southern Baptist Association delayed acceptance of the 1953 standards only because of pressure from the Louisville and New Orleans contingents to add to the 1953 standards certain requirements for graduate degrees. The Winston-Salem supervisors urged the adoption of the 1953 standards without modification, and their wishes prevailed in the 1959 annual meeting.[37] Within a few years, however, the standards of the Association had been upgraded substantially. An entire section was added on the "Qualifications of the Teaching Supervisor." Continuing education for at least one quarter or semester every three years was expected, and the principle of full reciprocity with other accrediting agencies was adopted.[38]

The question of whether or not to accredit non-Baptists arose almost as soon as the Southern Baptist Association formed. It was settled on an inclusive basis in 1960. By 1967 approximately 25 percent of the membership were identified with other denominations.[39]

In the person of Oates, the Southern Baptist Association for Clinical Pastoral Education traced its connection with the Committee of

Twelve to 1951. Oates was on the program of the Second National Conference on Clinical Pastoral Training in Boston in October, 1951, and became one of the original members of the Committee of Twelve as a representative of the Association of Seminary Professors in the Practical Fields. When the Committee of Twelve became the Advisory Committee in 1957, Southard and Young were added as regional representatives. Oates, Price, and Young became the official representatives of the Southern Baptist Association to the Advisory Committee in 1958, and Young was subsequently made a member of the Steering Committee.

In spite of adequate representation, the Southern Baptist Association was minimally involved in the Advisory Committee on Clinical Pastoral Education from 1957 to 1960. This was only partly because of the negative attitudes of some Advisory Committee members toward the appearance of a Southern Baptist Association. The Southern Baptist Association was preoccupied with its internal development as a professional association. In this they were much like the Council for Clinical Training and the Institute of Pastoral Care during the late forties and early fifties. A time lag of approximately one decade was perhaps the basic difference after all between the Council and the Institute, on the one hand, and the Southern Baptist Association on the other. In 1957, however, the Southern Baptist Association seemed much more disruptive of efforts toward unification than proved to be the case.

The Warming Climate of Theological Education

Positive attitudes toward clinical pastoral education evidenced by the Southern Baptist Theological Seminary were duplicated by seminaries in every region of the country by the mid-fifties. The American Association of Theological Schools continued to foster a professional model for theological education and consequently welcomed the influence of clinical pastoral educators in the fifties as they had in the twenties and thirties. Leadership in clinical pastoral education from seminary professors who grew up in the movement multiplied geometrically. The high mark of the warming climate was made by the Niebuhr, Williams, and Gustafson studies sponsored by the American Association of Theological Schools and the Carnegie Corporation.[40] Richard Niebuhr urged the integration of the practical and classical fields, saying that theological educators have had "inadequate theories of the relations of action and reflection." He concluded that theological education is not simply the attaining of "intellectual comprehension" but is a process of nurturing students "into the measure of the stature of the fullness of Christ." [41] On the basis of this educational principle, Niebuhr and his associates affirmed that the new emphasis on psychology and pastoral counseling represented "a significant new turn in the education of the ministry." [42]

Reuel Howe became an effective interpreter of the educational philosophy undergirding clinical pastoral education and broke new ground in applying the method of dialogue to the classroom and the religious retreat.[43] Seward Hiltner's *Preface to Pastoral Theology* (1958) laid the foundation for theoretical work in pastoral theology. He identified a perspective on pastoral studies that transcends and thereby unifies the varied perspectives of pastoral shepherding, healing, guiding, and reconciling. Never again could informed spokesmen for clinical pastoral education set the shepherding and healing perspectives over against each other as mutually incompatible approaches to pastoral identity, as was done in the Committee of Twelve debate of 1952, for example. Besides Hiltner's work in the late fifties came major contributions toward the correlation of theological and psychological understandings by Wise, Johnson, Hulme, and Oates—representing coincidentally the Council, Institute, Lutherans, and Southern Baptists respectively.[44]

The Institute of Pastoral Care, Inc., 1953-60

The Council and the Institute experienced both a pull and a push for unification. The pull was from the new openness of seminaries and of society generally toward professional education for the ministry. The push was from that third force in the field: independent programs and the denominationally identified accrediting agencies. In spite of pressures for unification, both the Council and the Institute resisted the process about as much as they encouraged it. With respect to unification, the word that best characterized both of the old-line groups was ambivalence.

Nowhere was the ambivalence more dramatically enacted than by actions of the Board of Governors of the Institute of Pastoral Care, in April and October, 1960. On April 5 the Board went on record "supporting the creation of a national organization," but on October 25, just a few days before the incorporation of a national organization was to be accomplished, the Board gave their representatives "a directive . . . to vote against incorporation." [45]

The Institute was the least ambivalent about unification of all the constituent groups in 1956. The proposal of an Association for Clinical Pastoral Education that was drawn up by Klink and his committee was positively supported in three specific actions of the Institute's Board during 1956.[46] When the Southern Baptist Association was recognized by the Advisory Committee, the Institute supported the action. In February, 1959, Institute of Pastoral Care supervisors brought a recommendation to the Board "to consider the possibility of affiliation with the Lutheran Advisory Council and the Southwide (sic) Baptist Association." The Board was not willing to go along, however, being uneasy about what it would mean for an incorporated agency to affiliate with groups that were not legally incorporated.[47]

The two poles of the Institute's ambivalence afford an appropriate outline for discussing the Institute of Pastoral Care during the middle and late fifties. First, we shall consider factors delaying unification, and second, factors fostering positive attitudes toward federation.

One of the factors inhibiting movement toward the Council for Clinical Training, in particular, was the sense of distinctiveness that developed in the Institute of Pastoral Care under Fairbanks and Burns. Under Burns' executive leadership, 1950-54, members frequently presented themselves as defenders of a pastoral vs. a psychiatric orientation in the education of ministers. During the administration of Orlo Strunk, 1954-57, this sense of distinctiveness was expressed in only slightly modified form. Institute leaders saw the Council for Clinical Training limited by negative attitudes toward the seminaries and the church. The Institute of Pastoral Care saw itself emphasizing "the training of parish ministers, an emphasis not always stressed by the Council." [48]

The administration of Otis Maxfield lasted only one year, 1957-58. While he contributed to the administrative reorganization of the Institute of Pastoral Care, his impact on Institute-Council relationships was negligible. John I. Smith became Executive Secretary in 1958 and aligned himself with forces moving toward unification. He contributed substantially to the breakup of old stereotypes about the Council for Clinical Training and other clinical training agencies.

Attitudes change slowly, however. In January following Smith's election as Executive Secretary, twenty supervisors met in St. Louis and expressed themselves about possible merger with the Council for Clinical Training. The minutes of the conference sound like a broken record when the attitudinal phrases are extracted:

see no real value in the merger . . . for further explorations but with reservations . . . with caution . . . strong reservations . . . open for discussion but have reservations . . . caution . . . extreme caution . . . in principle yes, but have reservations . . . very strong reservations . . . real reservations . . . very strong reservations . . . need long and careful talks . . . we must not merge by surrendering our views . . . very serious questions . . . against the merger . . . proceed slowly and very cautiously . . . some sort of federation but no merger . . . see no real gain in merger . . . not in favor of merger . . . must maintain our own objectives and values.[49]

Amazing, is it not, that full unification was achieved in only eight more years.

Another factor in the resistance of Institute of Pastoral Care supervisors to schemes of merger was the rapid growth of the Institute, itself. With growth came a new group consciousness as a national rather than a strictly New England group. The Institute's growth was impressive between 1952 and 1960. The number of centers increased from six to thirty-three, supervisors from eight to fifty-one, students in the summer school from ninety-six to more than four hundred.[50] The Institute could take pride in the academic achievements of its supervisors as well. Billinsky noted in January, 1959, that out of thirty-five supervisors, sixteen held earned doctorates, fifteen had the master's degree in theology, and four the Bachelor of Divinity degree.[51]

Growth brought problems of organization, and the Institute of Pastoral Care was no exception. Internal developments occupied the attention of the Institute's leaders throughout the fifties, and this, too, diverted concern away from the need for unification of the entire field. The years from 1954 to 1956 were a time of adaptation to the demands of the standards adopted in 1953. Constitutional revision was followed by the problem of what to do about older supervisors who did not measure up to the requirements of the new standards, even though they had received the best training available in previous years.[52] New urgency about accreditation precipitated a struggle in the Board of Governors over the authority to grant accreditation. Johnson supported the prerogatives of the Training Committee in the matter against those who would have retained full authority within the Board of Governors. Then in October, 1954, the Board asked the Training Committee to come up with "ways to meet the emergency situation into which the adoption of the new standards for Chaplain Supervisors may have precipitated the Institute." [53] In responding to the crisis the authority of the Training Committee was substantially enhanced.

In 1955 the supervisors made plans to press for a stronger voice in the decision-making process within the Board of Governors. They decided to ask for two positions on the Board and two positions on the Training Committee of the Board to be filled by supervisors nominated by the supervisors, themselves. Daniel Sandstedt and John Smith were chosen to be their representatives.[54] By 1956 the conference of supervisors had presented a long list of motions to the Board.

Standards steadily rose, and the procedures for accreditation became gradually more refined. It was decided, for example, that an acting supervisor would become a full supervisor only after conducting one quarter of clinical pastoral education as an acting supervisor. This had not been required previously. No review of one's functioning as an acting supervisor was required, however. The supervisor's advancement was to be automatic.[55] The receipt of applications in 1958 from two men trained under Southern Baptist supervisors led to a policy that supervisors trained under other auspices must serve as Assistant Supervisors under the Institute of Pastoral Care auspices for one quarter prior to being considered by the Training Committee for certification.[56] Internships began to be approved by the Board in 1957, and the twelve-week unit became standard by 1958. A minimum of three students in an approved training program was established in 1960.[57] A comprehensive document containing standards and procedures for the Committee on Training was produced in December, 1960. While internal developments diverted some attention away from the cause of national unification, they also prepared the base on which the Institute of Pastoral Care could stand secure while beginning negotiations with the Council for Clinical Training.

Turning to factors contributing positive attitudes toward federation, the financial stability of the Institute of Pastoral Care must be cited. By 1956 the Institute was on firm financial footing. An appeal to the Danielson Foundation for funds to support participation in the Advisory Committee on Clinical Pastoral Education had been successful. The General Service Foundation made a grant of $5,000 in 1957 toward the search for national unity.[58] The Institute increased the percentage of student fees which supervisors were required to forward to the central office in 1957 and increased membership dues in 1958, maintaining, thereby, a balanced budget with modest reserves.[59]

The selection of John I. Smith as Executive Secretary in April, 1958, gave the Institute constructive and competent leadership plus the needed element of continuity. Smith remained in office until the formation of the Association for Clinical Pastoral Education in 1967. He then served as interim Executive Director of the new Association, 1967-68, while serving also as its first president. He united the Institute of Pastoral Care supervisors and its Board of Governors. He launched a successful program to enlist new members and won the confidence of the other clinical pastoral education agencies in the negotiations that led finally to full unification of the profession. The first meeting of supervisors following Smith's election as Executive Secretary set in motion a self-study process and a series of conferences that had beneficial results for the profession as a whole. The original proposal, presented by Richard J. Lehman and C. Charles Bachmann, was that "in addition to the regular student assessment, another ten percent of the fee paid to the center to be set aside for a four-day Conference for supervisors . . . to hammer out a clearer understanding of the Institute of Pastoral Care's concept of Clinical Pastoral Training." [60]

Twenty-six supervisors contributed brief essays on their personal goals and methods for clinical pastoral education, and the compilation of essays was published. Whatever remained of the old stereotypes about the Council for Clinical Training and the Institute of Pastoral Care died with the publication of this collection. The ratio of Institute supervisors who relied upon the so-called psychiatric orientation (previously ascribed exclusively to the Council) as over against the so-called pastoral orientation was three to one. The healing perspective was more in evidence than the shepherding perspective on pastoral care. An educational philosophy that accepted major responsibility for attitudinal and behavioral change in the personality of the student was espoused in preference to professional training strictly defined as mastery of skills. The goal of professional education was expressed by William B. Spofford, Jr. in these words:

Clinical pastoral training is a . . . fundamental part of education for the ministry. . . . The fundamental goal of clinical training (is) not so much the communication of philosophy or content, but involving the students . . .

163

deeply in a living situation, under supervision, against which he can see his real *self* . . . which, in other areas of education, he has not been able to deal with.[61]

Illustrative of the permissive educational methods used by Institute supervisors was this statement by John I. Smith:

Each morning is free for the student to use as he sees fit. He may be on his wards, reading, writing, in individual conference with his supervisor or sleeping. We do not tell the student where or how he should use his time, but *what* he does with his time is important to us and is discussed with his supervisor.[62]

The essays submitted by Institute of Pastoral Care supervisors in 1959 revealed clearly that the issues dividing the profession were not fundamentally whether one belonged to the Council, the Institute, the Lutherans, the Baptists, or the Seminary Professors in the Practical Fields. Paul R. Swanson, commenting on the theme of structured vs. unstructured programs of clinical training, said:

There are different theories of education, and then there are different educators. . . . All of this was formerly thought to indicate whether a supervisor was a "Council man" or an "Institute man." However, the thousand-word statements of the Institute supervisors indicate that such is not a valid ground for distinction.[63]

What became valid ground for distinction was one's philosophy and methodology of education. The Institute's exercise in self-study cut across the formal boundaries of separate organizations and struck to the roots of the entire profession's reason for being.

Before plans for federation were publicly buried, forces were set in motion that led ultimately toward organic union. As shown previously, these forces were loosed when Paul Johnson and Carroll Wise, as presidents respectively of the Institute of Pastoral Care and the Council for Clinical Training, renewed talk of merger in June, 1958. At a Joint Executive Committee meeting, December 1-2, 1960, a seven-point statement was adopted that launched negotiations in earnest.[64] Before examining these plans in detail, we turn to the Council for Clinical Training and events leading Council supervisors to adopt pro-merger proposals in 1960.

The Council for Clinical Training, Inc., 1953-60

The Council for Clinical Training, like the Institute of Pastoral Care was halfhearted at best about a federation of all the accrediting agencies. Council supervisors were investing most of their attention in continuing the transformation of their group from a fellowship of rebels to a profession of clinical pastoral educators. This was true from 1954 to 1957 in particular.

Problems were aggravated by the resignation of Kuether as Director of the Council for Clinical Training in Feburary, 1954. Kuether observed that since 1947 the number of supervisors in the Council had doubled, but the Director's time had been cut in half. There was not enough money for a full-time director and not enough time for fund-raising.[65]

Whether the Board attacked its problems from the standpoint of expanding the Council's financial base or from the standpoint of improving the quality of professional services, they came back to the issue of seminary relationships. Concern was expressed about the growing fragmentation of the clinical pastoral education field, but this too became a prod to improve seminary relationships. Most of the "fragmenting" or proliferation was occurring, as we have already seen, in relation to seminaries that were either distrustful of the Council for Clinical Training or simply uninformed about the resources that the Council had to offer. Some of the Board members were, themselves, unsure what it was that the Council had to offer to seminaries in return for membership and financial support. A special committee was appointed, therefore, to study the problem of seminary relationships." [66]

Bruder was given the task of doing for seminary relationships what he had done for standards, that is, of articulating the objectives and defining the criteria involved. His committee produced a comprehensive document in the summer of 1955. The Fall Conference of Supervisors in 1955 devoted itself exclusively to discussing and amending this document. Anxiety mounted as the meaning of "seminary memberships" came clear. Workshops were organized in midstream, and supervisors set to work facing the sources of threat that they were experiencing. Four topics were tackled:

1. What are the aspects of the Council's identity that realistically are likely to be sacrificed?
2. What are the specific problems that would be anticipated if administrative functions were given to seminary representatives?
3. How ought seminary membership fees and student fees to be determined?

4. What is meant by "integration of clinical pastoral training into the total seminary experience of the student"?

Reporting to a plenary session, the supervisors discovered that they had little to fear and much to gain from the proposal. After nearly two full days of discussion and many amendments, they voted to recommend to the Council's Board of Governors the adoption of the plan. In so doing, the Council for Clinical Training opened membership on the Committees of the Board to seminary representatives and defined the services and the fees to be given and received in the alliance.[67]

The next big step toward full professional identity was the formulation and distribution of a document on the Procedures and Criteria of Accreditation. Supervisors began calling for such a statement as early as the Fall Conference of 1953.[68] In November, 1954, in the last months of his tenure as Director, Kuether suspended another supervisor under circumstances reminiscent of the episode of 1948. An Advisory Committee of supervisors supported Kuether's judgment and then took responsibility for the fact that no regularized procedures had been developed and none had been published concerning any of the accrediting (or dis-accrediting) functions of the organization. For the next three years the Accreditation Committee worked on the problem. Under the chairmanship of Herman Eichorn, the job was completed in the fall of 1957.[69]

The statement on Procedures and Criteria of Accreditation was a milestone in the journey toward the unification of the field. For the first time since the thirties, the veil of secrecy and the aura of the inexpressible was lifted from the process of certifying supervisors. The way was opened for meaningful communication with non-Council groups about the distinctive goals of the Council for Clinical Training. Council supervisors discovered that their innovations in educational philosophy and methodology could be articulated in spite of the subjective realities involved.

When Kuether resigned as Director, the Board of Governors found that they were not able to afford a successor on a full-time basis or to entice one on a part-time arrangement. Carroll Wise was offered the position of full-time Director but declined. Next the Board looked to the supervisors. The supervisors nominated several of their own number, but were unable to come to a final decision. It was not until 1962 that a part-time director was again employed in the person of

166

Maurice C. Clark. In the meantime late in 1954 the Board announced the employment of Miss Emily Spickler as Administrative Assistant. She was to become Executive Secretary within a few years and to remain with the Council for Clinical Training until 1961. The administrative solution involved the formation of regional organizations and the investment of executive responsibility in a committee of regional chairmen and officers of the Board.

By 1957 the Council for Clinical Training was functioning well with a fully developed structure as a professional association. The number of centers had increased from seventeen in 1947 to forty-three a decade later. More than fifty supervisors were actively engaged in clinical pastoral training. The number of student quarters had tripled during the decade, 1947-57.[70] Bigham's work on the Finance Committee was bearing ample fruit as well. From a budget of slightly more than seventeen thousand dollars in 1950, the 1957 budget exceeded forty-three thousand dollars, and by 1960 it was nearly fifty-seven thousand dollars.[71] Seminary relationships had been improved dramatically. The Standards Committee had prepared a handbook, and procedures for nominations and elections had been regularized. The Curriculum Committee took a giant step toward the articulation of the Council's distinctive educational philosophy in 1955, and their work was complemented by the Accreditation Committee's report in 1957.

A perennial debate flared up wherever supervisors discussed their educational philosophy during the fifties. The terms of the debate were whether clinical pastoral training was essentially education or therapy. Both sides stood opposed to the traditional model of theological education, but they often sounded more like enemies than allies as they waged the battle of education vs. therapy. Those who accented education defined the goals of clinical pastoral training in terms of a ministry to be performed with personal change or emotional growth as a secondary goal. The therapy camp saw professional understandings and the quality of professional functioning to be by-products of self-understanding and personal maturation. Academic degrees were valued by the educationists more than they were by the proponents of therapeutic goals. Investment in personal psychotherapy was considered more appropriate by the latter group than the acquisition of a doctorate, for example. Some structural differences were associated with the two positions. Most supervisors on the education end of the continuum looked to a constituency (such as a denomination), and institution (such as a seminary) , or to endowments from private donors for financial backing. They tended, therefore, to interpret their functioning in familiar didactic language acceptable to their sponsoring groups. Most supervisors on the therapy end of the continuum, including most of the Council for Clinical Training, relied heavily upon student tuition for their support as a professional group. By analogy with the doctor-patient relationship, they were prone to see their work primarily in the personal terms of supervisor and student.

The terms of the debate were false as subsequent experience has shown. Clinical pastoral education is education by definition. The debate was crucial to the profession, however, for fundamentally it was an effort to define a basic philosophy of education. At issue were the relative merits of the objective and the subjective dimensions of learning, the problem of assimilation and integration of new learning into one's total life-style, the nature of church and ministry, and the relative values of personal authenticity and professional role image. Clinical pastoral educators, particularly the Council supervisors, were arguing the merits of psychological education for theological education before the language of psychological education was well developed or generally understood.

Under the chairmanship of Keith Keidel, the Curriculum Committee addressed itself to the articulation of the Council's educational philosophy in 1955. The result was a definition of clinical pastoral education that was, first of all, balanced. The goals were two: "developing the personal attitudes and professional skills" enabling the student to effectively communicate the gospel. Secondly, the definition was bold. It affirmed the necessity of theological education to seek the integration of "the redemptive message of the Gospel" with "living experiences of individuals" so that learning occurs *on the level of the feeling of the individual student"* (italics mine) .

The Committee offered a clear statement of the educational principle that a student's progress must be determined by his own rate of development rather than by arbitrary grades or schemes of advancement. Though the normative time span was set at one year of fulltime training, the Curriculum Committee stated that some students would achieve the curricular goals in one or two quarters, whereas others might require a second year. The Committee also took some tentative steps toward designing a graded curriculum in which various levels of training would be correlated with increasing evidence of personal maturation and professional competence.[72]

The criteria developed by the Accreditation Committee reflected the educational philosophy of the Council for Clinical Training also. Professional competence and skill appeared in the criteria, but no methods of testing applicants were used. It was assumed "that an adequate minimum of formal learning has taken place in his year of study in the training programs he had undertaken in accordance with Council standards." Under "Emotional and Spiritual Stability" the criteria were more explicit. Key sentences include the following:

We expect him to be able to cope with unpredictable or unusual situations without his effectiveness becoming seriously limited by his own anxiety.

We look for freedom from obvious symptoms of anxiety or distress. Rather than defensiveness, we look for openness, honesty, calmness, spontaneity and strength.

We expect him to be neither apologetic nor rigidly stereotyped in his employment of traditional religious [terms]. . . . We expect him to have usable religious metaphors relevant to the interpersonal encounter rather than detached and isolated metaphors relevant only to "theology."

Under the criterion of qualitative relatedness, the Committee said that it looked for

an ability to communicate openly and fully with others; the courage and trust that underlies such communication and the kind of closeness that results. In short, we look for evidence of an ability to achieve a quality of relatedness that can be described as communion.

Maturing self-awareness meant that the Committee sought evidence of

a growing self-awareness, some knowledge of how closely or how distantly he works best in interpersonal relationships and a deepening appreciation of his own potentialities as a person and as a minister.

We want to gain some impression as to what the applicant has dedicated himself to, religiously and professionally. . . .

By direct questioning the Committee seeks to determine the candidate's awareness of his own attitudes, of his characteristic responses and of his defenses.

The interview itself gives an excellent opportunity for the Committee to see the applicant in the process of making decisions, forming judgments, and controlling or expressing his feelings. A clear impression of how he deals with authority can be formed from observing how he seems to see the Committee and from how he relates to the Committee.

The final section dealt with characterological qualities:

On the one hand we look for a person with honest personal and religious convictions. On the other hand we look for a person with some tolerance and flexibility.

We look for the kind of person who can see human needs and who is able to relate himself constructively to them. He should be able to judge when to move and when to wait . . . so that what has been distorted may be straightened out, so that what has been hurt may be healed, and so that what has been unloved may be loved.

We look for a character which includes a combination of flexibility, spontaneity and stability, when confronted . . . by a variety of dimensions such as aggressiveness, passivity, hostility, anger, rebellion, dependency and love.[73]

Kenneth Crofoot compiled evidence in 1959 that the criteria reviewed above were actualized to a substantial degree in the ten centers of clinical pastoral education that he studied.[74] Since he studied centers under auspices of the Southern Baptist Association as well as the Council for Clinical Training, we may conclude that the criteria articulated by the Council in 1957 were applicable to a wide cross-section of the profession. The essays by Institute of Pastoral Care supervisors published in 1959, which we reviewed in the previous section, support the view that goals of personal change were high on the value scale of supervisors throughout the nation by the late fifties.

One point at which the Council was unable to stretch its curriculum sufficiently to keep up with developments was in relation to specialized training in pastoral counseling. The story of Kuether's request for accreditation of his work at the American Foundation of Religion and Psychiatry has been told already. Another issue testing the flexibility of the Council in the fifties was application for certification by a Roman Catholic priest. The matter was under discussion in 1956 and was resolved in favor of opening the door to Roman Catholic clergy provided they were qualified under the standards and accrediting procedures that obtained for others.[75]

The years 1957 to 1960 were transitional for the Council for Clinical Training. A conflict erupted between Bruder and the Council's Board of Governors.[76] Wise was then president of the Council. Bruder had long championed the cause of delegating the authority and fees for training to the centers in which clinical pastoral education was offered. As Bruder saw it, the central organization of the Council for

Clinical Training should function as a standard-setting and certifying agency only. In writing the introduction to the published proceedings of the Sixth National Conference on Clinical Pastoral Education, dated June, 1959, Bruder expressed a loss of confidence in "leadership from the 'Training Organizations' which no longer have any 'training' function." He urged that "the broad areas of standards-making, certification, research and communication" be taken over "by a new organization concerned about these distinctives in clinical pastoral education." [77] One result of the conflict affecting the profession as a whole was a shift from the goal of federation to the goal of organic union between the Council for Clinical Training and the Institute of Pastoral Care.

Bruder was a major contributor to the plans for a federation of accrediting agencies. Just at the moment that federation seemed within grasp, the Southern Baptist Association for Clinical Pastoral Education appeared, and Bruder was unable to favor its inclusion. Ironically, therefore, the principle of federation was contradicted just when the profession appeared ready to accept it. At about the same time that plans for federation were faltering Bruder's differences with the Council's Board of Governor's came to a head. By the fall of 1959 Bruder's relationship with the Council for Clinical Training ended.

Concurrent with the Bruder-Wise affair, the Council for Clinical Training and the Institute of Pastoral Care moved into unilateral negotiations seeking merger. The result on the national scene was the final failure of efforts to form a federation of existing accrediting agencies. The Advisory Committee of the National Conference on Clinical Pastoral Education went through the motions of forming a federation during 1959 and 1960. Opposition grew within the Council for Clinical Training. Wise urged Council supervisors in the fall of 1959 to go on record opposing activity designed to form a national association.[78] Bruder was then chairman of the Advisory Committee. It was not surprising that the Council's Board and the Advisory Committee of the National Conference moved in divergent directions.

Even while Council for Clinical Training supervisors debated the character of the Council and the nature of the unification desired, the Council as a whole moved steadily toward unification. From 1960 to 1967 when the Association for Clinical Pastoral Education was incorporated, movement continued at an accelerating pace. How the Era of Unification reached its climax is the story of the next chapter.

8

THE BREAKTHROUGH TO UNION, 1960-1967

The Seventh National Conference on Clinical Pastoral Education (1960) marked the end of hope for a federation of accrediting agencies, but it disclosed surprising agreement about the educational philosophy undergirding the entire profession. Concensus about the objectives of clinical pastoral education helped to hold the profession together during the next five years, during which no national conferences were called. Theoretical unification of the field was not generally acknowledged in 1960, and no single interpreter contributed a unified exposition of the profession's distinctive philosophy of education. A careful reading of the proceedings of the 1960 Conference reveals that ideological unification had been achieved substantially even if it had not been adequately articulated.

Hiltner was the keynote speaker for the Conference. He wrestled with the issue of "what is and should be central and focal in clinical pastoral education." He offered a threefold definition: clinical pastoral education is essentially a method of professional theological education; it is a movement (which by implication is seeking to reform theological education), and it is a body of knowledge derived from systematic reflection upon its methods.[1] Hiltner's commentary was a hard-hitting critique of the field organized around three assertions:

(1) That while the essence of the profession is connoted by the word "clinical," the leaders of the field have mistakenly identified clinical with the health and welfare institutions in which clinical

pastoral education usually occurs. They have failed, thereby, to distinguish "the focal from the peripheral, or the crucial from the derivative within the method of clinical pastoral education." [2]

(2) That clinical pastoral education may never permeate theological education in the way psychoanalysis has the mental health field because "the chaplain supervisors . . . wavered between being a professional and training association within a larger profession . . . and being a kind of guild or operating trade union." Hiltner confessed his personal distress at finding that, as a seminary professor who came out of the clinical pastoral education movement, both he and others in his type of position were made to feel that "real clinical pastoral education was not ourselves but something to which we were outsiders." [3]

(3) That supervisors of clinical pastoral education have retreated from theory back to the method of the field, "even though tributes are paid to theory." Symptoms of this retreat are the absence of any test of knowledge as a part of the process of certifying supervisors and the tendency of some to devalue doctoral degrees as prerequisite preparation for the clinical pastoral educator.[4]

Those who responded to Hiltner on the spot generally avoided or rejected his appeal for a body of knowledge and for greater intellectual stature within theological education. It remained for those who presented papers on the objectives of clinical pastoral education to articulate an alternative to Hiltner in precise terms.

Speakers on the objectives of clinical pastoral education represented the four accrediting agencies. Without prior access to Hiltner's paper, they presented a remarkable concensus. In a word they said that clinical pastoral education is neither anti-intellectual nor inattentive to theory. Its theoretical concerns are simply of a different order than Hiltner's. The essence of clinical pastoral education is not to be found in the settings (health and welfare institutions) in which education occurs but in the students whose personal and professional maturation is intended. If the professors of pastoral theology feel out of touch with clinical pastoral education, it may be that in reality they are. It may be that seminary professors have not addressed themselves to the core concerns of the supervisors, i.e., how authenticity is nourished through educational processes and how the integration of the cognitive and affective dimensions of theological inquiry may best be achieved. The supervisors identified their theoretical concerns with what may be called psychological education for ministry. Educational processes are properly clinical, therefore, when theological education is programmed to occur "at the experiential level," when the human development and professional competence of the student are the essential objectives, and when confrontation of existential issues precedes integration theologically and operationally within the student.[5]

What emerged from the totality of the conference was a concensus that the *sine qua non* of clinical pastoral education has to do with the new profession's service to theological education. The service consists of offering basic psychological education to seminarians. Psychological education seeks the human development of the student. It employs educational means (as distinct from psychiatric means) to foster growth toward emotional and spiritual maturity.

Specifically, growth objectives are the following: growth toward expanding awareness of self, others, the universe, and God; growth toward authenticity in one's feeling experience and the flexibility needed to enjoy intimacy or to maintain distance in relationship with others; growth toward a constructive resolution of the "authority problem" so that one becomes secure in his authority over others without abdicating or becoming authoritarian; growth toward identity and the freedom to commit oneself to persons and groups in mutually fulfilling ways.[6]

Psychological education is distinguishable from psychotherapy both in the methods employed and in the context of its functioning. Psychological education seeks mental health goals as does psychotherapy. It seeks these goals not in the context of treatment for illness or for behavioral malfunctioning, but in the context of graduate, professional education. It seeks mental health goals for the great majority of the student population (approximately 85 to 90 percent) who are not experiencing major psychological difficulty in living. The assumption is made that "these individuals grow psychologically more rapidly in guided learning situations," just as it has long been assumed "that individuals learn academically more rapidly in educational settings than when left on their own." Psychological educators are not therapists attached to schools. They are, in the seminary context, theological educators who teach (supervise) in the realm of emotional and spiritual experiencing in order to assure improved professional functioning in ministry.[7]

Specialists in clinical pastoral education were building a body of knowledge by 1960. They were building in the field of educational theory as befits a profession of educators. The origins of this theoretical work may be found in the conferences of the New England group in 1941 and 1943; in the first National Conference of 1944 and in successive national conferences; in the Council for Clinical Training's Curriculum Committee report of 1955; and in the articulation of criteria for accreditation by all the accrediting agencies since 1957. The proceedings of the conference of 1960 left no doubt that clinical pastoral education as a field was still waiting for the person who would penetrate the methodological know-how of the supervisors and articulate a coherent body of educational theory. Intimations, fragments, and hopes there were in abundance. But not yet was there a theory that had been operationally validated in effecting the attitudinal and personality changes needed for effective ministry in the contemporary world. Not yet had the methods of clinical pastoral education been interpreted within the framework of a comprehensive theory of psychological education for ministry.

To what extent a consensus on educational theory was felt by the members of the profession is impossible to determine. From 1960 to 1967 the action of individuals and agencies in the field left no doubt that something had changed. Motivation for merger between the Council for Clinical Training and the Institute of Pastoral Care began to grow, and structures for unification began to appear.

The Structures for Merger of the Council and the Institute

December 1-2, 1960, the Executive Committees of the Council for Clinical Training and the Institute of Pastoral Care hammered out a seven-point program launching unilateral negotiations with the possibility of a merger clearly in view. In brief the representatives agreed to recommend to their Boards the following:

1. that the 1961 Supervisors Fall Conferences of the Council and the Institute be in the same place at the same time and that the Program Committees of both groups work together.
2. that through the Presidents of each Board, individuals of comparable committees in each group be invited to any significant meetings of the other organization's committees as participating observers.

3. that a joint committee be established to explore the possibility of a joint training program announcement.
4. that there be an exploration of the possibility of joint staff personnel.
5. that the Finance Committees of both groups be in consultation.
6. that the Executive Committees of the Council and the Institute meet jointly semi-annually.
7. that the Joint Executive Committees appoint a group of people whose primary concern would be to consider the future of Clinical Pastoral Training. . . . Their considerations should not be related to the two respective groups but to Clinical Pastoral Training as a part of theological education, the broader concern of Clinical Pastoral Training as a movement rather than its relation to any particular organization.[8]

The two Boards approved these recommendations promptly, and negotiations were begun formally in April, 1961. An indication of the hope that resulted from the early talks is an action by the Council's Board in mid-1962 relative to the selection of an executive director. They selected Maurice C. Clark, one of the Council's veteran supervisors, as part-time Executive Director. In so doing the Council gave up plans to secure full-time executive leadership—a dream that had been kept alive since Kuether's resignation in 1954.[9]

Goals of the merger talks remained tentative and very limited for another year. Council supervisors expected some kind of solution for their problem of executive leadership to come out of the merger talks, but they were talking about a "federated assembly of supervisors" rather than organic merger in 1962.[10] Billinsky told the Fall Conference of the Institute of Pastoral Care in 1963 that perhaps the most realistic solution at that time would be "some kind of federation" between Institute and Council.[11] While he was deeply concerned to be inclusive of all those engaged in clinical pastoral education, Billinsky saw no way to achieve such an ambitious goal. He concluded his remarks on the merger question:

In my own heart I am committed to the ultimate unity of all in Clinical Pastoral Education. But what is the best way to bring this unity about? I must confess that so far I know not in which direction we must go. I firmly believe that if our desire to merge is coupled with patience and understanding we shall be able to reach our goals, not in spite of but because of questions that are presently being raised.[12]

A characteristic of the Council-Institute merger talks was the determination that unification "ought to be allowed rather than programmed." [13] In fidelity to this principle, the unification efforts of the sixties benefited from the unhappy experience of the fifties. John I. Smith described the merger process in 1962 as not unlike that of two people "who, little by little, grow in their maturity to the point where defenses are no longer necessary. They can meet together in a healthy way for discussion, even though there may still remain some inner conflict that affects the relationship." [14] During the 1962 Fall Conference, a physician appealed to the Institute of Pastoral Care and the Council for Clinical Training to "set aside their differences and unite into one great body." He held out the model of medicine which "became a powerful and progressive science when Homopaths (sic) and Alopaths (sic) united." These groups "had good reasons for their stand," said Dr. Elia, but they "merged themselves for the good of the medical profession." [15]

The combination of wise leadership and repeated application of pressure from the outside kept the merger fire burning. The formation of the Committee on Clinical Pastoral Education of the American Association of Theological Schools was one source of continuous and constructive pressure.[16] Joint meetings at many levels were proving useful in solving problems within the respective groups as well as between them. This, too, provided motivation for their continuation.

The Institute of Pastoral Care, for example, was facing the problems of regional organization and seminary memberships in the early sixties. Regional organization had been pending since Robert Leslie's report of November 3, 1953. It was accomplished in 1961 and 1962 in relation to joint regional meetings with the Council for Clinical Training.[17] Seminary memberships were especially vexing for the Institute of Pastoral Care since the four founding seminaries of Boston had a unique position in the Institute. The Council for Clinical Training had devised a model with two levels of seminary membership, and this was adapted by the Institute of Pastoral Care in 1961.[18] Benefits of this order flowing from joint meetings strongly motivated the continuation and intensification of the merger process.

The breakthrough from thinking federation to thinking organic union occurred when joint accreditation proved workable. In retrospect it was obvious that organic union of separate agencies could never have occurred apart from a jointure of the separate accreditation committees. Discussion in the previous chapter highlighted the sensitive nature of accreditation and its centrality to the whole clinical pastoral education enterprise. We saw also that the idea of joint accreditation was alive and operative in the late fifties when the Eastern Region of the National Conference staged a role play of the accreditation interview. Resistence to joint accreditation delayed progress toward merger until 1962-63.

John Smith attacked the problem head on in the 1962 Fall Conference. Addressing both Council for Clinical Training and Institute of Pastoral Care supervisors, he said:

> I am sure all of us would agree that the only way we can understand the accreditation practice of each other's group is to share in the process. That is the only way of getting the "feel" of what takes place. It is only in this kind of sharing that we can establish both trust and confidence in the process. . . .
> To my mind, then, an immediate and essential need in our consideration of a closer relationship is mutual sharing in the accreditation process. We have been talking of doing this for at least two years, but for some reason a sharing has yet to take place. I suggest that the reason for this involves more than matters of time and space. It is my guess that our loyalties to a particular group may have more bearing on our failure in this direction than we like to believe. Surely we ought by now to have outgrown the restrictions imposed on us by little loyalties! [19]

Charles E. Hall, Jr., and Richard J. Lehman were the chairmen of the accreditation committees of the Council for Clinical Training and Institute of Pastoral Care, respectively, at the time. They took Smith's challenge seriously and engineered three joint meetings during the next year. Lehman recalled, in a speech to the 1963 Fall Conference, that when he and Hall presided over the first joint meeting they were both "playing it safe." They quickly came to grips with the controversial issues, however, and discovered "a basis of trust on which we could build." He confessed that "some of the prejudices which have helped us all to be confident that we had joined the 'right camp' " fell away in the discovery that "neither side has a monopoly on all the sharpest guys or right methods." [20]

The formula for successful joint accreditation was discovered in a mid-winter meeting in New York City (1963). On the first day two students were interviewed. The first student was interviewed by a committee of Council for Clinical Training supervisors while an Institute of Pastoral Care committee looked on. The second student was interviewed by Institute supervisors while the Council men observed. On the first night everyone was anxious, critical, and hostile. The formula had not worked. The second day each interviewing committee was mixed—consisting of both Council and Institute supervisors. The observers were also a mixed group. Again one committee conducted the interview while the other observed, but this time both Council and Institute men were interviewing and observing simultaneously. When the second day ended the spirit among the supervisors was cooperative. In reflecting on the experience, John Smith said that this was the real beginning of the momentum that eventually brought union to the field.[21]

Using the mixed committee formula, joint accreditation proceeded apace. Initially the prerogatives of each agency were protected by the ruling that voting would be done only by Council for Clinical Training supervisors on Council-sponsored candidates and vice versa. Even though an examining committee contained both Council for Clinical Training and Institute of Pastoral Care supervisors, only the Council men would vote on the Council's candidates, for example. Lehman reported that he received the impression throughout that the interview process would have been little different had committees not been mixed and that the decisions would have been no different had the voting been done by the entire mixed committee. Such differences as might have occurred would not "have been because it was an Institute committee or a Council committee, but far more because of the personalities . . . of the men comprising the committees." [22]

The next big breakthrough occurred the following year. The W. Clement and Jessie V. Stone Foundation announced a decision to invest $97,500 in the search for unification of the profession. Between March 30, 1965, and March 13, 1967, the Stone Foundation contributed the designated funds to the Council for Clinical Training and the Institute of Pastoral Care to underwrite meetings of the two groups. Mr. Stone required no commitment that a merger would result. He shared deeply in the risk of Council and Institute participants in the merger talks. His faith and the efforts of many members of joint committees found fulfillment not only in a merger of the Council for Clinical Training and the Institute of Pastoral Care but also in the unification of the whole field.[23]

From Merger of Council and Institute to Unification of the Whole Field

Early in 1966 the goal shifted from merger of the Council for Clinical Training and the Institute of Pastoral Care to the unifica-

179

tion of the entire field of clinical pastoral education. Unification of the entire field meant, concretely, the assimilation of the Lutheran and Southern Baptist accrediting agencies and formal relationships with the American Association of Theological Schools and the National Council of the Churches of Christ in the U. S. A.

The Council for Clinical Training and the Institute of Pastoral Care considered themselves functionally merged by December, 1965. While plans for merger had received no official approval, the operational committees were meeting jointly and the climate for merger had become favorable. At this juncture the National Council of Churches convened a consultation on accreditation and certification for clinical pastoral education. For the first time since 1960, members of all four accrediting agencies met together to discuss the unification of the field. The National Council of Churches, the denominational representatives, and the executive leadership of the American Association of Theological Schools spoke with one voice advocating a national board for accrediting chaplains and supervisors of clinical pastoral education. They were clearly running out of patience with the leaders of clinical pastoral education for repeated postponement of the day when unification would be achieved.[24]

Council for Clinical Training and Institute of Pastoral Care supervisors who were present spoke of their progress toward merger, but declined to present their working plan to the consultation. Their respective boards were afraid that an exposure of merger plans at that point might interfere with the continuation of the merger process. The consultation was unanimous (including Council and Institute supervisors in attendance) in recommending to the Council for Clinical Training and the Institute of Pastoral Care that they invite the Lutheran and Southern Baptist groups to consult with them at an early date with a view to formation of a unified accrediting agency. As the consultation adjourned, the feeling of most non-Council and non-Institute participants was that implementation was doubtful.[25]

Implementation came within a few months, hastened by the strong support of Hall and Billinsky. The Joint Executive Committee invited Lutheran and Baptist representatives to the April, 1966, meeting of the Joint Structure Committee "to hear a report of the work done to date and to discuss ways by which the Council and Institute merger may become as inclusive of the movement as is possible." [26] The report in a word was this: the Council for Clinical Training and Institute of Pastoral Care are already merged functionally. We want your reactions and possibly your participation in the new association we are designing. A timetable has been set. The Council and Institute will go out of business on January 1, 1968, and a new Association for Clinical Pastoral Education will come into being. If you, as the Lutheran and Baptist groups, like what is taking form and can get aboard and help us complete the work we have begun, you are welcome.[27]

Reporting on the meeting to the Southern Baptist Association for Clinical Pastoral Education, Verdery and Thornton wrote:

We tested the spirits of the men on the Joint Structure Committee and found that they were truly inclusive in their attitude toward the Southern Baptist Association for Clinical Pastoral Education. . . . We are not facing a merger of the Council and the Institute so much as the creation of a new association for clinical pastoral education. Since the principles for this new association are (1) inclusiveness of all supervisors presently accredited for CPE, (2) regional organization and functioning, and (3) local autonomy of centers and supervisors, the possibility for the Southern Baptist Association for Clinical Pastoral Education to enter the new organization is great.[28]

The response of Lutheran participants was equally positive. Council for Clinical Training and Institute of Pastoral Care representatives warmed to the idea of creating a broader base of participation as the April, 1966, meeting came to a close. The session had shown that inclusiveness would mean an even more creative design for the new organization.

Lutheran and Baptist groups participated in the Standards Committee next and proved to be helpful participants. The Committee on Clinical Pastoral Education of the Department of Ministry of the National Council of Churches studied the preliminary structure document and gave a positive reaction to the Joint Structure Committee in June, 1966. The only negative report from outside groups came from the Chaplain's Service of the Veterans Administration and the St. Elizabeth's Hospital in Washington, D.C. The preference of these chaplains was for a federation of accrediting agencies rather than organic union.[29]

Lutheran and Baptist groups were invited to send participant observers to a Joint Accreditation Committee in October, 1966. They became full participants in two successive meetings prior to the incorporation of the Association for Clinical Pastoral Education. The

Southern Baptist Association for Clinical Pastoral Education invited Council for Clinical Training and Institute of Pastoral Care supervisors to be full participants in the final meeting of their accreditation committee in Nashville, Tennessee, September 23-25, 1967. Joint accreditation involving the four groups occurred four times prior to organic union. A Personnel and Site Committee, Finance Committee, and Executive Committee met in the winter of 1967 bringing the four groups into full collaboration in the widest possible way.[30]

The new structure was based on a representative form of government in contrast to the Board of Governors' model of the Council for Clinical Training and the Institute of Pastoral Care. The center of power lay in the regions. Each region sent four delegates to constitute a House of Delegates. With nine regions, this meant thirty-six delegates. To the representatives of the regions were added fourteen delegates as follows: two from the American Association of Theological Schools; one from the Department of Ministry of the National Council of Churches; six from denominations, the Roman Catholic, and the Jewish faith; and five delegates at large elected by the House of Delegates. Since regional representatives consisted primarily of the certified supervisors, the control of the national Association was placed firmly in the hands of the supervisors. Seminary and denominational representatives were given the privilege of membership in the regions as well as at the national level, thus assuring them representation commensurate with their involvement at the grass roots of the profession.[31]

We can see the origin of the move from a self-perpetuating Board of Governors to a delegated legislative body in several historic moments. The financial crisis of the Council in 1940-41 was resolved by the assumption of full control of the Board of Governors by the supervisors. While the centralized structure was maintained, the effective control of the organization passed to the supervisors. In 1955 Institute supervisors made their first move to gain representation and authority on the Board of the Institute of Pastoral Care. The Lutheran Council was an arm of ecclesiastical authority of necessity, but most Lutheran-approved supervisors were members of either the Council for Clinical Training or the Institute of Pastoral Care as well. When the Southern Baptist Association for Clinical Pastoral Education was formed in 1957, it functioned as a pure democracy with the members attending the annual meeting as the final authority. Only the decisions of the accreditation committee pertaining to supervisory status were exempt from ratification by the annual meeting of supervisors.

A difficult structural problem was that of balancing authority between the national office and the local center. This was focused financially in the issue of funding the annual Fall Conference of Supervisors. Both the Council for Clinical Training and the Institute of Pastoral Care had developed a policy of paying the supervisor's expenses for attending the Fall Conference. The financial burden that this posed for the new Association made it impossible to project a balanced budget. The representatives from the Southern Baptist Association for Clinical Pastoral Education suggested eliminating this expense item totally and expecting each supervisor to finance his own attendance at the Fall Conference. This solution was seen at once to fit the new understanding that the unified Association was not a training agency, that responsibility for attendance at professional meetings lay with the local training center. Each supervisor would receive and retain tuition from students in his own program. Funds would be available to active supervisors even in centers where monies were not budgeted by the administrator to pay for the supervisor's attendance at Fall Conferences.

The problem of how to balance authority and financial support between the national and the regional organizations was even more difficult. The national organization developed its own system of fees and relegated the problem of financing regional programs to the regions, themselves. This became one of the basic unresolved issues facing the new Association for Clinical Pastoral Education upon its incorporation.

The new structure aroused a great deal of anxiety about the designation of tuition charges for clinical pastoral education. Many supervisors were adamant that setting fees was the prerogative of the center, itself. This was true especially of supervisors whose training programs were tied administratively to seminaries. No seminary would allow an outside accrediting agency to stipulate its tuition scale. Yet, the absence of a nationally set fee raised the possibility of a "price war." Supervisors who worked alone in locations geographically remote from the major teaching centers were especially concerned about how they would survive the competition with seminary programs and large clusters in the major urban areas. The solution of the problem was to make no stipulation of any kind concerning fees at the national level. Whether this proved to be a solution or merely a postponement of the problem remained to be seen.

A final structural element of the Association for Clinical Pastoral Education needing comment at this point is the cluster. The Joint Structure Committee was unanimous in feeling that clusters of clinical pastoral education centers integrally related to one or more seminaries in the same geographical region were desirable and ought to be encouraged in the new Association for Clinical Pastoral Education. The cluster of centers was designated as a separate membership category, therefore, and a financial incentive was added to stimulate the formation of clusters. At the same time high standards were written into the Bylaws governing the formation of clusters. Approval of a cluster was based on the following criteria:

1. Evidence of there being not less than three accredited centers within the same region responsibly related to theological education, ordinarily with at least one seminary, the cluster functioning as a unified educational unit.
2. Evidence of a responsible Committee or Board that has general oversight of the training offered in the cluster.
3. Evidence of having integrated clinical pastoral education into the total curriculum of theological education.
4. Evidence of the integration of other theological disciplines into the clinical pastoral education offered in the training centers.
5. Evidence of offering integrated programs of study for trainees, utilizing the resources and facilities of the training centers within the cluster.
6. Evidence of having established a program for the continued education of the supervisors in the clusters.
7. Evidence of geographic accessibility of the participating training center and seminaries.[32]

Strong objection to the cluster features of the proposed structure was registered by some regional meetings. Regional Executive Directors pressed the issue in May, 1967. The fee scale was modified as a result, but the basic design remained and was accepted by the constituent groups.

The Georgia Association for Pastoral Care, Inc.

The cluster that provided the primary model for development of the criteria listed above was the Georgia Association for Pastoral Care,

Inc. The Georgia Association united the Christian Council of Metropolitan Atlanta with three theological schools, a medical school, and nearly a dozen clinical centers offering chaplaincy services to the public and clinical pastoral education to seminarians and clergy. Its purpose: to offer persons "undergoing some of the common crises of life" the benefit of "a ministry that is both true to the Christian Gospel and knowledgeable about modern scientific approaches to healing." [33]

The Georgia Association for Pastoral Care arose in response to local needs. The initiative came from Charles V. Gerkin who was a Council for Clinical Training chaplain supervisor of the Grady Memorial Hospital in Atlanta. Ecumenical cooperation began with the selection of Gerkin in 1957. Dr. Monroe Swilley, pastor of the Second-Ponce de Leon Baptist Church, enlisted representatives of Columbia Theological Seminary and Candler School of Theology in planning a clinical pastoral education program for Grady Memorial Hospital. A twenty-six-million-dollar addition to Grady Hospital was under construction at the time, including the John Newton Goddard Memorial Chapel. Gerkin began the chaplaincy program just prior to the opening of the new facilities.

Clinical pastoral education was already underway at Georgia Baptist Hospital under E. A. Verdery who was a supervisor in the Southern Baptist Association for Clinical Pastoral Education. From 1957 to 1962 the two programs steadily developed strength and increased their involvement with the theological seminaries of Greater Atlanta.

A twofold crisis in 1961 precipitated the creation of the Georgia Association for Pastoral Care. One issue was whether the chaplaincy program being established at the Central State Hospital in Milledgeville would be a Baptist program or a Council for Clinical Training program related to the Christian Council of Atlanta and the Grady Memorial Hospital chaplaincy. Dr. Louie Newton, Pastor of the Druid Hills Baptist Church in Atlanta, was chairman of the campaign to raise approximately one million dollars to build chapels for the twelve-thousand-bed Milledgeville hospital. He and many others in the state preferred the selection of a Baptist as Chief Chaplain. Seminary affiliations were already operative through the Christian Council of Atlanta, however.

The Christian Council of Atlanta was in a state of crisis itself at the time because of acute problems of leadership. The Grady Chaplaincy Committee was prompted to consider establishing some independence for its program from the direct control of the Christian Council. Gerkin recalled that "in the midst of this crisis atmosphere the idea of the Georgia Association for Pastoral Care was born." [34]

Gerkin found confirmation of his idea for an association of clinical pastoral educators during a luncheon meeting in January, 1962. He met with Dr. Allison Williams, Pastor of Trinity Presbyterian Church and Chairman of the Grady Chaplaincy Committee of the Christian Council of Atlanta; Dr. J. McDowell Richards, President of Columbia Theological Seminary; and Dr. Thomas H. McDill of the Columbia Seminary faculty. These four men were the first "to catch hold of the idea of an ecumenical organization that would cut across a lot of lines"—seminary, denominational, health and welfare institution systems, and accreditation structures.[35] In rapid succession they were joined by Verdery and the Georgia Baptist Hospital, by the Emory University School of Medicine and Candler School of Theology, by the Interdenominational Theological Center, and by the Georgia Department of Public Health.

The Georgia Association for Pastoral Care was incorporated on September 26, 1962. Dual affiliations became operative with the Southern Baptist Association for Clinical Pastoral Education in September, 1963, and with the Council for Clinical Training on January 1, 1964. The Council for Clinical Training created the category of "Independent Affiliated Centers" during its search for ways to resolve the conflict with Bruder and St. Elizabeth's Hospital. Gerkin used this category in establishing affiliation with the Council.[36]

Within five years of its incorporation, the Georgia Association for Pastoral Care was offering service and education in health and welfare institutions and through a Pastoral Counseling and Referral Service. The Annual Report for 1967 showed that 105 seminary students received basic clinical pastoral education, 33 clergymen received a year of full-time training as pastoral interns, and 9 men were engaged in residency programs leading toward certification as supervisors. Clinical pastoral education was offered by the staffs of 7 affiliated centers: Central State Hospital of Milledgeville, the Emory University Chaplaincy (functioning in three centers), Georgia Baptist Hospital, the Georgian Clinic, the Georgia Mental Health Institute, Grady Memorial Hospital, and the Youth Development Center.[37]

The Pastoral Counseling and Referral Service was begun in 1964 under Joe E. Caldwell. It provided nearly 3,000 counseling hours to 365 persons during 1967. Training in pastoral counseling was made available to 7 men engaged in Th.M. programs at Columbia Theological Seminary. The permanent staff in 1967 consisted of John Patten, the new director, and 9 part-time staff counselors. The Georgia Association for Pastoral Care was undergirded by a budget of nearly $75,000, an amount equal to the budget proposed for the national Association for Clinical Pastoral Education.[38]

From the perspective of the unification of clinical pastoral education, the Georgia Association for Pastoral Care inspired hope that collaboration on the basis of full equality between an old-line group, such as the Council for Clinical Training, and a "third force" group—the Southern Baptist Association for Clinical Pastoral Education—could occur with mutual benefit. It created an impressive example of the benefits of collaboration between ecclesiastical, theological, and medical institutions concerned with pastoral care and clinical pastoral education. Regional and ecumenical principles of organization were implemented. Ecumenical cooperation at the local level had proved itself during the thirties in Boston and during the fifties in the alliance of the Institute of Religion in Houston with the Texas Medical Center, a medical and a nursing college and five theological seminaries. The creators of the Georgia Association were mindful of both of these models for their regional, ecumenical, and inter-institutional structure. What was instructive for the profession as a whole in the creation of the Georgia Association of Pastoral Care was that competitive accrediting agencies could work together, could reciprocate in the certification of training, and could demonstrate substantial gains for everyone concerned.

The appearance of the Southern Baptist Association for Clinical Pastoral Education in a unified regional structure raises the question of its place on the national scene. How may we account for the readiness of the Southern Baptist Association to enter the merger plans of the Council for Clinical Training and the Institute of Pastoral Care at such a late date and with such little difficulty?

The Southern Baptist Association for Clinical Pastoral Education Renamed

One impulse was dominant in the formation of the Southern Baptist Association: the desire to become visible and influential on the national scene. In 1956, at the Fifth National Conference in Atlantic City, Southern Baptist professors and chaplains active in clinical pastoral education discovered with a jolt that the movement was headed toward unification without them. They saw that representation at the national level would be possible only for supervisors whose affiliations transcended their local seminaries and medical centers.

One objective stated in the Constitution of the Southern Baptist Association for Clinical Pastoral Education was "to provide a channel of communication with regional and national professional organizations in the field." [39] So important was representation to the Advisory Committee on Clinical Pastoral Education to the framers of the Constitution that the representatives of the Southern Baptist Association were "empowered to speak for the Association." [40] The Constitution was drafted by Southard, and it was Southard who presented the credentials for the Southern Baptist Association to the Advisory Committee in 1957. Out of personal experience at the national level, Southard urged giving the strongest possible hand to the group's representatives.

Once an Association had been formed, interaction with supervisors of other groups intensified. Regional meetings provided a start toward such interaction. Especially significant for the development of the Southern Baptist Association were regional activities centering in Houston, Texas, and Atlanta, Georgia. In Houston, supervisors of the Southern Baptist Association who were connected with the Institute of Religion were under the scrutiny of several Council for Clinical Training supervisors and Council-affiliated seminary professors. The Institute of Religion's policy of certifying supervisors on the authority of its affiliated seminaries provoked Council supervisors to challenge the procedures, criteria, and competence of the staff at every turn. Because dialogue remained open and continued for several years the program of the Institute of Religion was enriched, and indirectly benefit accrued to the Southern Baptist Association for Clinical Pastoral Education.

In Atlanta several leading Southern Baptist supervisors became a part of the Georgia Association for Pastoral Care, and there, too, a creative interaction with Council for Clinical Training supervisors resulted. The Southern Baptist Association acquired a debt of gratitude to the Council for Clinical Training not only for the initial training provided for Oates and Young in the mid-forties, but also for stimulation of development as a professional association in the late fifties and early sixties. It may be more than coincidental that the two representatives to the Joint Structure Committee who were most active in facilitating the inclusion of the Southern Baptist Association for Clinical Pastoral Education in the unified Association for Clinical Pastoral Education (Verdery and Thornton) were located in Atlanta and Houston respectively during the critical years under review.

The period from 1960 to 1965 saw a metamorphosis resulting in a professional association that could with integrity change its name to the Association of Clinical Pastoral Educators. From a small group of Southern Baptists, the Association became national in scope, ecumenical in membership, cohesive and well disciplined as a professional society. The record of this growing up duplicates in many ways the story told already of the Council for Clinical Training and the Institute of Pastoral Care in the fifties.

Not unexpectedly the Accreditation Committee was in the vanguard. A showdown with some of the founding supervisors over the procedures and criteria of accreditation and with others over enforcement of standards was inevitable. At one point the threat of secession was in the air. By 1962 the Accreditation Committee had established its authority in the Southern Baptist Association for Clinical Pastoral Education, and threats of secession abated.

Standards were upgraded in some respects and compromised in others from 1959 to 1961. Southard won consent in 1961 to an "equivalence" clause in the national standards that would allow candidates to enter supervisory training with only two units of clinical pastoral education provided the clinical work was received in the context of a graduate degree program (Th.M., Th.D., or D.R.E.). In the same meeting (1961) the Standards Committee, under the leadership of Kenneth Pepper, moved beyond national standards by making stipulations governing supervisors of advanced clinical pastoral education. A supervisor was required to have offered three units of accredited training at the introductory level before offering training for interns. Teaching supervisors were required to have offered six units of accredited training before accepting responsibility for an Assistant Supervisor. A center offering a program for assistant supervisors was required to have a minimum enrollment of six students in addition to the supervisory staff.[41]

In 1965 standards for teaching supervisors were made even more

189

stringent, and in 1966 the equivalence clause discussed above was rejected. No exceptions were made in the standards for seminary programs once the equivalence clause was rejected. Teaching supervisors were to be seminary related, however. They were required to function in a center where a graduate degree program was in progress. At least one member of a staff of teaching supervisors was required to hold a graduate theological degree. All teaching supervisors were to have had at least three years' experience in supervision of interns before beginning a program for supervisors-in-training. The center in which such training was offered was required to have been in operation at least one year and the teaching supervisor employed in his center at least one year. A minimum of six students remained standard. Procedures for certification of professors as supervisors were tightened up, making them identical with procedures for chaplain supervisors.[42]

The transition from a regional, denominational group to a national, ecumenical group became clear in 1963. The principle of full reciprocity with other clinical pastoral education agencies was adopted simultaneous with recognition of the Georgia Association for Pastoral Care, Inc. Regional organization of the Southern Baptist Association took place in 1963. The Association divided its seventy-one supervisors into five regions, stretching from Pennsylvania to California and from Ohio and Kentucky to the Gulf of Mexico.[43]

The percentage of non-Baptists was growing steadily. Add to this the number of Baptist supervisors employed in state and federal institutions, and a substantial majority of the membership were experiencing problems with the Southern Baptist name by 1963. Upon the motion of E. A. Verdery, Chaplain of the Georgia Baptist Hospital in Atlanta, a committee was appointed to study the question of a change of name.[44] The committee proposed in 1964 that the name be changed to "The Baptist Association for Clinical Pastoral Education." The report was tabled and a new committee appointed with a broader base of representation. In the annual meeting of 1965 the Association amended the Constitution to rename itself "The Association of Clinical Pastoral Educators." [45]

Three weeks later the Council for Clinical Training and the Institute of Pastoral Care in Joint Fall Conference adopted the name "Association for Clinical Pastoral Education" for the organization they were projecting as the consummation of their merger. The former Southern

Baptist Association did not know in September, 1965, that the Council and the Institute were proposing to become an A.C.P.E., too. The profession faced the prospect in October, 1965, of two associations, each designated A.C.P.E., differentiated by the final syllable of the last word—Educa*tors* and Educa*tion*. The manipulation of words in the titles was symbolic of just how close the several accrediting agencies were in reality. It was not surprising that six months later the former Southern Baptist Association was sitting down with Council for Clinical Training, the Institute of Pastoral Care, and Lutheran representatives to explore the feasibility of getting on board the merger train.

In September, 1966, the Association of Clinical Pastoral Educa*tors* gave their representatives in joint committees wholehearted endorsement and full authority to act as delegates in forwarding the "formation of an Association for Clinical Pastoral Education." [46] The following year, the members overwhelmingly approved resolutions that accreditation activity be delegated to the Association for Clinical Pastoral Education, and subsequently "that the Association of Clinical Pastoral Educators be dissolved at the close of the annual meeting in 1967 in the interest of full participation in the new Association for Clinical Pastoral Education." Advocates of unification were surprised that only two negative votes were cast.[47] In retrospect it appeared that the basic issues had been resolved in the debates about the change of name from 1963 to 1965.

The Association for Clinical Pastoral Education, 1967

A final burst of effort in joint committees and in regional meetings during 1966-67 prepared the way for the first meeting of the constituting agencies of the Association for Clinical Pastoral Education in October, 1967.

The House of Delegates met unofficially following the Fall Conference to ratify the Constitution and By-laws. Their actions were taken with the understanding that they were subject to final approval after legal incorporation on November 17, 1967. I was privileged to observe the first session of the House of Delegates as the Constitution and Bylaws were discussed and voted item by item. Being a nominee for an office, I was invited to attend but was not qualified to participate or vote until after the ratification of the Constitution and Bylaws and the election of officers. This afforded me the opportunity of functioning as an observer in a group dynamics process. I recorded the feelings communicated in the discussion and have analyzed my notes as follows.[48]

An inclusive spirit prevailed over separatist attitudes in at least seven issues. Concern about the status of inactive supervisors, of supervisors in centers outside the United States, and of membership for councils of churches provided the clearest instances of the attitude of inclusiveness. A humanistic stance prevailed in discussing the relationship of the Association for Clinical Pastoral Education to so-called secular centers for clinical pastoral education. An effort to stress the churchly character of clinical pastoral education in the statement of purpose (Article II) was soundly defeated. Delegates were concerned to avoid church-state conflicts as well as to avoid the separatism implicit in stressing the churchly identity of the profession.

The relationship of the national to the regional centers of the Association for Clinical Pastoral Education appeared in six distinct issues. In half of the instances the focus of concern was to effect a clear division of authority and responsibility in the interest of good order, clear responsibility, and fair represenation. In other instances the House of Delegates firmly rejected the patterned dependency of supervisors who were asking for a continuation of the paternalism once characteristic of a national office.

The issue of clusters appeared in connection with the Bylaws (Article I, Section 4-C). The House of Delegates came down strongly in favor of the cluster concept and in support of the financial inducements offered to those centers that unite in clusters around one or more theological schools. A minor struggle erupted over the division of authority between the Standards Committee and the Structure Committee in writing the section on clusters. Aside from this, no evidence of bad feeling stemming from the merger process itself appeared in the House of Delegates meeting.

Analysis of representation in the Association for Clinical Pastoral Education showed a remarkable balance of the constituting agencies. Based on statistics reported by the nine regional meetings during the spring of 1967, the Association for Clinical Pastoral Education formed with 256 supervisors divided approximately in thirds: 90 from the Council, 74 from the Institute, and 92 from the former Southern Baptist Association and those supervisors in the Lutheran Council who were not dually affiliated with the Council for Clinical Training or the Institute of Pastoral Care.

Examining regional distribution, I found Council for Clinical Training supervisors with a strong majority in two regions (Eastern and Pacific), Institute of Pastoral Care supervisors with a majority in two regions (Northeast and East Central), the former Southern Baptist Association with a majority in two regions (mid-Atlantic and Southwest), and the Lutheran Council a majority in one region (North Central). In the Southeast Region the Council for Clinical Training and the former Southern Baptist Association had approximately equal numbers, and in the South Central Region the Council for Clinical Training and the Institute of Pastoral Care were equally represented. The ratio of former Southern Baptist Association members to others dropped somewhat when the membership of the House of Delegates was examined. The slight decrease in Southern Baptist Association representation in the 1967-68 House of Delegates probably reflected the relative lateness of this group's participation at regional levels of the new Association for Clinical Pastoral Education.[49] Perhaps the most remarkable aspect of the first meeting of the Association for Clinical Pastoral Education was the absence from view of group consciousness associated with previous affiliations. A sense of being united in spirit as well as in organizational structure was evident.

During the following winter the selection for Executive Director fell upon Charles E. Hall, Jr. Hall was a Kansan who assumed executive leadership of the Association for Clinical Pastoral Education from his position as Chaplain Supervisor at Topeka State Hospital. Hall began his career as a Council for Clinical Training Supervisor in 1953. He appeared in the history of clinical pastoral education as chairman of the accreditation committee at the time the Council for Clinical Training and the Institute of Pastoral Care effectively merged their accrediting functions. He became President of the Council for Clinical Training next. He was deeply involved in the creation of the Association for Clinical Pastoral Education from the early sixties until he was chosen to be its first full-time Executive Director in December, 1967.

Early in November, 1967, John Smith, the President and Interim Executive Director for the Association for Clinical Pastoral Education, was a guest in the Board of Governors' meeting of the American Association of Pastoral Counselors. He found there an interest in coordinating times and places for annual meetings and, further, an interest in the joint accreditation of centers.[50] Whether this would be predictive of subsequent developments remained to be seen.

The Association for Clinical Pastoral Education was not ready to pay serious attention to additional mergers or the formation of new joint committees during 1967-68. These matters were reported during the November 16-17 meeting of the Executive Committee in Boston. Preempting such issues, however, was the formal Incorporation Meeting of the Association for Clinical Pastoral Education, Inc. Just before noon on November 17, 1967, the unification of the profession was accomplished in a brief legal ceremony. Incorporation was accomplished with the assistance of Mr. Lloyd Anderson, attorney, from Worcester, Massachusetts. The incorporators were John I. Smith, Arthur M. Tingue, Emil M. Hartl, Charles V. Gerkin, Edward E. Thornton, Thomas L. H. Collin, Orwoll O. Anderson, Lowell G. Colston, Charles E. Hall, Jr., Armen D. Jorjorian, E. Augustus Verdery, Lloyd Anderson, John M. Billinsky, Henry C. Brooks, James W. Dykens, Bardwell H. Flower, Judson D. Howard, Homer L. Jernigan, Rollin J. Fairbanks.

With incorporation of the Association for Clinical Pastoral Education completed, the efforts of two decades found organizational fulfillment. The hopes of nearly a half-century were actualized. The prospects had never been better for the wholesale re-formation of theological education on a professional model.

Professional Maturity at Age Forty-four

Clinical pastoral education was born in 1923 when the physician, Keller, and theologues from Bexley Hall plunged into the social problems of Cincinnati's inner-city. The profession reached maturity in 1967, at the ripe age of forty-four years. The internal dynamic of its maturation had to do with the relationship of clinical pastoral education to theological education. As the separate groups moved toward theological education, they moved toward each other. As they accepted each other, they became more fully accepted by theological education. Theological education became the unifying commitment of the field. The word chaplain was dropped from the label "chaplain supervisor," and "clinical pastoral educator" emerged as the appropriate professional identity of the supervisor.

The new Association for Clinical Pastoral Education broadened its base both in clinical centers and in seminary support. Eighty-one seminaries sought membership within three months of incorporation. This was 27 more than had affiliated with all the separate agencies combined. Clinical centers were functioning in 6 parishes and 11 community service agencies and clinics, as well as 64 psychiatric hospitals, 113 general hospitals and medical centers, 18 correctional institutions, and 5 mental retardation schools.[51]

Theological education was expected to be the major preoccupation of the new profession as it moved beyond unification. W. Paul Jones, Dean of the Saint Paul School of Theology in Kansas City, told the 1967 Fall Conference: "For me, it goes almost without saying that you are the wave of the future. The new curricula will be coming in your direction." Jones stated categorically: "As we move educationally into the methods of colloquys, team teaching, exposure requiring competent supervision . . . there is no faculty member that dare be without special training in these skills that you use." [52]

Indicative of an educational philosophy coming of age was the concluding presentation to the 1967 Fall Conference. Thomas W. Klink and colleagues from the Division of Religion and Psychiatry of the Menninger Foundation presented a study of "Critical Incidents in Supervision" with the subtitle "Toward a General Theory of Learning in Practicum-Based Education." [53] Directions for the future of the profession were clearly given by both Jones and Klink in the Conference at which unification occurred.

The developmental history of any profession reaches its maturity, according to Freeman, when a synthesis of specializations is devised. Its next developmental task is "to determine whether to surrender a part of its function to others or encompass a new social problem." [54] Of the many social problems confronting clinical pastoral educators in their first year as a unified profession, none seemed more ripe for solution than the problem of radically reforming theological education. Leaders of the American Association of Theological Schools were committed to drastic redeployment of resources and to curriculum revisions that would give at least one full year to professional education in clinical centers of many kinds." [55]

Could it be that the promise of clinical pastoral education announced by Keller, Cabot, and Boisen nearly a half-century before was about to be realized for all seminarians rather than for a select few only? The question was a persistent one in 1967-68. It called for vision, flexibility, and educational statesmanship. It put the maturity of the profession to the test. The test was one of ultimate loyalties. Which was higher on the clinical pastoral educator's hierarchy of values: to protect the hard-won gains of professional identity in a unified association, or to risk losing those gains by joining wholeheartedly in the fast-breaking, revolutionary remaking of theological education? The answer to the question will be told in the history of the next half-century of clinical pastoral education, perhaps, but not in this volume.

Curiosity about what lies beyond unification cannot be put to rest entirely. I do not presume to read the future in the past, but I believe that one may with integrity find hints of the future in the dynamic realities of the present. A careful reading of the structure and dynamics of a developing organism is a fairly reliable method for predicting subsequent behavior. Part IV is based on the assumption that a depth analysis of specific programs of clinical pastoral education will yield valid clues to understanding the future. In a fundamental sense what is beyond unification is as yet undetermined. It is being shaped, however, in the decisions that clinical pastoral educators make about the hard questions of the present. The case studies that follow point up both the questions and some of the alternative solutions out of which the future will be turned into a new era in the history of clinical pastoral education.

Part IV

Beyond Unification

9

DYNAMICS AND DEVELOPMENT

Clinical pastoral education offered its founders and early developers the excitement and fascination of an adventure. It was a venturing into little-known countries. It was discovering how to learn from one's own experience. It was learning to survive and to minister on the frontiers of interpersonal involvement under crisis conditions. For Boisen and many who followed him into mental hospitals, it was exploration of the inner world. For Keller and the many who have gone in his direction, it was exploration of the outer world—the world of social structures and the dynamics of social change. For theological educators it was engagement with the institution of the seminary—a wager that revolutionary educational processes would prove effective in growing seminarians more free to love and more competent as professional persons than before.

The history of clinical pastoral education would not be complete if it presented only a chronicle of organizational events at the national level. The heart of the profession is in the local institutions where clinical pastoral education actually occurs. It is bi-focal, including both the clinical centers where ministers make their way with other professional persons and the theological faculties where the future of religious communities is given shape.

In order to add a dimension of depth to the history of the profession and to show the development that has occurred over several decades, I shall present case studies from both a hospital and a seminary. Samples will be presented from the twenties and thirties and from the sixties.

The first study is the Worcester State Hospital where Boisen launched clinical training in a mental hospital. Boisen's program will be examined in its fourth year, 1928-29. In 1928 Boisen was at the full flower of his distinctive style of training. Phil Guiles, Don Beatty, and Alex Dodd of subsequent note were engaged in their first summer of training. Four decades later the program at Worcester State Hospital was under the direction of John I. Smith. Smith completed his twentieth year at Worcester in 1968. Not only was he director of an extensive and highly sophisticated program of professional education, but also he had moved from executive leadership of the Institute of Pastoral Care to become the first president of the Association for Clinical Pastoral Education.

The second case study will be a double-exposure in the Philadelphia area. I shall present Philadelphia Divinity School (Episcopal), which was the most highly developed seminary program of clinical pastoral education in the thirties, and Crozer Theological Seminary (American Baptist) a school that has made notable progress in the psychological education of seminarians in the sixties. Reuel L. Howe directed the program of the Philadelphia Divinity School, and I have been closely related to the program at Crozer.

Worcester State Hospital, 1928

Anton Boisen prepared an illustrated booklet on the Summer Program of 1928 that tells the story so well, I shall reproduce it in its entirety (see insert following page 208).[1] The pictures are from photographs Boisen, himself, took and developed. He included these in the booklet much as one might put together a family scrapbook. The booklets were produced in some quantity, although few are extant. Presumably Boisen used them in recruiting students as well as for remembering groups from year to year.

Perhaps the best description of the content of the training experience in 1928 was given by Donald C. Beatty, who was Boisen's assistant chaplain in 1927-28 and was a member of the 1928 summer group:

"We had to justify our place and indeed our presence in the hospital by assuming many responsibilities now shared or carried on by other workers. In addition to worship services, pastoral calling, and individual interviewing, we conducted choirs, managed ball teams, promoted plays and pageants and outdoor carnivals for patients, published the hospital newspaper, took patients out for walks and hikes, managed the hospital library, sometimes the canteen, and generally made ourselves useful. The theological students we brought to the hospitals to study human personality problems sometimes worked as ward attendants, supervised recreation or otherwise contributed to the leisure-time activity of the patients. Our 'study' in those days may have been short on theory, lectures, and conferences, but it was long on first-hand contact with people in trouble . . . and we learned a lot in the process." [2]

In Beatty's words, the 1928 program was "long on first-hand contact with people in trouble." *Doing* was the way of ministering in the early days of clinical training. Boisen and his students lived out the theology of "a cup of cold water" given in Jesus' name.

In a real sense the training program was an extension of Boisen's own experience as a patient after remission of his symptoms in 1921. Boisen preserved the memo he sent to Dr. Chambers on June 15, 1921, a few days after being transferred to a convalescent ward. In it he told the doctor of his problem finding a way to spend his energy "to good advantage." He observed a *"lack of occupation for most of the men during the major part of the day."* He presented the doctor an inventory of the recreational equipment on the ward, consisting of one victrola, one set of checkers accessible only by grace of the attendant, six books, and a few periodicals. In conclusion Boisen proposed a lengthy list of supplies and recreational equipment and a program of activities including daily walks, talks on mental hygiene, and the like. In subsequent memos Boisen proposed doing photographic work, a Fourth of July festival with ball games, track events, and musical programs.[3]

When we compare Boisen's memos of 1921 with his program descriptions from the early years of clinical training, the similarities are striking. Boisen described the 1933 program at Elgin State Hospital, for example, under ward work, recreational work, educational work, religious work, and instruction. Under recreation he listed: softball, volley ball, bowling, and play festivals; under educational work; home talent programs, special class for convalescent catatonics, the Hospital Messenger, the Hospital Pictorial, the choir, the Orchestra, mental health conferences, and the Hospital Interprter (a paper for the relatives and friends of patients).[4]

Boisen and his students acted out their ministerial identity in the conduct of public worship primarily. They gave little attention to counseling as a significant method of ministry. Concerning worship in a mental hospital, Boisen wrote that its aim was not merely to reawaken faith known in times past. For this faith was often based on erroneous presuppositions. Its aim was to "substitute a wholesome religion for one which may have been associated with the patient's difficulties." The problem of worship, Boisen continued, "is how to make use of all available resources . . . to re-inforce therapeutically valuable suggestions. Religious emotion was not to be looked upon as an end in itself, but as a means of re-making and stabilizing character."[5] To facilitate his goals in worship, Boisen found it necessary to publish his own hymnal. In *Hymns of Hope and Courage* (1937), he eliminated references to enemies, magic, a sense of fear and isolation, and inappropriate moods of joy. He focused on the consciousness of sin and aspiration for a better life; on the love and forgiveness of God; on resignation and faith, courage, action, and the future life.[6]

The neglect of counseling as a means of ministry may be understood in part by recalling that Boisen was pre-Carl Rogers. Even post-Rogers, however, Boisen modified his training program only slightly. In 1948, Boisen saw "neither the possibility nor the desirability of establishing a new profession of religious counselors." He pinned his hopes on "the well-trained minister in the quiet discharge of his duties as pastor and preacher."[7] In 1932 Boisen developed what he called "Group Therapy" for patients. It consisted of open discussion groups conducted on a Bible class model and dealing with the problems of everyday living which patients faced within a hospital setting. In this, too, he relied on traditional models of ministry and avoided the challenge of the counseling field.[8]

Boisen's students in 1928 were infused with a strong sense of interprofessional collaboration in their service to patients. Guiles was assigned to Dr. Sleeper and Dr. Hoskins as a research assistant during the year 1928-29. Boisen was already publishing research articles in the *American Journal of Psychiatry* (1926) and the *American Journal of Sociology* (1928).[9]

Clinical training at Worcester in 1928 was, indeed, "short on theory." Theory sessions consisted of two seminars per week on the "interrelationship between religious experience and mental disorder." Boisen said the seminars were under the direction of "our brilliant young assistant superintendent," Dr. Lewis B. Hill, who was assisted by staff psychiatrists Spafford Ackerly and Henry B. Moyle.[10] Necessity dictated the curriculum in 1928. In the first place students were employed as orderlies and had little free time for class sessions, and in the second place not much theory had developed from the pastoral perspective. More classroom work was introduced after 1930. Wise, who succeeded Boisen at Worcester State Hospital in 1931, reduced ward work to five hours a day for the first two weeks and eliminated ward work altogether thereafter.[11] Boisen made similar changes at Elgin after 1932. The number of hours devoted to conferences during the summer term was increased from twenty-two in 1932 to eighty in 1937. Many theological professors from Chicago shared leadership of the seminars with Boisen and representatives of the psychiatric staff of Elgin State Hospital.[12]

The financial base for clinical training in 1928 was the hospital budget from which Boisen drew his salary, plus contributions from private individuals and a few Congregational churches in the Boston area. Boisen reported supplementary income for the training program as follows:

1926	$ 300
1927	$ 680
1928	$2,500
1929	$1,660
1930	$6,450

These figures do not reflect the contributions from Boisen's own earnings. In 1932 receipts for the teaching program at Elgin State Hospital were $221, while expenses were $925. The balance of $704 came out of Boisen's pocket.[13]

Insofar as the inadequacies of the instructional program were due to the necessity of students being employed as orderlies, improvements in the curriculum awaited a more adequate financial base. Guiles understood this in 1928, and a year later delivered the monies necessary to underwrite the program, as we have seen in an earlier chapter.

The identity of the Worcester program of 1928 was reflected in correspondence between Boisen and Cabot in 1929 concerning a name for the incorporation that would receive the Earheart Foundation grant. Boisen proposed the name, "Committee for Religious Work among the Mentally Ill." Cabot's suggestions were two: (1) Committee for educational, occupational, recreational, and religious work among the mentally ill, and (2) Committee for social work among the mentally ill. Boisen countered with "Committee on Ministry among the Mentally Ill." Clearly Boisen stressed the religious and ministerial purposes of his work, whereas Cabot saw primarily the educational, occupational, recreational, and social work methods that Boisen employed.[14]

Paul Johnson's comment is apropos to the character of clinical training both in 1928 and in 1968. He saw a characteristic of the stance of the church in America (as distinct from Europe) to be involvement in society, wherever society is in need of service. Boisen, therefore, plunged into an activity program at Worcester State Hospital, while Dicks, for example, organized his students to carry bed pans at Massachusetts General Hospital. Both saw their activities as religiously significant even though observers on the outside might see only the secular meaning.[15]

Worcester State Hospital, 1968

Boisen's term as chaplain at Worcester State Hospital ended in 1931 with his move to Elgin. He was succeeded by Carroll A. Wise, 1931-42. From 1942 to 1945 no chaplain was appointed, and no clinical training occurred at Worcester. An Episcopal clergyman, Al Greene, became chaplain from 1945 to 1949.[16] In cooperation with Fairbanks at Episcopal Theological School, Greene offered a six-week unit of training in the summer of 1948. The Minutes of the Board of Governors of the Institute of Pastoral Care record that Worcester became the first mental hospital center to open under auspices of the Institute of Pastoral Care, Inc. and that members of the Board were anxious lest this lead to a shift away from the study of "normal people." [17]

John I. Smith became chaplain at Worcester in 1948 as Greene's associate. In the summer of 1950, Green moved to Western Massachusetts and left Smith with a class of students to supervise on his own. Smith was accredited by the Institute of Pastoral Care in 1952 and remained at Worcester to the time of this writing.[18] He became a member of the Institute's Training Committee in 1955, joined the Andover Newton cluster in 1956, and became Executive Director of the Institute of Pastoral Care in the Spring of 1958.[19] Smith has been a leading supervisor throughout his tenure at Worcester.

The Summer School in Clinical Pastoral Education at Worcester State Hospital, 1968, was under the auspices of Andover Newton Theological School and accredited by the Association for Clinical Pastoral Education, Inc. The staff consisted, in addition to Smith, of four assistant supervisors and four course assistants. Whereas Boisen and Beatty had ten students in 1928, Smith and his eight assistants had twenty students in 1968. Students included five Roman Catholics, five American Baptists, four Episcopalians, two Sweden Borgians, and the rest from the United Church of Christ, Methodist, and Lutheran denominations.

Goals for the 1968 Summer School were four: (1) "to enable the student to gain an understanding of people, their deeper motivations and difficulties, their emotional and spiritual strengths and weaknesses"; (2) to "develop effective pastoral methods for ministering to people," giving special attention to the "unique resources, responsibilities, and limitations" attendant upon the role of clergyman; (3) "to help the student learn how to work cooperatively with representatives of other professions and to utilize community resources toward achieving more effective living"; and (4) to "encourage a desire for further understanding," that is, to stimulate research interests. Underlying all these objectives, according to Smith and his staff, "is the hope that the student will grow to have a better understanding of himself." [20]

The student's time was divided approximately fifty-fifty between direct patient contact and formal learning situations. The verbatim had long since become standard in mental hospital centers as well as general hospitals where the method was developed. Students at Worcester in 1968 wrote fifteen verbatims at approximately two per week, plus three book reviews, and two case studies. The case study involved a detailed analysis of the patient's history, present functioning, pastoral conversations over a period of several weeks, evaluation, prognosis, and plan for further ministry. The following guide for verbatim writing was given the students at the beginning of the training period:[21]

Record of Pastoral Interview

Date _____

Counselor _____

No. _____

Code _____

Comments: _____

I. *Known Facts:*

Summarize here what factual information you have learned about the person before the interview. Describe the person, situation, and occasion for the interview.

Note three-inch margin for the supervisor's comments.

II. *Preparation:*

Knowing what you do about the person, prepare your mind for the visit. Note what you do not wish to do. Then list the specific things you would like to see result from the interview. Avoid pressing your agenda on him.

What is the value of such preparation?

III. *Observations:*

What do you find at the beginning of the visit? Observe situation in which you find the person. Note appearance of the person as to posture and gestures, facial expressions and attitudes, nervous mannerisms and calm poise.

Such observations are clues as to how to proceed.

IV. *Interview:*

The pastoral role usually prevents taking notes during the interview but immediately after, a stream of key words may be jotted down. Then at first opportunity, type-write interview as verbatim as possible. Avoid third person summaries. Enter only direct quotations, each speech as a separate paragraph led in by letter for the one speaking. Nonverbal communications may also be noted. Listen with full attention, and you will find that memory grows with interest and practice.

Reserve all interpretations for conclusion, keeping this part for text without commentary.

V. *Conclusion:*

1. *Analysis* of what took place. Note association of ideas, repetition, hidden implications, unconscious revelations, etc. State insights gained by the counselee and interpretations that occur to you.

2. *Criticism* of your own responses. Note what you might have done better. Consider successful methods worth using again.

3. *Opportunity* for positive steps by the counselee and further service by the pastor or others who might be helpful.

4. *Time* of the visit in minutes. Next appointment if any, or plan for follow-up.

Arrange this part in four numbered paragraphs.

Use of the verbatim presupposes a commitment by Smith and his staff to Boisen's thesis that the living documents are the primary

206

sources of data in clinical pastoral training. Empirical observation is obviously the basic methodology in the Worcester program of 1968, as it was in 1928. This is seen in the ratio of fifteen verbatims to three book reviews. Differences between the presuppositions of Smith and of Boisen appear in the fact that 1968 students functioned at all times in a pastoral role, whereas 1928 students were seen most often as orderlies assigned to recreational, occupational, or musical activities. Pastoral counseling in one-to-one relationships was the primary method of ministry in 1968. Boisen's students were defined as "religious workers" only when they conducted public worship. Smith's program moved far beyond the Boisen model in regard to the pastoral role identity of students. The 1968 summer program at Worcester had not yet begun to place students in the emerging new training roles associated with community mental health centers. Such roles as community organizers, equippers of the laity for community mental health functioning, and consultants to community clergy with respect to parish administration, small group leadership, and the like were being developed for interns and residents but not for summer students in 1968.[22]

The classroom was the scene of clinical pastoral education about 50 percent of the time for Smith; it occupied less than 10 percent of the time for Boisen. Approximately thirty hours were given to orientation lectures during the early weeks of the course. Themes included the functioning of other professionals and the goals and methods of pastoral care in a mental hospital and the types of mental illness that students were seeing. Hospital personnel representing all the professional disciplines were used as lecturers. Four seminars were scheduled on a formal basis with course outlines and recommended readings. Each seminar continued for variable periods of three to seven sessions. Themes and leaders were (1) Interpersonal Relationships by Roger Bibace, Ph.D., Assistant Professor, Psychology Department of Clark University; (2) Adolescent Behavior by Miriam Gavarin, M.D., Psychiatrist at the Youth Guidance Center, assisted by the chaplain and psychologist of the juvenile court and the Detention-Reception Center; (3) Group Psychotherapy and Group Work by Richard Rablen, Ph.D., Director of Training, Psychology Department of Worcester State Hospital; and (4) Phenomenological Theology by John M. Billinsky, Guiles Professor of Psychology, Andover Newton Theological School, assisted by Meredith B. Handspicker, Assistant Professor of Practical Theology at Andover Newton.[23]

Students in the 1968 Summer School participated in small group meetings with an Assistant Supervisor and Course Assistant four times each week. One of the four sessions was used for a case seminar with material being presented by the students, and the other three sessions were unstructured. Each student was required to have one conference per week with his own supervisor and more if needed. Verbatims were discussed and any concerns related to the student's relationships at any level could be explored in these individual supervisory sessions.[24]

Assistant supervisors met with Smith as a group twice weekly. In addition, Smith met weekly with each of the eight staff members for an individual supervisory session. Course assistants had separate small group meetings with Smith two times each week. The total staff met weekly, and all the students met with the total staff once each week also. Chaplain Smith's time was devoted almost exclusively to the supervison of his eight staff assistants, who in turn supervised the twenty students.[25] While Boisen had one assistant chaplain in Don Beatty, nothing of the present-day understanding of the philosophy and methodology of training assistant supervisors had appeared in 1928. Not until the late thirties and early forties did experienced chaplain supervisors become self-conscious about their work in training other supervisors. Formal standards for supervisory training did not approximate present-day standards until the mid-fifties. In these respects Smith was the inheritor of the many gains associated with the development of clinical pastoral education from a movement to a profession.

Summary Evaluation

In summary, the 1968 Summer School in Clinical Pastoral Education was characterized by balance between the perspectives of the behavioral sciences and of pastoral care and counseling. It made use of many resource people from the staffs of the Worcester State Hospital, Andover Newton Theological School, and also community clergymen with special competencies. Teaching methods reflected a balanced use of lectures, visual aids, case studies, seminar discussions based on independent study, and student-centered seminars designed

CLINICAL EXPERIENCE FOR THEOLOGICAL STUDENTS

WORCESTER STATE HOSPITAL

Worcester, Massachusetts

1928

FOREWORD

For four years the Worcester State Hospital has been offering to students in theology an opportunity to get clinical experience in dealing with maladies of the personality. This rather unusual project has proceeded from the view that in very many cases such maladies are spiritual problems in the strict sense of that term, disorders of emotion and volition, of belief and attitude, rooted not in cerebral disease or in intellectual deterioration, but in the age-old conflict which the Apostle Paul so vividly describes, the conflict between the law that is in our minds and that which is in our members. When such conflicts result happily we recognize them as religious experiences, as in the cases of John Bunyan and George Fox and Augustine; when they result unhappily we send the sufferer to such a hospital as ours and speak of him as insane.

It is our belief that the religious worker ought to be able to do a good deal more to help such sufferers than he is now doing and that in their experiences he has an unequalled opportunity to chart the little-known country of the inner world in which such sufferers have lost their way. Certainly the experience of the medical profession has shown that the study of the pathological is one of the best approaches to the understanding of the normal. And those who are not physicians know that it is when our cars get out of order that we are most apt to learn something about the machinery which runs them. We hope therefore thru this approach to gain new understanding into the deep forces of the religious life and of the laws with which theology deals.

The pages which follow summarize in word and in picture the activities, the responsibilities and the opportunities afforded the students who have taken advantage of our offer.

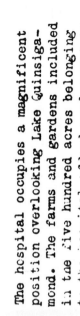

The Worcester State Hospital was founded in 1833. It is the oldest state hospital in Massachusetts and the third oldest in the U.S.A. It bears a long and distinguished record as a teaching institution and many of those now prominent in American psychiatry have received training here.

The hospital occupies a magnificent position overlooking Lake Quinsigamond. The farms and gardens included in the five hundred acres belonging to the hospital afford employment to many of the 1700 patients housed under its single roof. In this view, all that you see above the bridge belongs to the hospital.

Dr. William A. Bryan, superintendent, whose broad-minded policy has made this project possible. Dr. Bryan is one of those rare executives who can keep men with very different views working together harmoniously at a common task.

The medical staff of the hospital, for the summer of 1928. In addition to the executive officers and the regular medical staff, this picture includes six medical internes who spend some months here in clinical psychiatry.

Mr. Anton T. Boisen, under whose direction the chaplain's department of the hospital has been developed, divides his time between the hospital, where he spends nine months as chaplain, and the Chicago Theological Seminary, where he spends three months as a member of the faculty. He also teaches this year in the Boston University School of Theology.

These students comprised the summer group of 1928. They are (front row, left to right) Rice, Crozer; Akers, B.U.; Miss Grant, Yale; Boisen, chaplain; Dodd, Union; Beatty, associate chaplain; (rear) Carter, Chicago Theological; Brockelbank, Alexandria; Guiles, Union; Schilling, B.U.; Bennett, Columbia; Smith, B.U.

Dr. Lewis B. Hill, until September assistant superintendent of the hospital, a capable executive and a brilliant and stimulating teacher, has given generously of his time and strength to the conferences which the theological group has held twice each week. In conjunction with Mr. Boisen Dr. Hill will give this year a seminar course in the Boston University School of Theology.

Students are privileged to attend staff sessions where individual cases are presented and discussed. The example of careful and exhaustive study from different angles, so typical of the best hospitals for mental disorder has been stimulating and instructive.

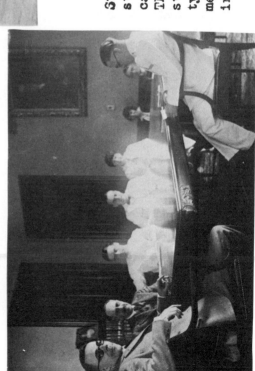

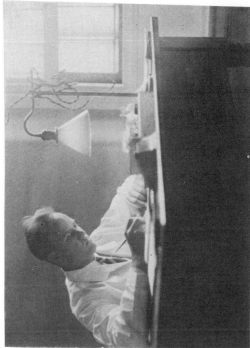

is valuable as any of the varied duties assigned the students, is that of making careful and detailed notes of the conduct and progress of the patients. This training in careful observation and accurate recording of findings should be of decided value in their later work.

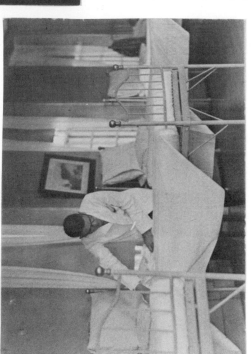

This year six of the students have served as ward attendants. There is no greater opportunity in the hospital either to help or to study the patient than such service affords. The welfare of the patient probably depends more on the attendant with whom he is in constant daily association than on any other worker in the hospital.

The chaplain's department sponsors the recreational program both indoors and out. This picture was taken near the "finals" of a checker tournament. The department distributes in the course of the year dozens of packs of playing cards as well as many checker sets and other games.

The "Hospital Herald" and the "Hospital Pictorial" - mimeograph news-sheets which are posted thruout the hospital - have become a valuable part of the summer's work. Smith and Akers were the editors this year and made "the paper" a very real part of the institutional life.

A typical group of patients out for
an airing. These men, under the
leadership of Mr. Guiles, had just
completed a three-mile hike and were
refreshing themselves before returning to the ward.

Conferences with individual patients give opportunities to understand and to help. There is
no more important feature of our
work - either from the standpoint
of the patient or the student -
than these personal talks.

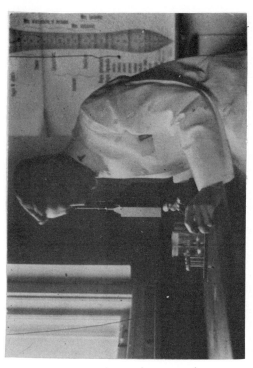

The hospital is participating in a very important research project for the study of catatonic dementia praecox. The aim is to study cases of this type from every possible angle: physiological, psychiatric and social. Dr. Sleeper and Dr. R.G. Hoskins are in charge of the project for our hospital, and welcome any contribution which we may be able to make. Mr. Guiles is to be directly associated with Dr. Sleeper (pictured) through the coming year.

The student is made acquainted with the significance of the laboratory tests and the other physical findings. About one-third of the newly admitted cases have a demonstrable physical basis for the disorder on account of which they have been sent to our hospital.

The occupational therapy department each year has students from
the Boston School of Occupational
Therapy who complete their practical training here. Thus with the
medical internes, the student
nurses and the theologues, the hospital is a training center for
five allied groups of students.

The Smith College School of Social
Work sends four students here for
their institutional training. The
group here pictured constitutes the
Social Service Staff for the year
1928-1929.

Mr. Donald C. Beatty, a graduate of the Boston University School of Theology, is now serving his second year as associate chaplain and musical director. Mr. Beatty's marked ability as a singer and leader of choral music and his great versatility make him a valuable man in the hospital.

Mr. Justin Philip Guiles, Union Seminary 1925, is to spend the entire year in research work at the hospital. Mr. Guiles has been doing some effective psychotherapeutic work with individuals. His skill as a musician makes him of great assistance in our musical program.

EXCERPTS FROM LETTERS OF SUMMER THEOLOGICAL STUDENTS

"That month at the hospital has meant a great deal to me.... The thoughts and emotions stirred by the experiences there have done as much to broaden and quicken me as any one term of college work has done. It is impossible to estimate the significance of that month of training, but certainly it will be a factor in the formation of whatever philosophy I finally emerge with."

"The value of such an experience simply cannot be put into words and it seems as if the insights gained in the hospital are going to make definite and permanent changes in my ministry."

"I felt quite unprepared on leaving Seminary to deal with the personal problems of the people who would come under my ministry - partly because many of my own problems were not happily solved and partly because I had not known enough of the lives and difficulties of people to know what to do in difficult situations. While I am still humble in the face of trouble of any serious sort I am not nearly so appalled by the difficulties that lie therein.- I will know how to go about finding the trouble and will be able to advise and counsel much more sanely and effectively than before my hospital experience. I can never adequately express my gratitude for the opportunity afforded me at Worcester.

LETTERS OF ENDORSEMENT

From Professor George A. Coe
Department of Religious Education, Teachers' College, Columbia University.

May I tell you why I am interested in Mr. Boisen's undertaking?

First, the problem which he is working upon is an important one. It affects many individuals and, what is more important, any results which he reaches are almost certain to be widely applicable both by physicians and by ministers and teachers of religion.

Second, as far as I know, no one else is working upon this problem. Further I know of few persons anywhere who are equipped for doing so. Mr. Boisen is clearly so equipped both by study and by preliminary practice. The reason for the neglect of so important a field is precisely that neither the physician nor the minister, except in the rarest instances, combines the necessary knowledge and outlook in the two aspects of the matter. The minister either bungles because he does not know psychiatry or else he turns the afflicted one over to psychiatrists who do not understand the psychology of religion.

From Dr. William A. Bryan
Superintendent, Worcester (Mass.) State Hospital.

The work which Mr. Boisen has been doing at this hospital has been productive of a great deal of good. The close personal observation of the students who have been at the hospital has helped us in arriving at an understanding of the difficulties of many of our patients, and their presence here has increased our facilities for intensive case work, has multiplied the recreational activities and has given an impetus to the religious services.

From Dr. William Healy
Judge Baker Foundation, Boston, Mass.

I am profoundly impressed by Mr. Boisen's attitude toward the intensely important problems he is trying to understand and by the deeply thoughtful and indeed ingenious approach to them. He has a certain fearlessness, bred of his own experience, and the ability to categorize the facts of human lives in ways most pregnant for practical understanding and treatment of situations. His recently developed attempt at the classification of personality changes and upheavals is to my mind one of the most suggestive contributions that I have recently seen in psychology and psychiatry.

. . . .

To my thinking Mr. Boisen's contribution stands the chance of being great not so much in psychiatry itself and in the dealing with abnormal minds as in the gaining of a better knowledge of normal mental life and experience. He is wise in understanding that time and again it has been pathology which has led to the understanding of the normal.

to facilitate the emotional assimilation of the student's new experiences. Learning at the affective level remained a pervasive concern of the Worcester program. Smith saw clinical training as an aid to the process in which a person becomes internally free to allow the image and likeness of God in which he is created to be expressed through him in all his relationships.[26]

Contrasts at Worcester State Hospital between 1928 and 1968 extended also to the programs of the academic year. Boisen's first "intern" was Beatty, who remained as an Assistant Chaplain in 1927-28. Guiles became Boisen's Assistant in 1928-29. They collaborated with psychiatrists in research projects, provided interim chaplaincy functions during Boisen's one-quarter absence each fall, and assisted Boisen in his activity programs the rest of the year.

Year-long training under Smith centered on the education of supervisors. Four to six positions were filled each year, even though no funding was provided by the hospital. Assistant supervisors filled part-time pastorates in the area in order to participate in the Worcester program. Their experience was graded with increasing levels of responsibility during the year. During the academic year, they assisted in part-time clinical pastoral education (on a two-day-per-week basis) with graduate students engaged in the S.T.M. program at Andover Newton Theological School and with candidates for a Masters Degree in Psychology, Counseling, and Guidance at Assumption College (Roman Catholic). They also conducted orientation programs for community clergymen on an interfaith basis and worked with the Director of Research of the Worcester State Hospital. During the summer, assistant supervisors carried major responsibility for the supervision of five first-unit students and one course assistant in the full-time program of clinical pastoral education previously described. Trainees at the supervisory level were typically engaged in their own psychotherapy during the year. The psychiatric resources of the hospital were available as well as those of the surrounding area.[27]

Smith was employed by the State of Massachusetts on the basis of a thirty-hour-per-week contract (an arrangement mandatory for all chaplains in Massachusetts as of 1968). His work as clinical pastoral educator was remunerated by affiliation with Andover Newton Theological School. The entire cost of the Summer School was underwritten by Andover Newton, and student fees were paid to the Seminary. Smith's program enjoyed obvious advantages over Boisen's.

Not only was the 1968 program fully accredited academically and professionally, but also it was subsidized financially by a theological school.[28]

Other benefits of professional maturation among clinical training groups appear in the comparison of Worcester in 1928 and 1968. Boisen was a self-certified supervisor, as were all the founding fathers and elder brothers of the movement. As I have shown in the chapter on Boisen, his role was highly instrumental but not intentional so far as present-day clinical pastoral education is concerned. He was never able to turn the corner from movement to profession, to enlarge his concerns, and to enter the mainstream of the seminary task of educating men both for personal authenticity and for functional competence. Smith was a second-generation supervisor who entered the field as it became a new profession. He had been immersed in the tasks of setting standards; certifying supervisors; and accrediting centers; in clarifying relationships with medical administrators, ecclesiastical authorities, and seminary faculties. While Boisen resisted the professionalizing trends, Smith pushed them along and directed them. The appearance of an interfaith rather than merely a pan-Protestant ecumenism in the training group of Worcester in 1968 is further tribute to the maturation of the profession of which the Worcester program is only one instance among many that could have been cited.

Boisen repeatedly said that he was not introducing a new content into theological education but only a new method of theological inquiry. He failed to describe the extent to which methods of inquiry in any field shape the conceptualizations of the field. From Boisen's single-minded study of religious experience in relation to mental disorder in 1928, the field moved in 1968 to a curriculum that opened students to the growth sciences and to sophisticated theories and methods of ministry, to a curriculum that culminated in the articulation of a phenomenological theology. Boisen's original concern to explore the inner world became an exploration both of the inner world of psychic dynamics and of the outer world of interpersonal relationships, of pastoral identity and pastoral role functions.

Pastoral work continued to be considered primarily in the shepherding and healing perspectives. The persistence of these two perspectives in clinical training was one strand of continuity between 1928 and 1968. It reflected the dependence of clinical pastoral education upon hospital centers and upon medical colleagues. As community mental health centers grow and as social engineering becomes better organized for training purposes, new breakthroughs may be expected to occur in the study of pastoral work from the perspectives of community organization, reconciling of groups in conflict, and the leadership of local congregations for constructive social action.

Clinical pastoral educators have talked about taking training into local churches since the early thirties, but tangible achievements have been few and far between. The problems of financing and supervising clinical training in local churches were matched by the difficulty in motivating students to go into congregational settings in preference to hospitals. A basic incompatibility is just now coming to light. So long as the controlling perspective of clinical pastoral education was shepherding and healing, the hospital and agency provided a superior laboratory for learning. Once training is undertaken from a fundamentally different perspective—that is, on the theoretical foundation of social psychology, community organization, and social change—the congregation and community at large may become an optimal setting for functional learning.

Hospital settings have predominated for over forty years, and not without reason. The empirical study of man and of religious experience was the primary educational goal of clinical training initially. Hospital settings provided protection against the deductive methods and idealistic styles of theological thinking that dominated most seminaries right down to the fifties and sixties. Separate medical institutions and a powerful medical profession wholeheartedly committed to inductive methods and realistic philosophical presuppositions constituted a needed bulwark behind which clinical pastoral education could develop. As the profession developed over the past four decades, new advances in educational method and in the articulation of educational philosophy were made. Leaders become secure enough as educators to take their methodological tools out of the hospitals in which they were designed and built and put them to work on the campuses of old-line seminaries and in the urban locations of action training programs.

The sophistication in educational method that makes new experimentation possible was evident in the Worcester curriculum of 1968. Gone were the teacher-centered methods of Boisen and the canned case studies with their psychology of religion preoccupation. Student-centered learning was the norm with verbatims reflecting the immediate experiencing of the students. Boisen's affiliation with faraway Chicago Theological Seminary had given place to the direct educational supervision and funding of the Worcester program by the nearby Andover Newton Theological School in connection with a cluster of five hospital centers.

Interns and residents were becoming involved in community mental health centers. The staff at Worcester, like clinical pastoral educators in many centers in 1968, had no interest in defending the prerogatives of hospital-based training. New thrusts were everywhere apparent. The profession awaited only the development of the organizing and reconciling perspective on pastoral functioning in the congregation and its larger community. Then proven supervisory methods could be applied to the community context. Clinical pastoral educators at Worcester State Hospital were ready in 1968 to enlarge the locus of their functioning in order to continue the adventure of offering theological education in the midst of the major conflicts of the age.

The dynamics and development of clinical pastoral education have been seen within a single hospital center by taking cross-sectional samples from the Worcester State Hospital programs of 1928 and 1968. But what are the dynamics, and what has been the fate of clinical pastoral education in theological seminaries? To answer this question we turn in the next chapter to two Philadelphia area seminaries and take cross-sectional samples from the late thirties and from the sixties. We shall see the turmoil and the hope that resulted from the juxtaposition of psychological and theological education for ministry.

10

PROFESSIONAL EDUCATION FOR MINISTRY

Theological educators have been alternately fascinated and repelled by clinical pastoral education during the past several decades. Many patterns of seminary-supervisor relationship have been tried, but no one pattern has emerged as the unanimous choice of those involved. A continuum measuring the degree of involvement between seminary faculty and clinical supervisors would show three major groupings.

The least involvement occurred when supervisors and seminary officials met only through the mediating services of an association of clinical pastoral educators. A student was recruited by brochures, as it were, screened by supervisors adjacent to the school, and met for the first time by his supervisor on the opening day of the summer program. Reports were sent to the student's seminary if requested, but with no face-to-face meeting of supervisor and faculty. The school exercised control over the curriculum of the center only indirectly through representation in the agency that certified the supervisor. The school had no choice in the employment of the supervisor, and the supervisor had no choice in shaping the curriculum within the seminary from which his student came.

A medium degree of involvement occurred when a seminary affiliated directly with one or more centers in which its students received clinical training. Often the training would be required, though not necessarily. Supervisors characteristically received a salary supplement from the affiliated seminary. The seminary faculty exercised, thereby, direct supervision of the curriculum offered in the clinical setting, and in some instances had a voice in the employment of the supervisor. The supervisor had faculty status in the affiliated school. This pattern was seen in Worcester State Hospital, for example.

Maximum involvement occurred when a seminary employed certified supervisors on its full-time faculty in the context of a thoroughly professional curriculum. Supervision would be practicum-based and could relate to a student's functioning in field education, homiletics, religious education, or social action, as well as pastoral care and counseling. Typically a school that sought maximum integration of clinical supervision into its curriculum also would maintain affiliations of the middle type described above. Interaction between supervisors and other faculty members was more intense, and more students came under the supervisory process. Clinical learning occurred the year around rather than primarily during a summer school in clinical pastoral education. Guiles developed this pattern early in the thirties, and a few other schools have adopted it subsequently.[1]

The two seminaries in the Philadelphia area selected for case study have tried all three patterns at various times. They should stimulate insight into both the problems and the possibilities of using clinical methods for theological learning.

Philadelphia Divinity School in the Thirties and Sixties

The vitality of the clinical training movement was nowhere more evident during the thirties than in a bold and creative experiment begun in the Protestant Episcopal Divinity School in Philadelphia in 1937. The school closed in 1933 because of financial problems attending the depression. Allan Evans was appointed Dean in 1935-36. He entered into consultation with Dunbar and Hiltner of the Council for the Clinical Training of Theological Students in order to design a radically new plan of theological education.

Hiltner prepared a prospectus on "Clinical Training as an Integral Part of the Curriculum of aTheological Seminary." [2] He bolstered his case by appealing to the successful experience of two Episcopal clergymen who received clinical training during the summer of 1935 under Leon R. Robison, Jr., at the Franklin School, a division of the Institute of Pennsylvania Hospital. Earl D. Bond, M. D., who became President of the Council for the Clinical Training of Theological Students in 1935, was Director of the Institute of Pennsylvania Hospital. He employed Robison as Assistant Principal of the Franklin School for emotionally disturbed children in 1933, and Robison offered training in the summers of 1934 and 1935. Robison's Episcopal trainees were older than most seminarians and very positive about the relevance of clinical training for parish functioning.[3]

Reuel L. Howe dominated the scene of the experiment. Evans employed him as a professor in the pastoral field while the New Plan was under construction, and Howe contributed to the design along with Evans and Hiltner. The origins of Reuel Howe's interest in psychiatry and in clinical training date to 1930-31. Howe described the events that led to his entrance into the field as follows:

It was at the end of my senior year, as a result of reading several books about the contribution of psychological insights to the ministry, that I fell into conversation with Dean Bartlett by accident and expressed my interest in further study along this line. . . . As a result of his interest, I was given a year's fellowship for study. This I did at the Institute of Mental Hygiene of the Pennsylvania Mental Hospital in Philadelphia and the University of Pennsylvania. My work was supervised by Dr. Earl D. Bond, President of the American Psychiatric Association, at that time. My work was also supervised by Dean Bartlett and W. Arthur Warner, on the faculty of the Divinity School and also director of a social agency in Philadelphia.[4]

The Rev. Dr. W. Arthur Warner, the Rev. Dr. Daniel McGregor, and Dr. Dunbar were in the forefront of the committee that encouraged the Board of the Divinity School to undertake the New Plan of Theological Education. What was new about the New Plan was that for the first time "full-time clinical training became an integral part of the curriculum." The Rev. J. Arnold Purdie joined Howe early in 1938 to help establish the first training program.[5]

Two plans were used from 1937-44. The first plan required all students to spend ten weeks in full-time clinical training each year. First-year men were in a general hospital, second-year men in a mental hospital, and third-year men in parish work. The Philadelphia Divinity School operated on a four-quarter system allowing clinical work to be done during the first, second, and third quarters for the juniors, middlers, and seniors respectivelly. The center at Pennsylvania Hospital continued to function under Purdie. Arthur P. Noyes, M.D., Superintendent of Norristown State Hospital, opened his institution for training in 1938-39. Senior placements were all made initially in South Philadelphia, making supervision relatively easy.[6]

Experience with the first plan was basically positive, but improvements were needed. In the fall of 1942 a second plan was launched. A three-semester system replaced the quarter system with the fall semester designated as the training period for all students simultaneously. Fifteen weeks instead of ten were then available for clinical training each year, and the program of academic studies was not interrupted by clinical work as under the first plan.

Robert D. Morris became chaplain superviso at Pennsylvania Hospital in January, 1940, and in the fall of 1941 moved (ne Episcopal Hospital taking the training program for juniors with him. Ernest E. Bruder succeeded Morris at Pennsylvania Hospital but shifted to Norristown in 1942. Bruder offered training for the middlers. Robert N. Stretch became supervisor of parish work in 1940 and expanded the field placements as the student body increased. All three men were given appointment as part-time instructors at the Divinity School where they assisted students in assimilating their training experience and relating it to their other seminary studies. A senior colloquy during the last two weeks of the senior year brought all the faculty and seniors together for two hours every day "to review and integrate the total seminary experience." Supervisors participated with other faculty and students. Howe credits the clinical training program with stimulating this integrative effort.[7]

Howe's evaluation of the New Plan of Theological Education may be organized under three headings: (1) it enhanced theological learning in the classical as well as the practical fields; (2) it provided professional training for pastoral functioning in ministry to persons. Training was found to be relevant to preaching, teaching, and the administration of the sacraments, as well as to pastoral care and counseling. (3) The New Plan stimulated the students' growth as persons.

In terms of clinical pastoral training, the experience with general and mental hospital centers proved more satisfactory than the parish context. Two problems proved insurmountable in the parish centers: (a) the students were time-limited (only one semester per year), and they were not ordained. In the Episcopal Church this was a serious handicap. (b) Supervision was extremely difficult under the second plan, not because of any deficiencies on the part of the supervisors, but because the work was so widespread and diverse it was hard to keep up with what students were doing.[8]

216

The faculty affirmed to a man that clinical training enabled students to begin their studies in the classical disciplines better motivated and with a greater sense of reality than ordinarily was true. Students gained a new open-mindedness and a new freedom to question the faculty as well as themselves. They were stimulated to attempt the correlation of theological and psychological understandings with greater seriousness than would otherwise have been the case.[9]

Howe and his staff made a concerted effort to explicate for students the relation of clinical pastoral training to classical theological subjects. Howe affirmed, for example, that "the Bible is not religious experience: It is the record of religious experience." The experience of which the Bible is witness involves the processes of human development, human action and interaction. "An understanding of these processes is essential to a full understanding of Biblical study." Once a student discovers something of the way theology grows out of life, he is prepared to see that theology is applicable to life.[10]

Monological teaching gave way to dialogical teaching in Howe's experience with the New Plan. He articulated in 1944 the theme that became a central contribution to theological education in Howe's later writings, the theme of dialogue: "drawing out and utilizing the students' thinking and experience." [11]

The testimony of students who graduated under the New Plan led Howe to claim that substantial gains had been made in the effectiveness of educating for professional functioning. After observing recent graduates, he said "their increased ability to employ themselves as objective agents in the relationships and work of the ministry was most gratifying." [12] They were more clear as to their purpose in ministry, and they demonstrated appropriate skills, especially the ability to seek out and cooperate with other community agencies. An unusual number of recent graduates were being appointed to membership on Boards of community agencies as a direct result of their interest and their proven competence. Howe offered a pointed aside in discussing the professional competence of seminarians. "It is essential," he said, "that the professor of pastoral theology have had as nearly as possible the same type of training as his students, and be familiar with their experience in training and with its significance for theological education in general and for pastoral practice in particular." [13]

A final return from the investment of the Philadelphia Divinity

School in clinical training was its contribution to the student's personal maturation. Howe called it "education for a relevant use of Christian personality." [14] Involvement of the supervisors with the total faculty enabled them to interpret the growth needs of students and to deepen, thereby, the faculty members' understanding and appreciation of each student. The Divinity School was able to exercise responsibility with respect to the student's vocational planning. Howe observed that "the School has been able to eliminate candidates for the ministry who under a purely academic system would have been graduated and who might have been ineffective in the ministry." [15]

In spite of these positive achievements the New Plan was bitterly opposed and finally abandoned by the Philadelphia Divinity School in 1944. The failure of the New Plan may be interpreted with reference to several factors. As one might suppose, the New Plan posed a threat to proponents of traditional theological education and a pre-scientific understanding of pastoral ministry. Howe found that his efforts to integrate clinical training into the theological curriculum appeared to many to be a corruption of the training of men for the ministry. Opposition arose from the suspicions of many clergymen and from political factors within the structure of the school and the denomination.

Since the Philadelphia Divinity School did not prosper under the New Plan with respect to enrollment and finances, many theological educators concluded that the emphasis on clinical pastoral training caused the comparative failure of the School. Hiltner did an autopsy, as it were, of the New Plan from the vantage point of his position as Executive Secretary of the Commission on Religion and Health of the Federal Council of Churches. He wrote on April 7, 1947:

After careful study of the facts, I am convinced that it was only the clinical pastoral training program which kept the school going as it has—and that it was in no way the clinical program which led to the School's slipping backwards. The failure of the School to meet expectations many of us had had was due to a complex series of factors, mainly administrative and personal, involving faculty members other than those teaching clinical training.[16]

Howe's interpretation of the collapse of the New Plan places major responsibility upon himself and his staff. He noted first, a structural flaw, namely, that clinical training was identified exclusively with one department of the seminary. His attempts to demonstrate that

218

clinical settings were as relevant to biblical, historical, and theological studies as to the practical fields were doomed to failure because his own department, pastoral theology, received a disproportionate amount of time or, as the saying goes, the largest slice of the curriculum pie.[17]

A second factor was impatience, defensiveness, and relative inexperience in school administration on the part of Howe and his staff to carry through such a far-reaching innovation. Howe confessed: "The leadership was not strong enough for this conflict with the result that the situation deteriorated. I contributed to its deterioration by being too impatient and too defensive.[18]

Howe moved to Virginia Theological Seminary in Alexandria in 1944 where his contribution to the clinical training enterprise continued to grow, as we have seen. A reaction against clinical methods of theological learning persisted at the Philadelphia Divinity School, however. Examination of the school's curriculum in 1968 disclosed that clinical training was a minor and optional ingredient. Students intending to enter the parish ministry were required to take six courses in the Practicum plus field education. One of these six courses was Pastoral Ministry to Individuals. It could be taken during the academic year at which time the student spent three hours per week in a clinical setting for a semester. Summer clinical pastoral training could be substituted for the part-time training if a student were motivated in this direction.[19]

Crozer Theological Seminary in the Thirties and Sixties

A striking reversal of patterns appears when we place Crozer Theological Seminary in Chester, Pennsylvania, beside the Philadelphia Divinity School. The two schools are only minutes apart in travel time, but three decades apart in curriculum development. While the Philadelphia Divinity School was breaking new curricular ground in the late thirties, Crozer was squeezing into a curricular box that very nearly became her tomb. When Crozer Theological Seminary came alive to the professional model of theological education in 1964, the Philadelphia Divinity School had returned to the graduate school of religion model. Both schools became inventive in the face of massive threats to their institutional survival. Philadelphia Divinity had suspended operations entirely for two years prior to unveiling the

New Plan of Theological Education. In the opinion of many observers Crozer Theological Seminary was marked for extinction by the report of the American Baptist Convention's Committee of Seventeen, released in June, 1962.[20] Two years later, under the leadership of President Ronald V. Wells, one of the initiators of the Committee of Seventeen Report, the Crozer faculty launched a new curriculum comparable in many ways to the New Plan of 1937. The New Plan of 1937 functioned well, achieving its objectives in large measure, but it survived only seven years. Crozer's new design is only five years old at the time of this writing, and it remains to be seen whether or not it will enjoy a longer life than the New Plan or make a more durable contribution to theological education generally.

A decisive moment in the development of Crozer's educational philosophy occurred in January, 1935. A proposed new curriculum built on the principles of progressive education was rejected, and advocates of the classical position won control of the curriculum. The difference between Crozer Theological Seminary and many other seminaries of the day was not that the classical position became ascendant. The difference was that at Crozer there was a contest at all between the classicists and exponents of a professional model of theological education as early as 1935.

Progressive education became conspicuous at Crozer Theological Seminary in 1924, riding on the wings of religious education. Stewart G. Cole, a product of the Chicago Divinity School, was professor of religious education at Crozer from 1924 to 1936. He broke the authoritarian tradition in educational methodology by the warmth and informality of his own person and by making use of the "project method," as it was then called. An example of the project method was a religious education program that Cole organized in the fifth, sixth, seventh, and eighth grades of a nearby public school. He recruited a few professors and students and conducted a kind of clinical training program in the teaching of religion in the public schools. Cole regularly placed his students in community agencies for field education and he, himself, formed a new agency, the Chester Goodwill Council, to foster understanding among religious and racial groups of the area. He became a volunteer chaplain for the County Prison, taking his students with him. He directed a survey and long-range planning program for the recreational services of Delaware County and taught his more advanced students how to use survey techniques in projecting their ministry into the larger community.[21]

Cole was chairman of the Curriculum Committee in 1934 when a new president began his duties. One of the first acts of President Franklin was to instruct the Curriculum Committee to draw up principles for a new curriculum. Using the recently published three-volume study of theological education edited by Mark A. May, Cole and his committee presented the faculty in January, 1935, with a curriculum that was functional, imaginative, and wide open with respect to the future. A group led by the biblical professors of the seminary defeated the proposal, accepting only some minor adaptations in the form of catalogue listings.[22] Since this event shaped Crozer's educational style for the next quarter of a century, and since the Cole document was actualized almost totally in Crozer's new curriculum of 1964, a brief analysis of it is in order.

Five principles deserve mention: (1) that the new curriculum be designed to fit the goal of "vocational" or professional education. The product of the Seminary was held to be men who could function effectively in the parish ministry. The work of the existing ten departments was to be reorganized into three fields in order to foster the integration of separate fields of knowledge into a unified and essentially functional perspective. The stated goal of departmental reorganization was that "individualism would yield to faculty cooperation."

(2) Under the rubric of "orientation" courses, an effort was to be made to take seriously the questions that junior seminarians brought with them and to shape course offerings not by a logical principle but according to established psychological data on how learning occurs.

(3) Cole's committee proposed a reduction in the number of courses from five or six to three per term.

(4) The need for increased specialization in vocational areas was stressed. To allow for specialization, Cole urged that all required courses be packed into the first year, leaving second and third years for electives.

(5) Cole proposed, finally, that no grades be given at all and no minimum number of hours be required. Instead, a series of comprehensive examinations was suggested, one series at the end of the junior year and another prior to graduation. These exams would be both written and oral and would focus both upon academic and professional fitness for the ministry.[23]

The resemblance between this proposal and the 1964 curriculum of Crozer Theological Seminary is uncanny. The Cole proposal had been forgotten by 1964, but the needs to which it was addressed were even more acute. Before examining these more recent inventions, however, note should be taken of the consequences of the 1935 decision.

The consequences of the faculty decision to stand firm on a classical, individualistic, and authoritarian style of education were focused most dramatically in the career of Professor William Roy McNutt. McNutt came to Crozer Theological Seminary in 1928 as Professor of Practical Theology. He retired in 1944 protesting that he had been "circumscribed, hedged in and humiliated" during the later years of his term.[24] McNutt left the pastorate of the First Baptist Church of Worcester, Massachusetts, in 1928, to begin his seminary duties. Boisen was known to McNutt and was an occasional visitor in McNutt's classes.

McNutt's inaugural address put him on record supporting a professional model of theological education—a curriculum shaped by the needs of the churches. His method of choice was, like Cole's "the project method." "As far as possible," said McNutt, "we shall aim to teach by affording opportunities *to do under our supervision*" (italics mine). He noted that Professor Cole was already moving in this direction, and he promised more of the same. The "Crozer Man" whom McNutt wanted to graduate would be a balanced, healthy pastor who was free to function effectively both as prophet and as priest. The pastoral function demands wholeness, said McNutt, for the minister "who heals must himself be full of health." [25]

McNutt's problems at Crozer stemmed in large measure from two facts: first, he did not have a terminal academic degree and was not seen as a scholar in the accepted understanding of the term. Second, he did not know when to stop growing as a person and as a professor. In a climate that was becoming increasingly hostile to growth and change, McNutt was on collision course. He expanded his interests and commitments to the emerging field of clinical pastoral education. Between 1938 and 1942, while Reuel Howe was developing the New Plan, McNutt brought a steady stream of clinicians into his classes, including Rollo May. A few Crozer students each year took clinical training during the summers. But President Franklin intervened with the dictate: "No psychiatry may be taught at Crozer so long as I am President." [26]

The most remarkable event in McNutt's career at Crozer Theological Seminary may well have been his decision in 1942 to devote his sabbatical to clinical pastoral training. This, too, was stubbornly opposed by the president. Only after the faculty Instruction Committee approved did the president acquiesce. In a blatant violation of academic freedom, Franklin pushed through the board of trustees in June, 1942, a ruling aimed at McNutt specifically, "that no changes in or additions to courses of instruction be made except as approved by the President of the Faculty and the Board of Trustees." Franklin's action not only raised the issue of academic freedom but also flew in the face of evidence that McNutt had presented to the faculty that pastoral counseling was being offered in most seminaries already and that students were clamoring for it to be offered at Crozer.[27]

In spite of the reactionary stance of his president and some of his colleagues, McNutt strode into the future again. At sixty-three years years of age he began a nine-month training program under the auspices of the Council for Clinical Training. He followed the recommendation which, said McNutt, "the Council holds to be the ideal for the well-trained minister of the future." [28] He spent the summer of 1942 at the New Jersey State Hospital in Greystone Park where he was related to Robert Brinkman; the fall quarter in Boston City Hospital under Philip Guiles and his associates from Andover Newton Theological School; and the spring quarter in the U. S. Penitentiary in Atlanta, Georgia, under Chaplain Supervisor Robert A. Preston.

In reporting to the board of trustees on April 14, 1943, McNutt identified his chief learning from the experience as understanding "the structure and the working of the human personality, and what, if anything, may be done about it." He saw the major challenge to theological educators to inhere in a minister's need to achieve a level of competence comparable to that of medical and related professionals and to save the churches, thereby, from men who are "bunglers in their high calling." He concluded the report with the poignant words: "I even have a faint hope that some of our students may find therein [at the Crozer Hospital which is adjacent to the Seminary] an opportunity for a bit of supervised 'clinical training.' " [29] His hopes were not to be realized for nearly twenty years.

The larger context in which McNutt and the Crozer faculty of the thirties might best be placed is the shift from a prescientific to a scientific base for the vocational or professional education of ministers.

Prior to 1930 almost all instruction in the practical fields was of the "helps and hints" variety. A seasoned pastor who had proved himself effective in the parish ministry would be invited to return to his alma mater as professor of practical theology. He was expected to pass on the accumulated wisdom of his own experience. By 1968 most of the seminaries in America were building their offerings in pastoral theology upon the foundation of specialized training in the behavioral sciences. McNutt anticipated these changes in the thirties and tried unsuccessfully to bring the Crozer faculty and president along in the acceptance and implementation of the scientific orientation to practical theology. Ironically, the decision-makers on the Crozer Theological Seminary faculty built their entire professional careers on the use of scientific method in biblical scholarship and then unwittingly turned back the clock on curriculum development because of their fear of the scientific method in the practical fields. During the very years that Philadelphia Divinity School was making educational history with its New Plan, from 1937 to 1944, President Franklin and a strong clique within the Crozer faculty temporized with practical theology and delayed the school's emergence out of a nineteenth-century helps-and-hints style into a professional style of theological education.

Twenty years later Crozer Theological Seminary moved in a single step all the way across the continuum from minimal to maximal involvement in clinical methods of theological learning. Curriculum revision began in 1962 with a concern to enlarge offerings in the practical fields and reshuffle the sequence of courses a bit. By 1965 the unexpected began to occur: a concensus began to appear among the faculty that theological education ought to be unequivocally professional education and that serious attention to the human development of students and faculty need not compromise academic excellence.

Changes in faculty perceptions contributed to this concensus. Several professors began to think of themselves as educators as well as specialists in a field of study. To accept "educator" into one's professional self-concept was to become responsible for the mastery of learning theory; for continuing education in the use of new educational methods; and for disciplined observation, analysis, and evaluation of one's own functioning as an educator. One sought to master the teaching-learning process as well as his own specialized discipline.

The meaning of a professional model gradually became clear in the daily interaction with faculty supervisors and students engaged in clinical pastoral education throughout the academic year. Two professors joined the faculty in 1963 and 1964 who were also certified supervisors of clinical pastoral education, and a basic unit of clinical training was required of middler seminarians. Graduate students engaged in advanced units of clinical pastoral education and a post-Th.M. resident in supervision helped to interpret by action as well as by word the theological relevance of supervised clinical experience. The faculty was surprised to discover that the professional model delivered them from the old dilemma of trying to choose between a graduate school and a trade school model. They discovered that motivation was heightened, comprehension increased, and academic excellence generally was enhanced, not compromised, when basic theoretical disciplines were related directly to the rewards of professional problem-solving.

The consensus that resulted centered ultimately on a shared commitment to the human development of both students and faculty. It led to the building of a "covenant community" in which the meaning of the life of faith would be lived authentically, not merely talked eruditely.

Human development goals were served to a remarkable degree by Charles D. Flory, Ph.D., a psychological consultant. Flory was added to the faculty of Crozer Theological Seminary on a part-time basis in 1964. He entered the picture ostensibly to provide guidance counseling for entering students, and he performed this function well. He rapidly became consultant and counselor for members of the administration and faculty. Within four years nearly all the administration and faculty had used Flory's consultation in their personal and professional growth. The combination of Flory's consultation with intensive professional education in clinical settings stimulated within the total seminary community a heightened sensitivity to the dynamics of communication and the conditions of emotional growth. An exhilarating freedom from crippling inhibitions, increased openness toward the future, engagement with the social revolution of the times, and a healthy appreciation of differences within a common commitment to a professional model of theological education became hallmarks of the Seminary.

A third certified supervisor of clinical pastoral education was added to the faculty in 1965. Affiliations with two nearby mental hospitals and with the Hahnemann Medical College provided psychiatric settings for clinical learning. The original clinical facility and the first to be developed was the Crozer Chester Medical Center, located on the same hill with the Seminary. Supervised learning was inaugurated at Glenn Mills School for delinquent boys in 1967 and in three community mental health centers—the University of Pennsylvania, Temple, and Hahnemann—in 1968. Field education provided the curricular structure for supervised clinical learning of juniors. Clinical pastoral education was required for middlers and elective for seniors and for graduate students (in pursuit of the Th.M. in pastoral counseling). Post-Th.M. candidates seeking certification as supervisors of clinical pastoral education shared the instructional and supervisory load of the program. A series of integrating courses culminating in a senior colloquy brought teams of Crozer faculty members together on a cross-field basis from the first to the final year of the student's seminary career.

One of the felicitous turns in the unfolding process was the decision by the faculty to establish the category of Candidacy for the M.Div. degree. Students could achieve candidacy after their junior year. They must be so recognized by the end of their middler year if they were to continue. Candidacy for the degree entailed an evaluation of the student's intellectual and professional functioning. If a student displayed adequate functioning and emotional health, the question became whether student and faculty were prepared to commit themselves to each other for the remainder of the student's career in the ministry. The relationship could be severed after candidacy had been awarded, but the decision-making process assumed for the faculty, at least, a kind of "for better or worse" quality.

At this point the entire faculty became involved in depth in the human development of students. At the end of each school year, the faculty went on retreat and spent a major portion of the time discussing recommendations prepared by a faculty committee concerning the human and professional development of the rising middler class. The faculty made decisions ranging from deferral of candidacy pending remedial reading to deferral pending intensive psychotherapy. What the faculty achieved by implementing the candidacy policy was a growing sense of common identity as educators who must collaborate for the student's growth as a whole person rather than compete for

226

the student's loyalty. The student who becomes a fragmented apprentice in a professorial subspecialty was less and less in evidence at Crozer as the new curriculum developed.

Charles Feilding's challenge in "Education for Ministry" (1966) expressed a judgment about what was needed in theological education, and by implication, a view of what was accomplished in the Crozer Theological Seminary's curriculum of the sixties.

The system . . . must contain responsible teachers whose business it is to decide whether students have achieved agreed levels of competence. And these decisions must be communicated to students as human decisions which they can consider and test for themselves in their own experience as far as they are able. There is a certain cowardice in a system of education which can tell a student only that he knows enough church history or not enough systematic theology, but remains unable to inform him courteously and show him reasonably that he is too repressed, hostile, aggressive, or dependent to be allowed yet to exercise a particular ministry. Good students of the highest potential who could be helped at all on these points may be lost because of educational naivety or cowardice, or turned out into the world to bring disaster on themselves and others which might have been avoided in a more professionally oriented system of education.[30]

What was bold in the decision of the Crozer faculty to foster the human development of seminarians was their readiness to accept responsibility to foster emotional growth as well as cognitive understandings. What was original was their reliance upon the growth sciences for guidelines. What was religious was their seriousness in applying the disciplines of human development to themselves as well as to their students. They dared to act on the premise that neurosis limits ministry as severely as ignorance. They recognized, in fact, that neurosis is a form of ignorance—ignorance of one's self—and that personality growth may be nourished through educational procedures. The faculty decided not merely to offer improved professional training. They decided to try to cultivate a growth-stimulating milieu in which it would be possible to reduce the debilitating and distorting effects of ignorance in behavioral as well as in traditional didactic terms.[31]

Summary Evaluation

Clinical pastoral education was a rough-hewn experiment in Worcester State Hospital in 1928. It posed a massive threat to the traditional educational philosophy of Crozer Theological Seminary in 1935. From then to now the change has been phenomenal. Worcester State Hospital offered in 1968 a sophisticated program of education for the profession of ministry to an interfaith group of twenty beginning students and eight supervisors-in-training. Its curriculum was under the auspices of Andover Newton Theological School and accredited by an international professional association. Crozer Theological Seminary offered in 1968 the whole range of accredited clinical pastoral education from basic units to supervisory training in the context of standard theological degrees. Furthermore, the faculty as a whole had become maximally involved in clinical methods of theological learning and had invested sizably in professional education designed to foster both the human development of seminarians and their professional competence.

At Worcester State Hospital students functioned as orderlies in 1928, but in the sixties they functioned as pastoral counselors under the auspices of an established chaplains' department. In the Philadelphia Divinity School clinical pastoral training became an integral part of the basic professional degree program in 1937 with a staff that was supervising men in pastoral role functioning and facilitating the integration of psychological and theological realms of thought.

The seminary scene has been marked by much greater ambivalence about clinical pastoral education than the hospital. Experimentalism is perhaps more congenial to twentieth-century medicine, social work, and the behavioral sciences generally than to theology. Pragmatism is indigenous to American culture and congruent with progressivism in education. Theology in America remained strongly tied to Europe during the first half of the century and understandably resistive to pragmatism in philosophy and progressivism in education. Thus a school like Philadelphia Divinity could embrace clinical methods wholeheartedly in one decade and reject them almost totally in another. At the same time Philadelphia Divinity School moved toward deeper involvement with the University of Pennsylvania and toward an ecumenical stance ecclesiastically. Crozer Theological Seminary contradicted the liberal theological position that it espoused in the twenties and thirties when it rejected progressivism in educational method and did not reconcile the gap between its theory and practice until faced with institutional annihilation in the sixties.

Pastoral functioning has been studied from the perspectives of shepherding and healing more than from the equally important perspectives of communicating, organizing, reconciling, and social engineering. One exception is that clinical pastoral educators have engaged in a ministry to the structures of theological education and institutionalized medical service. Within the four-decade range of this chapter, radical social change has occurred both in the hopsital and in the theological world as a direct result of clinical pastoral education. The remaking of the Crozer curriculum, for example, began with a shift from the classroom to community agencies as the setting for learning. Its objectives expanded from cognitive to include affective development. Within a few years, students, faculty, administrators, and even the Board of Trustees, cooperated in replacing authoritarian with democratized decision-making processes. Students were added to all faculty committees, and the center of control shifted toward the community as a true partner with the professional educators. Though the remaking of theological education on a professional model had much to show in 1968, the fact remained that pastoral education built on a scientific base had only begun.

Beyond Unification

What is beyond unification of clinical pastoral education agencies? The search for an answer to this question raises several other questions to which I shall address myself in turn.

Question One: Where are we developmentally as a professional group of clinical pastoral educators?

As seen in the Preface, clinical pastoral education is at the threshold of its development as a full-grown profession. According to Freeman's analysis of the developmental stages of all professions, clinical pastoral education is already struggling with stage nine of a ten-stage scale. Stage nine is "a synthesis of specializations." Tentative explorations are already underway between the Association for Clinical Pastoral Education, Inc. and the American Association of Pastoral Counselors, Inc. Conferential exchange is occurring at an accelerating rate among clinical pastoral educators and representatives of associations similarly concerned with the professionalization of the ministry. The question becomes one of goals and commitments now that professional maturity has been substantially achieved.

Question Two: To whom does clinical pastoral education belong?
Who needs clinical pastoral education? Where do supervisors restrict

their freedom in order to be responsibly related? Does the profession belong ultimately to medicine, to theological education, or to itself? By what criteria are its priorities to be established?

In its early days clinical training received sponsorship and guidance from a number of renowned physicians, best known of whom were Richard C. Cabot and Helen Flanders Dunbar. Supervisors were supported by hospital budgets. They found their rewards in alliance with physicians as part of the vanguard of comprehensive medicine or as apprentice psychotherapists. Boisen, in contrast, commuted from Worcester, Massachusetts, to Chicago for years in order to maintain a seminary appointment. Supervisors were as dependent on farsighted seminary deans and professors to send them students as they were upon hospitals for the development of training programs. But, organizationally, clinical pastoral education remained answerable, finally, to itself.

In a sense seminaries and hospitals have been mother and father for the new profession. At one stage, clinical pastoral education was a free spirit, seeming to belong responsibly to no one but itself. As services have become more readily marketable and as codes and standards have been developed, clinical pastoral education has become identified more and more unambiguously with theological education. Twenty years ago the question of identity posed a choice between the behavioral sciences and psychotherapy, on the one hand, and on the other, theology and a ministry of shepherding. In some quarters this was an issue as recently as the early sixties. Today clinical pastoral education is unambiguously committed to theological education. The homework in pastoral theology is being done faithfully and well, and the profession has found hearty acceptance within the educational establishment of Protestant churches and initial acceptance in Roman Catholic and Jewish seminaries.

The question of identity has changed, but it is not resolved. Given a primary commitment to theological education, what function should clinical pastoral education perform? Will it remain peripherally related to the seminaries like some forms of continuing education, or will it move steadily toward integrated patterns of relationship? Will all the trappings of its past programs be retained, such as insistance upon hospital settings and full-time student involvement, or will supervisory methodology be separated from the hospital setting in the interest of engaging more and more seminarians in supervised learning? Within a seminary, should supervisors develop sophisticated field education, offer basic professional training, specialize with graduate students, seek to become masters of team-teaching techniques developing the image of "integrator" within the faculty, compete with classicists by developing the content dimensions of Christian anthropology, or juggle all these items? Many decisions about loyalties and priorities remain to be made.

Question Three: Why is clinical pastoral education committed to theological education? Toward what end does it move?

This question assumes that clinical pastoral educators are less ultimately concerned about self-development and self-perpetuation as a group than about a corporate mission. It assumes that the mission has to do with being educators for the leadership of religious communities.

Clinical pastoral education has been working a quiet revolution (almost bloodless!) in theological education. We want to belong to theological education in order to make it over (but not to take it over—and that is an important difference). This never works in marriage. Nor did the Trojan Horse win many friends in Troy. The difference in theological education is that supervisors of clinical pastoral education have found as many seminary faculty people who are emotionally in the Trojan Horse as there are professors and deans on the outside defending the *status quo*. Clinical pastoral education is only one of many currents sweeping away the nonfunctional accretions of the past.

The part clinical pastoral education plays in provoking a crisis of purpose within a traditionally oriented seminary is substantial. To accommodate clinical training, a school must shift away from an exclusive identification with the arts and humanities toward the social and behavioral sciences. It must risk becoming a professional school and abandoning the graduate school of religion model. A radical reevaluation of educational methods follows. Students exposed to clinical pastoral education press for change from didactic to experiential styles of teaching, from the abstract and grand generalization to the concrete and particular—to cases; from mass groupings and the lecture method to small groups with individualized supervision of the learning process.

Lowell Colston shows why clinical pastoral education has a revolutionary impact in the teaching of theology. He concluded, after

231

visiting fifty-seven clinical pastoral education centers in eighteen cities, that the theological method characteristically employed is "developmental, existential and phenomenological."

Developmental because the focus is on process-learning rather than upon the impartation of content; existential because the concern is for present experiencing in which the student's self-consciousness is expanded and enhanced; phenomenological because the student's own uniqueness, the struggle for his own identity is at the heart of this educational enterprise.[32]

Supervisors see their revolutionary intent. The preamble to the Constitution of the Association for Clinical Pastoral Education sounds bland enough on first reading:

Historically it has been the responsibility of the church to provide for the education of her ministers. This task from time to time required new structures, new methods, new and creative efforts to insure the proper preparation of the clergy both in the historic faith and tradition and in emerging areas of knowledge in the world. Clinical pastoral education is one such creative movement within the church.[33]

But to require new structures and new methods means finally to abolish not only the old methods but also the old structures of theological education. In the hands of men of deep purpose and courage this polite language could be a revolutionary document.

Ten years ago when I first began writing a history of clinical pastoral education, my hidden agenda was to prove that clinical pastoral education really ought to be domesticated by affiliation with theological education. Today, my now open agenda is to fan the fires of adventuresomeness, to encourage the mavericks, to tend the radical spirit in those seminarians who may read a history of clinical pastoral education only because they are required to take the course in "clinical." We may affiliate with theological education for our own security, to enjoy the privileges of the establishment, or we may affiliate in order to accomplish the revolution that fired the imagination of the founding fathers.

Question Four: What is the essential of clinical pastoral education?

The need to discriminate essential from nonessential aspects of clinical pastoral education is being forced from two sides. The theological schools are demanding the know-how of certified supervisors but rejecting many of their accustomed structures.[34] The social actionists

232

sometimes discredit the profession indiscriminately. Peggy Way summarized the past ten to fifteen years of the "pastoral care movement" in the phrase "from *avant-grade* to *status quo*." [35] Are we inattentive to the dynamics of personal transformation inherent in organized efforts to change the structures of society?

The specialists in political solutions to man's problems are not asking for our help in any clear way. Political and personal "bettering" are discrete fields, as Halmos has shown. Individuals must decide on their own primary and secondary commitments among these fields, but the conclusion is inescapable that clinical pastoral educators ought to take the risks of involvement. Cooperation will enhance not only the happiness of the people served but also the maturity of the respective professional disciplines.

One way of putting the question of essentials is to ask whether hospitals are necessary to clinical pastoral education or merely historical accidents. Gibson Winter, more than a decade ago, argued that the chaplain-patient model ill equipped a pastor as an effective enabler of the laity in his ministry in the world. He saw hope of "little or no further significant progress until the chaplain-patient framework is seen as *the special case*." [36]

Seward Hiltner and others have urged the same point, in terms of defining the proper *context* of ministry. Hiltner resisted the trend toward specialization in pastoral counseling centers and encouraged the development of clinical pastoral education in local churches. [37] Prophetically, Hiltner wrote in 1960 that "pastoral psychology is much more likely to be damned for what it fails to do than for what it does" in the years ahead. [38] Clinical pastoral educators have failed to make clear to those outside the field just what is the essential of the profession. Our critics are not opposed to person-centeredness; only a few are afraid of psychology as a discipline. Our critics resent what they experience as our exclusiveness and our security within the walls of established institutions.

Much in the history of clinical pastoral education speaks to the other side of the question. Its educational superiority to fieldwork, for example, inheres partially in the insistence of early supervisors upon the "controlled laboratory" that hospitals provide in contrast to the open character of fieldwork placements. Both testimonials and research studies support the claim that attitudinal learning gained in a hospital may be transferred with little loss to the open settings of parish or community organization. The ultimate argument for considering the institutional setting as a necessity for clinical pastoral education is the quality of supervision that is possible when training occurs in the very presence, as it were, of the supervisor himself.

More radical than the appeal for a parish or community context for clinical pastoral education is the suggestion that supervision may not be the *sine qua non* of the specialty. In an article, "Consultation: An Alternative to Supervision," Henry B. Adams described the limitations of supervision for meeting the wide-scale educational needs of pastors. He identified "the *essential elements* of clinical learning" as "learning the practice from the practice." With this definition he made a case for consultation as it is used in medicine and industry as the essential element of clinical learning.[39]

And so the question of context or of the essential of clinical pastoral education remains open. It may be that the criticism from the left —from the social actionists—will force us into decision about our essentials. We have postponed an official declaration for a rather long time in spite of the prodding from the right—from advocates of parish prerogatives.

Question Five: What does professional competence mean within the field of personal ministries?

Turning from the outside relations of clinical pastoral education to its internal relationships, we face the question of competence. Supervisors take pride in the high standards hammered out during the past two decades. In response to high standards, clinical pastoral education is being required by more and more seminaries. But, ordinarily, the requirement is for one quarter or less.

Gratifying though this kind of seminary approval may be, is it enough? Will one quarter of clinical pastoral education set a seminarian on the road toward an effective ministry? The easy answer is to say yes. Besides, to say no is to ask the hard question: What more is needed, and how can it be provided?

An even harder question inheres in the stuff of life as a minister. No theological educator with integrity can long avoid this question: What does it take to live an authentic and meaningful life as a minister in today's world? Clearly, one quarter of clinical pastoral education grafted into standard theological education is not the answer.

Seasoned supervisors and counselors confess privately that in their experience nothing has been adequate, finally, short of the threefold formula of the psychoanalyst: mastery of the conceptual tools of the profession, plus extended supervised training in professional functioning, plus an intensive discipline of personal maturation, namely, psychotherapy.

Ministry by definition is a people-related profession. In people-related, helping professions, not only one's knowledge and skills but also one's person determines the quality of one's ministry. Neurosis limits and distorts one's ministry as severely as ignorance of the theological, biblical, historical, or practical fields. Neurosis is ignorance —ignorance of one's self and of one's true interpersonal world. Theological education must overcome ignorance in intrapsychic and interpersonal as well as in the cognitive areas of the minister's life. Recovery of the inherent authority of the minister awaits the acceptance of this hard reality.

No one has dared press the goal of emotional maturation of seminarians upon theological education until recently. University educators are only now gaining the tools to effect what some are calling "psychological education." [40] Clinical pastoral educators have been out in front of most other groups in developing psychological education for professional functioning.[41] We have been almost timid, however, in pressing the claims of our proven methodological findings upon theological deans.

I am not trying to blur the line between education and therapy in this discussion. We got clear on the need to discriminate education from therapy in our literature, at least, in the fifties. I want, instead, to challenge the rationalization that a seminary's job is to provide the intellectual leadership for the church but not to be responsible for the personal and spiritual development of the minister. I am asking that we be honest about what we know of learning theory. We know, for example, that learning—whether it is learning to run a maze or learning a doctrine of God—is the product of perception as well as of memory; of attitudes, experiences, relationships, and of metabolism as well as of reasoning. The tools of psychological education are at hand. The goals of personal and spiritual maturation may be enhanced thereby. Theological educators cannot be expected to hold a higher standard of personal maturity and of professional competence for graduating seminarians than clinical pastoral educators recommend. We must decide, therefore, what standard of professional competence in personal ministries we will settle for when it comes to our expectations of seminary education.

We have come a long way. Harry Emerson Fosdick wrote, near the end of his ministry:

When I began my ministry a journal devoted to pastoral psychology would have been inconceivable. During my years of preparation in two theological seminaries I cannot recall hearing personal counseling mentioned. It was not thought of as a ministerial function important enough to require any training. . . . Reared in a church-centered family I never in my life thought of such a thing as going to a minister for personal consultation—not even when I had a nervous breakdown and desperately needed help. . . . [The] "growing congeniality" [of psychotherapy and religion] is one of the most vitally important movements in the church's life in my generation.[42]

We can rest on these laurels and rationalize that, after all, one quarter of clinical pastoral education will equip seminarians for "general practice" in ministry. We can urge some to specialize in counseling and provide them more rigorous training plus the discipline of therapy. But the haunting question remains whether the stuff of human existence in an urban world will permit such an easy solution.

If clinical pastoral education follows the pattern of other professions, no single answer will emerge for any of these questions. Multiple answers are being tested. But we need to know our history and let it illumine our present situation. We may then move forward, more aware than before of the courage and confusion, the imagination and rigidity, the hope and the failure of hope that have characterized those who laid the foundations and did the framing for a profession of clinical pastoral educators.

appendix a.

Clinical Pastoral Education's Genealogical Chart

The Fathers	Keller—Cincinnati	Cabot—Boston	Boisen—Worcester, Mass., and Elgin, Ill.
1923	Bexley Hall Plan		
24	Clinical training begins in social agencies		Chaplain at Worcester
25		Seminar at ETS "A Plea for a Clinical Year in the Course of Theological Study"	Professor at CTS / Clinical training begins at Worcester
26	Summer school in social service for theology students and junior clergy		
27			
28			Guiles enters C.P.E. at Worcester
29			
1930		The Council for the Clinical Training of Theological Students, Inc.	Guiles — Schism — Dunbar
31			
32		The New England Group (The Earhart Foundation)	CCTTS (NYC)
33			The Chicago CCTTS / Boisen at Elgin
34		Cabot to ANTS / Cabot & Dicks leave CCTTS, Inc.	
35	Grad. School of Applied Rel. (Joseph Fletcher, Dean)		Hiltner, Executive Secretary
36			
37			Brinkman, Director
38		The New England Theological School's Committee on Clinical Training and the Cabot Club	The Council for Clinical Training / schism
39			
1940			CCT (NYC) Financial crisis / The Chicago CCTTS
41		1st Biennial Conf. of Supvrs.	
42			Supervisors take over Board of Governors / Boisen separates from CCT in NYC
43		2nd Biennial Conf. of Supvrs.	
44		1st National Conference on Clinical Training	

Beginnings   The Era of Separatism

Year	Related Associations	Institute of Pastoral Care	Council for Clin. Trng.	Third Force
	Chap.'s Sec. A.P.H.A.	Fairbanks, Exec. Director	Kuether, Director	Oates to SBTS
1945 & 46				
47			Kuether, Director	Mahnke to C.P.E. and Concordia Theo. Sem.
48	Association Mental Hospital Chaplains	Negotiations for merger of Journals		Young to N.C.B.H.
49	A.S.P.P.F.	Joint Fall Conference: IPC and CCT		Lutheran Advisory Council
1950		Burns, Exec. Dir. Merger: *Journ. Pastoral Care*		Price and Corley, N. O.
51	Am. Fndn. Rel. & Psy.		The Committee of Twelve	
52	B.U.S.T. Counseling Center			
53		Adoption of Standards for Clinical Pastoral Education		
54		Strunk, Executive Director	Kuether resigned	Institute of Religion at Houston
55	Acad. Rel. & Ment. Health			
56		5th National Conference on Clinical Pastoral Education		
57	Inst. for Advanced Pastoral Studies / Pastoral Inst., D.C.	Committee of 12 becomes Advisory Committee on C.P.E.	Maxfield, Executive Director '57	SBACPE
58			Unilateral negotiations: Johnson (IPC) and Wise (CCT) / Smith, Executive Director '58	
59				
1960		7th National Conference on Clinical Pastoral Education		
61		Joint Executive Committee: IPC and CCT		
62		Clark, Executive Director		Georgia Association for Pastoral Care (CCT and SBACPE)
63	A.A.P.C.	Joint Accreditation Committee: IPC and CCT		
64				SBACPE becomes A.C.P.E.
65		Consultn. on Accred. & Cert. for C.P.E. called by N.C.C. W. Clement & Jessie V. Stone Found. Grant		
66		Joint Structure and Joint Accreditation Committees become inclusive		
67		The Association for Clinical Pastoral Education, Inc.		

The Era of Unification

appendix b.

Standards for Clinical Pastoral Education, 1953

Adopted by the National Conference on Clinical Pastoral Training
October 13, 1953

I. Definition of Clinical Pastoral Education

Clinical pastoral education is an opportunity for a theological student or pastor to learn pastoral care through interpersonal relations in an appropriate center, such as a hospital, correctional institution, or other clinical situation, where an integrated program of theory and practice is individually supervised by a qualified chaplain-supervisor, with the collaboration of an interprofessional staff.

II. Qualifications of the Chaplain Supervisor

1. Graduation from an accredited theological school, upon the completion of a three-year graduate course beyond the bachelor's degree or its equivalent.

2. Ordination, an adequate period of pastoral experience, and denominational approval.

3. At least one year full time of clinical pastoral education and in addition, three months of supervised clinical teaching.

4. Professional competence, including graduate studies, past experience, and demonstrated performance. Graduate degrees in appropriate fields with clinical orientation are recommended and may be evaluated as follows: six months' credit toward clinical education may be given for an appropriate doctor's degree. Three months' credit may be given for an appropriate master's degree.

5. Personal qualifications to be appraised by the accrediting committee in a face-to-face interview.

III. Requirements for the Clinical Training Center

1. A chaplaincy service which is well established and recognized as a functioning part of the center, with a chaplain accredited as a supervisor.

2. A progressive institution, oriented toward therapy or rehabilitation, serving an adequate number of patients or inmates accessible to the chaplain's program, maintaining an interprofessional staff available for continuous teaching of theological students.

    a. General appreciation within the institution of the role of a chaplain, recognition of theological students as functioning members of the Chaplain's Department, and adequate opportunity for them to work in significant and appropriate clinical tasks.

    b. An alert and cooperative administration and staff, who will be ready to assume responsibility for implementing the clinical program.

3. Maintenance should be provided for students in training or such provisions as may be comparable to the internship programs of other professional groups in the institution.

IV. Minimum Essentials of Clinical Pastoral Education

1. A supervised practicum in interpersonal relations.

2. Writing of clinical notes for consultation with the chaplain-supervisor.

3. A continuing evaluation of the student's experience and growth to be offered during the training period.

4. Frequent association with an interprofessional staff who are genuinely interested and qualified to teach students.

5. Adequate provision for group discussions, seminars, and other group experience for all students.

6. A continuing concern for an integration of psychological, ethical, and theological theory with practical understanding of the dynamics of personality and facility in interpersonal relations.

7. A written evaluation of this experience to be made by the student to his chaplain-supervisor at the end of the training period.

8. A final summary evaluation of the student's work and capacities to be written at the end of the training period by the chaplain-supervisor, discussed with the student, and, with his knowldege, made available to the appropriate responsible parties.

V. Minimum Program Recommended for Clinical Pastoral Education

1. For the theological student who is preparing for the parish ministry:

    a. An introductory course to clinical pastoral care during the entire academic year, with one day per week at an accredited center and under the direction of an accredited chaplain-supervisor who is a functioning member of the staff of the center; and/or

    b. Clinical pastoral education for twelve weeks, full time.

2. For the student who is seeking a master's degree in pastoral care, at least six months' clinical pastoral education, full time.

3. For the advanced student preparing for the teaching of pastoral theology

and pastoral care, an appropriate doctor's degree with at least nine months, full time, of clinical pastoral education and in addition, three months of supervised teaching of pastoral care.

VI. Special Recommendations

1. For pastors and other religious workers seeking additional training.
   a. Full-time participation in clinical pastoral education for six to twelve weeks is recommended.
   b. Where this is not possible, participation in orientation programs at an accredited center is recommended.

2. For chaplains serving full-time, at least twelve months of full-time clinical pastoral education is recommended, six months of which to be in the type of institution which he serves. Where this standard has not yet been attained, institutional administrators are encouraged to release their chaplains periodically for the necessary training.

appendix c.

Standards for Clinical Pastoral Education, 1968

Clinical Pastoral Education is a method of theological education whereby a student learns pastoral skills within a context of responsible relationship to people and under the direct supervision of a trained clergyman. It provides a learning situation for a theological student and continuing education for a clergyman in which they may develop awareness of the theological and psychosocial concerns of persons in crisis. Clinical Pastoral Education also confronts the student with the human predicament. It supplies the nuturing milieu for him to understand himself as a person, to know himself as a pastor, to integrate his theology more meaningfully with life, and to become more aware of human worth and potential.

Clinical Pastoral Education provides a milieu for the student to enter more fully into relationships with God and man. Through the evaluation of pastoral relationships, it offers him opportunities to find purpose and meaning which can result in a more mature grasp of his Christian faith. It provides the process whereby knowledge, insight, feeling, and experience undergo assimilation and integration, and are transformed into understanding skill and competence in the pastoral function. This experience seeks to clarify in understanding and practice the resources, methods, and meaning of religion as expressed in pastoral care.

Clinical Pastoral Education provides for supervision of this experience by a clergyman. He brings to the learning situation his own unique personal contributions and competence which stimulate individual initiative and growth. His supervision encourages the unfolding of the student's warmth, native ability, and personhood, which the student can channel into meaningful pastoral relationships.

Clinical Pastoral Education is offered in a multidisciplinary center which supports a functioning religious ministry. The center provides a community in which creative theological and psychosocial education occurs.

I. Clinical Pastoral Education I

CPE I is a learning experience for seminarians and clergymen who wish to increase their competence in pastoral care, to fulfill prerequisites for CPE II or III, and/or to meet requirements of theological seminaries.

Admission Is Based on the Following:
  A. Graduation from college.
  B. Completion of at least one academic year of theological education.
  C. Adequate physical and emotional health.
  D. Admission interview by a qualified examiner.
  E. Acceptance by the Supervisor of a Training Center.

Program Objectives

This program level confronts the student with personal and pastoral situations within a setting providing responsibility for a ministry to persons. This confrontation offers a learning experience under pastoral supervision and in the context of a peer group in which the student explores and evaluates his:
  A. Personal and pastoral identity.
  B. Understanding of the dimensions of pastoral care.
  C. Pastoral function.
  D. Relationships to other professional disciplines.
  E. Ability to think theologically about his experiences.
  F. Ability to communicate meaningfully his faith.
  G. Interpersonal relationships.
  H. Attitudes and values, and the processes by which he grows, learns, relates, and communicates.
  I. Assumptions about life.
  J. Ability to integrate his experiences and knowledge into a frame of reference within which he perceives himself and others.

II. Clinical Pastoral Education II

CPE II is a program in one center for a full year. The program provides for a minimum of one unit of peer group experience. No more than two units of CPE may be certifiable when a peer group is not available. CPE II may provide prerequisites for admission to either CPE III or IV upon evaluation of the student by the appropriate committee in the region.

Admission Is Based on the Following:
  A. Graduation from college.
  B. Completion of at least two academic years of theological education.
  C. Completion and supervisor's evaluation of one certified unit of CPE I in an accredited center.
  D. Adequate physical and emotional health.
  E. Ecclesiastical endorsement.
  F. Acceptance by the Supervisor of a Training Center.

Program Objectives

The program objectives of CPE I are fundamental to CPE II. However, because of the length and intensity of CPE II, along with differing individual abilities, more precise objectives may be defined and pursued by student and supervisor. Therefore, in some selected instances the objectives of CPE III may apply.

III. Clinical Pastoral Education III

CPE III provides an opportunity in continuing education for the clergyman who desires to function in areas such as parish ministry, institutional chaplaincy, pastoral counseling, and the teaching ministry.

Admission Is Based on the Following:

A. Graduating from an accredited theolgical seminary.
B. Completion of not less than two units of certified CPE I in an accredited center. One of these units must have been full time.
C. Pastoral evperience
D. Ecclesiastical endorsement including ordination or certification in a religious vocation.
E. Written statement by the applicant of professional goals.
F. Demonstrated ability to function in an open and redemptive way in a religious vocation.
G. Acceptance by the Supervisor of a Training Center
   (The Regional Certification and Accreditation Committee is available for consultation on admission to CPE III.)

Program Objectives

CPE III gives the student firsthand contact with the range of pastoral opportunities represented in a training center. It also provides him opportunity to relate clinical data to personality theory and theology. Such objectives are to confront him with the problems and alternatives in structuring a ministry in a particular situation. The student will evaluate his training experience with a view to deciding his future training.

Professional goals may vary in CPE III, but there are certain basic, common objectives for all students. Under pastoral supervision and in the context of a peer group the student will explore and evaluate his:

A. Participation, with increasing responsibility, in the pastoral ministry offered in the center.
B. Personal and pastoral identity.
C. Development of creative and meaningful pastoral relationships that operate at the deeper levels of the human personality.
D. Development and demonstration of a pastoral theology that is correlated with the pastoral function.
E. Increasing ability to work with the supervisor as an equal.
F. Development of realistic administrative relationships with institutional and ecclesiastical authorities.

G. Discernment of the limitations and uniqueness of the pastoral role in relation to other professional disciplines.

H. Engagement in varied extended pastoral care relationships.

I. Participation in a curriculum involving an interprofessional faculty offering deeper understanding of personality and pastoral care theories and techniques.

J. Sharing individual and group evaluations to validate the learning experience.

In addition to these objectives, which are intrinsic to CPE III, students moving toward specific professional goals will focus on those areas related to their vocational aims, such as the following ministries:

Parish

The student preparing for the parish ministry will have an opportunity to discern the principles of pastoral care in the center and their application to a parish setting. He will be confronted with the range and depth of human problems and their broader implications. Such an opportunity will include application of the clinical method of learning to pastoral care, preaching, teaching, and parish administration. His learning experience will also include emphasis upon the special needs of persons moving either to or from his center to the parish. Opportunities to participate in consultative relationships will be made available. He will become acquainted with community services and referral techniques, and the developing principle of community planning.

Institutional

The student preparing to be a chaplain in an institution will be given an opportunity for increasingly independent responsibility, involving the total range of religious ministry offered in the center. He will become acquainted with the administration as related to the chaplaincy, the uniqueness of institutional life and ministry, and the opportunities and limitations of the multidisciplinary team approach. He will be expected to develop and demonstrate his philosophy of the institutional ministry.

Pastoral Counseling

The student preparing for a pastoral counseling ministry will be given an opportunity to function with increasingly independent responsibility in a variety of extended and intensive pastoral relationships. He will receive continuing counseling supervision, and will have opportunity for interdisciplinary interaction and consultation. He may validate clinically his knowledge of personality theories, and various pastoral counseling approaches and techniques. He will have an opportunity to discern the distinctiveness of the pastoral counseling role, and both develop and demonstrate his philosophy of pastoral counseling.

Teaching

For the student preparing for the teaching ministry there will be increasingly independent participation in the educational program of the center's chaplaincy department. He will become acquainted with the theories and methods of clinical method of learning and research to theological education.

IV. Clinical Pastoral Education IV

CPE IV provides a learning opportunity for the qualified clergyman, with demonstrated personal, professional, and clinical competence, who desires to become a certified supervisor of clinical pastoral education. Admission to this program is based on evidence of his potential to assist others in the clinical method of learning, together with a capacity to acquire techniques and theories of supervision.

Admission Is Based on the Following:
  A. Graduation from an accredited theological school.
  B. Ecclesiastical endorsement and ordination.
  C. Pastoral experience.
  D. Completion of at least two units of certified CPE III.
  E. A written statement in which the applicant dynamically and systematically develops his interest in supervisory education.
  F. Consultative evaluation by the appropriate committee in the region of his readiness to engage in CPE IV.
  G. Acceptance for training by a supervisor qualified to offer CPE IV.

Program Objectives

CPE IV is designed to enable the supervisor-candidate to learn and develop skill through the actual practice of clinical supervision under a supervisor. The candidate will be confronted with a wide range of pastoral and supervisory situations and choices intrinsic to the method of clinical learning. CPE IV provides opportunities for the candidate to share in the responsibility for these training programs, beginning with close and intense supervision and progressing to a freedom of function on definable levels.

The Levels of Both Methodology and Time Sequence Are:

Level 1—Introduction to and acquisition of the theories and techniques of supervision through partial supervisory responsibility for students in short-term and part-time courses (This level may be integrated into the latter part of CPE III.)

Level 2—Under the direct supervision of a qualified supervisor, the candidate assumes appropriate supervisory responsibility for a minimum of one full-time unit of CPE.

Level 3—Independent responsibility for supervision of students engaged in a full-time unit of CPE.

The development of the training pattern and program content is the responsibility of the supervisor and appropriate committee in the region. The following guidelines are suggested:
  1. The candidate should be enabled to function fully in the pastoral ministry of a center (level 1-2-3).
  2. The candidate should participate in seminars and individual conferences to evaluate his progress (level 1-2).

3. The candidate will participate in the planning of his training program according to his developing ability (level 1-2).
4. The candidate should plan and maintain supervisory responsibility for a full-time program of clinical pastoral education under direct supervision of a qualified supervisor (level 2).
5. Upon completion of CPE IV, Level 2, the candidate will be reviewed by the appropriate committee in the region and may be granted approval to function as defined in Level 3.
6. The candidates will meet with the appropriate committees when assessment and evaluation are indicated or a request for certification is made (level 3).

Footnotes:
1. The appropriate regional and national committees will develop criteria for: certification of a supervisor qualified to offer CPE IV; curriculum content in supervisor-candidate training; evaluation of training and certification procedures for candidates desiring certified supervisor status.
2. The appropriate committee in the region certifies the training of the students under Level 3 on the request and recommendation of the supervisor candidate.

V. Certification as a Supervisor

A. Certification Process
   The supervisor-candidate, following one or more years of successful functioning as an acting supervisor, may apply to the Association's Committee on Certification and Accreditation for certification as a Supervisor of Clinical Pastoral Education.
B. Continuation of Certified Supervisor Status
   The continuation of certified supervisor status is based on: high standards of personal and professional ethics; personal, spiritual, and educational growth; continuing and regular supervision of students in accordance with standards; good standing in a recognized denomination; and membership in the Association.

VI. Accreditation of a Center

The purpose of accrediting training centers is to assure that the administration of a center provides evidence of a responsible relationship to the region and maintains the standards adopted by ACPE.

Guidelines for a training center applying for accreditation:
   A. A functioning religious ministry and a full-time staff clergyman certified as a Supervisor of CPE by the ACPE.
   B. Sufficient patients, inmates, or parishioner population to provide adequate learning opportunities.
   C. An atmosphere which encourages human concern, and promotes teaching, research, and a multidisciplinary approach.

D. A receptivity to the CPE of seminarians and clergymen through the provision of opportunities for pastoral functioning, staff relationships, lectures, and the necessary facilities.

E. Maintenance for CPE students on a basis comparable to assistance offered students in other professional training programs.

F. Support of the CPE program by providing the supervisor adequate staff, time, and budget, making it possible for him to fulfill his professional obligations within the center and ACPE.

G. Cooperation with the representative of the ACPE in a survey visit and periodic reviews of the status of the center and the training program.

H. Accreditation or approval by the appropriate accrediting agency or agencies in its field.

Glossary

Accreditation: The action taken on a regional or national level to verify the potential and capacity of an institution to serve as a clinical pastoral education center.

Certification of training: An action, usually taken by a supervisor of CPE, to validate the quantity and quality of a student's clinical pastoral education experience.

Certification as a supervisor: The action taken by the appropriate body to validate formally the completion of specialty training in supervision and to certify the competency of a clergyman to function as a supervisor.

Supervisor candidate: The clergyman accepted for or engaged in CPE IV.

Supervisor: The clergyman who has been certified as having completed CPE IV and judged by the appropriate committee to be competent to function as a supervisor in clinical pastoral education.

Clinical: The method of study or learning involving firsthand supervised participation with and observation of another human being.

Clinical pastoral education organization: The Association for Clinical Pastoral Education is the agency which promotes clinical pastoral education, accredits centers, certifies supervisors, and sets standards of clinical pastoral education for supervisors, centers, and regions.

Clinical pastoral education center: The ACPE-accredited center served by a supervisor offering a program of clinical pastoral education in accord with ACPE standards.

Ecclesiastical endorsement: To be in good standing in a denomination and to have approval from the appropriate denominational authority to perform stated pastoral functions and approved to accept training or chaplaincy assignments.

Objective: The defined goal at which clinical pastoral education programs are aimed in order to enable the intern or candidate to engage in a clinical learning experience and to enable the supervisor or designated committee to evaluate that experience.

Pastoral care: The professional and personal response of the pastor, in traditional and nontraditional modes, to the needs of people to whom he ministers.

Pastoral experience: To have experienced as a pastor the responsibility and opportunity to meet the religious needs of people over an extended time period. Acceptance of authority, delineation of the pastoral task, and personal pastoral identity are some aspects of this experience.

Peer group: The three to six students accepted for clinical pastoral education in a specific training program.

Region: A defined geographical area in which are located accredited training centers, certified chaplain supervisors, and participating theological schools, with regionally elected officers and stated committees.

Standards: The accepted norms of clinical pastoral education. The term can be applied to program, content, structure, and admissions.

Units of training:
> Unit—At least 400 hours of CPE in a sequence of 11 consecutive weeks.
> Half-unit—At least 240 hours of CPE I or III in a minimum of six consecutive weeks.
> Part-time—At least 16 hours per week for 30 weeks which shall be a unit of CPE I.

Guide for orientation to pastoral care

A limited clinical experience on a part-time or short-term basis is available in some training centers. Application is made directly to the training center. Orientation programs are defined as all structural learning experiences which are preliminary to and shorter than the initial unit of full-time clinical pastoral education.

The general purpose of orientation programs is an introduction to a new dimension of the pastoral care role, the nature and meaning of illness, the institution and its methods of treatment, personality theory and development. Such programs provide for supervised pastoral contacts with patients, inmates, or parishioners.

appendix d.

Constitution and Bylaws, The Association for
Clinical Pastoral Education, Inc.
1967

CONSTITUTION
The Association for Clinical Pastoral Education, Inc., November, 1967

Preamble

Historically it has been the responsibility of the church to provide for the education of her ministers. This task from time to time required new structures, new methods, new and creative efforts to insure the proper preparation of the clergy both in the historic faith and tradition and in emerging areas of knowledge in the world. Clinical pastoral education is one such creative movement within the church. It has its roots in the efforts of pioneers who sought to bring the theological student into supervised encounter with man in crisis in order that "living human documents" might be studied, that the shepherding task of the ministry might be experienced, and that scientific knowledge of human relationships correlated with theological insights might be brought to bear on the pastoral task.

Out of this emerging emphasis within theological education has developed an increasingly complex network of relationships among theological seminaries, ecclesiastical bodies, health and welfare institutions, governmental, private, and church related agencies, and other professional persons either directly or indirectly engaged in the task of clinical pastoral education. Such a venture requires a coordinating agency that can provide a bridge by which these relationships may be fostered for the good of the church and the education of her clergy. It is for this broad purpose that the Association for Clinical Pastoral Education is formed.

The formation of this Association marks the culmination of efforts to bring together the work of the Association of Clinical Pastoral Educators; the Council for Clinical Training, Incorporated; the Institute of Pastoral Care,

250

Incorporated; and the Department of Institutional Chaplaincy and Clinical Pastoral Education, Lutheran Council in the U.S.A. with the intent that the Association for Clinical Pastoral Education be the successor corporation to the Council for Clinical Training, Incorporated, and the Institute of Pastoral Care, Incorporated.

Article I
Name

Section 1

The name of this organization shall be
The Association for Clinical Pastoral Education

Section 2

The Association for Clinical Pastoral Education shall be incorporated.

Section 3

For the purpose of this constitution and the accompanying by-laws, the Association for Clinical Pastoral Education is hereinafter designated as "this Association."

Article II
Purpose

Section 1

The general purpose of this Association is to foster clinical pastoral education.

Section 2

Its specific purposes are:

a. to promote clinical pastoral education as a part of theological education and of continuing education for the ministry;

b. to define and promulgate standards for clinical pastoral education;

c. to accredit clinical pastoral education centers and to certify clergymen as supervisors of clinical pastoral education;

d. to provide for development of professional concerns of supervisors of clinical pastoral education;

e. to provide conferences, publications, and research opportunities on behalf of the constituency;

f. to receive, maintain, administer, and spend funds for charitable, religious, or educational purposes.

Article III
Membership

Section 1

This Association shall consist, at its inception, of the individual members, the certified supervisors, the accredited training centers and clusters and the member seminaries of the Association of Clinical Pastoral Educators, the Council for Clinical Training, Incorporated, the Institute of Pastoral Care, Incorporated, and the Department of Institutional Chaplaincy and Clinical Pastoral Education, Lutheran Council in the U.S.A.

Section 2—Individual Membership
Individual membership shall be available to all persons interested in the purpose for which the Association is formed. Such membership shall have the right of participation in all regional and national conferences.

Section 3—Seminary Membership
Membership shall be available to any member seminary of the American Association of Theological Schools or seminaries recommended by a region. Such membership shall include the right to send a representative to regional and national conferences.

Section 4—Institution, Agency, and Parish Membership
An institution, agency, or parish may become a member of this Association by accreditation as a clinical pastoral education center. Each accredited institution, agency, or parish shall have the right to send a representative to regional and national conferences of this Association.

Section 5—Cluster Membership
A cluster of clinical pastoral education centers may become a member of this Association upon the recommendation of the Region and the approval of the Executive Committee. Such membership shall include the right to send a representative to regional and national conferences.

Section 6—Denominational Membership
A denomination and/or one of its representative agencies or departments may become a member of this Association upon request and with the approval of the Executive Committee. Such membership shall include the right to send a representative to regional and national conferences.

Section 7—Council of Churches Membership
A council of Churches may become a member of this Association upon request and with the approval of the Executive Committee. Such membership shall include the right to send a representative to regional and national conferences.

Article IV
Offices

Section 1
The principal office of this Association shall be located in the Commonwealth of Massachusetts in accordance with articles of organization.

Section 2
This Association may also have offices at such other places as the House of Delegates may from time to time designate.

Article V
House of Delegates

Section 1
The affairs of this Association shall be managed by the House of Delegates, which shall have the power and responsibility of carrying out the purposes according to the Constitution and Bylaws.

Section 2

The House of Delegates shall consist of:

a. Four delegates from each region of this Association who shall be members of this Association;

b. Two delegates selected by the American Association of Theological Schools;

c. One delegate from the staff of the Department of Ministry of the National Council of Churches of Christ in the U.S.A.

d. Six denominational representatives including one Roman Catholic and one Jewish representative chosen by the Department of Ministry of the National Council of Churches of Christ in the U.S.A.

e. Five delegates at large elected by the House of Delegates.

Article VI
Officers

Section 1

The officers of this Association shall be a President, a President-Elect, a Vice-President, a Secretary, a Treasurer, an Assistant Treasurer, and a Clerk.

Section 2

Each officer shall be elected by ballot by the House of Delegates.

Section 3

The President, President-Elect, and Vice-President shall be elected for terms of two years and shall not succeed themselves in office.

Section 4

The Secretary, Treasurer, Assistant-Treasurer, and Clerk shall be elected for terms of one year and may succeed themselves in office.

Article VII
Executive Director

Section 1

There shall be an Executive Director who shall be charged with carrying out the purposes for which this Association was formed.

Section 2

He shall be chosen by the Executive Committee and approved by the House of Delegates.

Article VIII
Executive Committee

Section 1

The Executive Committee shall consist of the President, President-Elect, Vice-President, Secretary, and Treasurer of this Association together with five members of the House of Delegates who shall be elected by ballot by the House of Delegates for a term of one year.

Section 2

During the interim between meetings of the House of Delegates and under the limitations imposed by the Constitution and the Bylaws, the

Executive Committee shall carry forward the work and policies of this Association and shall act on behalf of the House of Delegates, subject in all matters to review of its actions by the subsequent meeting of the House of Delegates.

Article IX
Committees

Section 1

Major administrative units of this Association which are charged with substantial segments of functional activity shall be called committees.

Section 2

The House of Delegates shall determine the responsibilities of the committees not inconsistent with the Bylaws.

Section 3

The chairman of each committee shall be an ex-officio member of the House of Delegates without voting privileges.

Section 4

Committees of this Association shall be constituted as follows:
a. Standards Committee
b. Committee on Certification and Accreditation
c. Finance Committee
d. Development Committee
e. Research Committee
f. Historical Committee
g. Nominating Committee
h. Judiciary Committee

Article X
Annual Conference

Section 1

There shall be an Annual Conference of this Association to deal with professional concerns on a conferential level.

Section 2

There shall be a Conference Chairman, a Secretary, a Treasurer, a Program Committee, and such other officers or committees deemed necessary, which shall be elected by the Conference.

Section 3

The Annual Conference shall be open to the membership of this Association.

Article XI
Regions

Section 1

This Association shall be divided into regions, whose number and boundaries are to be determined by the House of Delegates.

Section 2

The regions may be incorporated.

Section 3

Each region shall have a constitution and bylaws ratified by the House of Delegates. Amendments thereto shall be subjected to like ratification.

Section 4

The principal function of regions shall be:

a. to promote and facilitate development of clinical pastoral education;

b. to develop close working relationships among accredited centers of clinical pastoral education, the theological schools, and ecclesiastical bodies of this Association;

c. to admit institutions, agencies, and parishes to provisional accreditation status;

d. to consult with candidates for supervisory clinical pastoral education;

e. to certify candidates as acting supervisors;

f. to provide for fellowship and professional concerns of the constituency of this Association.

Section 5

Subject to other provisions of this Constitution and Bylaws, each region shall have jurisdiction in its own affairs.

Article XII
Periodical

Section 1

This Association shall publish a periodical, "Journal of Pastoral Care."

Section 2

The Editor of "The Journal of Pastoral Care" shall be chosen by the Board of Managers and approved by the House of Delegates.

Article XII
Amendments to Constitution

Section 1

Amendments to this Constitution must be presented in writing to the Secretary of the House of Delegates. Immediately upon receipt, the Secretary shall forward them to the Executive Committee for study and recommendation, which shall make a report thereon to the House of Delegates, if possible, but which shall not be required to do so until 48 hours have elapsed following the presentation.

Section 2

Adoption of an Amendment shall require passage at two successive meetings of the House of Delegates by a two-thirds vote of the delegates present and voting and the full text thereof shall be mailed to each delegate within 30 days after adjournment of the meeting of the House of Delegates first acting favorably thereon.

BYLAWS
Article I
Membership

Section 1—Individual Membership

A. Individual membership will be granted on receipt of application and payment of annual membership fees as follows:

Student (with Journal) .... $ 5.00
Annual (without Jounral) 10.00
Annual (with Journal) 15.00
Contributing (with Journal) 25.00
Sustaining (with Journal) .... 100.00 and over
Life (with Journal) .... 100.00 per year for
ten years

B. Any change in individual annual membership fees shall be voted by the House of Delegates.

Section 2—Seminary Membership

A. Membership will be granted by the Executive Committee to seminaries upon receipt of application and payment of the annual standard fee of one hundred fifty dollars ($150). Said fee may be changed by the House of Delegates.

Section 3—Institution, Agency, and Parish Membership

A. Provisional accreditation status may be granted upon request by an institution, agency, or parish to the Committee on Certification and Accreditation of the Region in which it is situated.

B. Accreditation may be granted by the House of Delegates upon recommendation of the National Committee on Certification and Accreditation.

C. There shall be an annual membership fee of two hundred dollars ($200). Said fee may be changed by the House of Delegates.

D. Any center having four or less student units in a given year may request an abatement of $100 from the Finance Committee of the Association. The said fee may be changed by the House of Delegates upon the recommendation of the Finance Committee.

Section 4—Cluster Membership

A. A Cluster is a group of not less than three accredited centers within the same Region responsibly related to theological education, ordinarily with at least one seminary, the cluster functioning as a unified educational unit.

B. Cluster membership is granted on the approval of the Executive Committee of the House of Delegates acting upon a recommendation from a Region, and payment of an annual affiliation fee of five hundred dollars ($500) in a cluster of from three to five centers and an additional one hundred dollars ($100) for each center over five in the cluster. Said fee may be changed by the House of Delegates.

C. Approval of a Cluster is based upon the following criteria:

1. Evidence of there being not less than three accredited centers within the same region responsibly related to theological education, ordinarily

256

with at least one seminary, the Cluster functioning as a unified educational unit.

2. Evidence of a responsible Committee or Board that has general oversight of the training offered in the cluster.

3. Evidence of having integrated clinical pastoral education into the total curriculum of theological education.

4. Evidence of the integration of other theological disciplines into the clinical pastoral education offered in the training centers.

5. Evidence of offering integrated programs of study for trainees, utilizing the resources and facilities of the training centers within the cluster.

6. Evidence of having established a program for the continued education of the supervisors in the cluster.

7. Evidence of geographic accessibility of the participating training center and seminaries.

Section 5—Denominational Membership

Membership will be granted to denominations and/or one of their representative agencies or departments upon request and receipt of payment of the annual fee of one hundred fifty dollars ($150). Said fee may be changed by the House of Delegates.

Section 6—Council of Churches Membership

Membership may be granted to Councils of Churches upon recommendation from a Region (with the exception of the N.C.C.) and payment of the annual standard fee of fifty dollars ($50). Said fee may be changed by the House of Delegates.

Article II
House of Delegates

Section 1—Meetings

A. All meetings of the House of Delegates shall be held at the principal office of this Association or at such other place as the Executive Committee from time to time may determine.

B. Notice of all meetings and of any unusual or important business to be transacted at the meeting shall be mailed or delivered not less than two weeks before such meeting by the Secretary.

C. The annual meeting of the House of Delegates shall be held on the third Friday in October or on some other day in said month as determined by the Executive Committee.

D. Special meetings of the House of Delegates may be called at any time by the President and Executive Director or by nine members of the House of Delegates.

Section 2—Quorum

The majority of all members of the House of Delegates shall constitute a quorum for the transaction of business at any meeting.

Section 3—Election of Delegates

A. The four delegates from each region shall be annually elected according to their individual constitution or bylaws. Two alternate delegates shall be annually elected by each region and their names submitted to the Executive Director upon election.

B. The two delegates selected by the American Association of Theological Schools shall be chosen annually. One alternate delegate shall be chosen annually and the name submitted to the Executive Director upon selection.

C. The delegate from the staff of the Department of Ministry of the National Council of Churches of Christ in the U.S.A. shall be annually selected by the Department of the Ministry.

D. The six denominational representatives shall be selected annually by the Department of Ministry of the National Council of Churches of Christ in the U.S.A. Two alternate representatives shall be selected annually by the Department of Ministry and their names submitted to the Executive Director upon selection.

E. The five delegates at large elected by the House of Delegates shall be elected annually.

Section 4—Duties of the House of Delegates

In addition to those duties described in the Constitution and Bylaws, the House of Delegates shall hear reports of the Executive Director, Regional Directors, Treasurer, committee chairmen and make whatever policy decisions are necessary to carry out the purposes of this Association.

Section 5—Publications

All publications of this Association shall be the responsibility of the House of Delegates.

Article III
Officers

Section 1—President

He shall preside at all meetings of the House of Delegates and the Executive Committee and shall see that the constitution and bylaws are observed. He shall appoint committees not otherwise provided for, and he shall discharge such other duties as are delegated to him by the House of Delegates or the Executive Committee. He shall sign or countersign all notes, contracts, and other instruments or documents including deeds, mortgages, and leases of this Association.

Section 2—President-Elect

The President-Elect shall serve on the Executive Committee and shall become the President, and in the absence of the President, or in the event of his inability or refusal to act (determined by the Executive Committee), the President-Elect shall act in his stead.

Section 3—Vice-President

In the absence of the President and the President-Elect, or in the event of their inability or refusal to act (determined by the executive committee), the Vice-President shall act in their stead.

Section 4—Secretary

He shall keep the minutes of the Executive Committee and send notices of all meetings of the executive committee and House of Delegates. He shall have charge of the membership books, papers, and other records belonging to or in the possession of the Association not otherwise kept by the clerk.

Section 5—Treasurer

He shall have custody of all funds and securities of the organization. He shall deposit in the name of the Association all funds together with notes, checks, or similar instruments as the House of Delegates may designate. Receipts and vouchers for payments shall be signed by him. Except as otherwise provided by resolution, he shall sign all checks and sign or countersign all notes, bonds, or other evidences of indebtedness. He shall keep complete books of account, and shall make reports to the House of Delegates at such times as requested, showing in detail the financial condition of the organization. He shall pay the obligations of the Association when due, and shall otherwise make distribution under the discretion and approval of the House of Delegates. He may be required to be bonded with a responsible surety company in such sums and forms as the House of Delegates may require.

Section 6—Assistant Treasurer

The Assistant Treasurer shall perform such duties listed under Section 5 as may be assigned by the Treasurer, or in the Treasurer's absence or in the event of his inability or refusal to act (determined by the Executive Committee), he shall act in his stead.

Section 7—Clerk

The Clerk shall be a resident of the Commonwealth of Massachusetts, and shall keep minutes of all meetings of the House of Delegates. He shall be custodian of all the official books, records, papers, and other records belonging to or in the possession of the Association.

Section 8

In the event of the death, resignation, or incapacity of an officer, the Executive Committee shall fill the vacancy until the next meeting of the House of Delegates elects a successor to fill the unexpired term.

Article IV
Executive Director

Section 1—Duties

A. He shall serve as the Administrative officer of this Association and function in such capacity as may be designated by the Executive Committee.

B. He shall be ex-officio member of all committees.

C. He shall have oversight of the office of secretary and the office of treasurer.

Article V
Committees of this Association

Section 1—Standards Committee

1. The Standards Committee shall recommend to the House of Delegates standards for clinical pastoral education, accreditation and certification based on broad principles, and suggestions of procedures and curriculum which may be used as resource material by regions and local centers.

2. The House of Delegates, on recommendation of the Standards Committee, shall set the standards for clinical pastoral education in programs accredited by the Association for Clinical Pastoral Education.

Section 2—Committee on Certification and Accreditation

1. The Committee on Certification and Accreditation shall recommend to the House of Delegates principles of Certification and Accreditation.

2. It shall serve as an examining board to recommend to the House of Delegates candidates for certification as Supervisors of Clinical Pastoral Education, following a period of one or more years of successful functioning as an acting supervisor.

3. It shall recommend to the House of Delegates institutions, agencies, and parishes that have completed one or more years of provisional accreditation as accredited training centers of this Association.

4. Each candidate appearing before the Committee shall pay a fee, set by the House of Delegates, based on cost, to begin with, $100 per appearance.

5. Upon certification each supervisor shall pay an annual certification fee of $25, a portion of which shall include his individual membership and function within the policies and procedures of both the national and regional constitutions and bylaws in order to maintain professional standing in this Association.

6. This committee shall consist of the Chairmen of the Regional Committees on Certification and Accreditation and nine additional members elected by the House of Delegates upon nomination from the nominating Committee of the Association. These nominees shall be selected from the two candidates elected from each of the nine regions.

Section 3—Finance Committee

1. The Finance Committee shall be charged with the responsibility of formulating the financial policies and procedures of the Association for the approval of the House of Delegates and to provide for an annual audit. It shall have the responsibility of preparing the annual budget to be presented to the House of Delegates for approval at the annual meeting. It shall have the responsibility of recommending to the House of Delegates the means of raising and disbursing funds and the responsibility to carry out such activities as are requested by the House of Delegates. It shall also serve as a review committee to review annually, within a reasonable time following the close of the fiscal year, all regional statements of cash receipts and disbursements for the previous year for the purpose of determining that

such cash receipts and disbursements have been made in accordance with the Constitution and Bylaws of this Association. It shall serve as a financial consultant to the Regional Finance Committees on request from the region. The Finance Committee eshall be empowered to appoint a subcommittee vested with the power, subject to the House of Delegates, to carry out the month-to-month management of the budget and financial affairs of this Association.

2. The Committee shall consist of the Treasurer of the Association and Chairmen of the Regional Finance Committees and five members at large elected by the House of Delegates upon nomination from the Association Nominating Committee.

Section 4—Development Committee

It shall be the responsibility of the Development Committee to further the growth and development of this Association as it relates to communications with individuals, ecclesiastical bodies, institutions, seminaries, and the general public. It shall develop and carry out suitable projects for the promotion of this Association as approved by the House of Delegates. It shall serve as a consultant to Regional Development Committees upon request from the regions.

Section 5—Research Committee

It shall be the Research Committee's responsibility to stimulate interest in research, to facilitate communications between researchers and centers promoting research activities. It shall foster rapprochement with relevant major fields allied with the interest of clinical pastoral education, i.e., psychology, psychiatry, medicine, social work, rehabilitation, sociology, anthropology, education, etc. It shall be appropriate for this committee to seek to innovate with respect to goals, methods, scope and assessment of the efficacy of programs, through pilot research and demonstration projects.

Section 6—Historical Committee

It shall be the responsibility of the Historical Committee to assemble historical documents in a central place or to record their existence in several places in order to establish a functionally useful archives. This committee shall encourage writing on historical issues, personalities, and influences upon the clinical pastoral education movement. The Committee shall be the permanent custodian of basic organizational records and provide for a secure repository for these.

Section 7—Nominating Committee

1. It shall be the duty of the Nominating Committee to present to the House of Delegates nominations for officers or members of committees as provided in the Constitution and Bylaws.

2. This Committee shall consist of one member from each region chosen by each region's elected delegates to the House of Delegates.

Section 8—Judiciary Committee

1. There shall be a Judiciary Committee of this Association.

2. The Judiciary Committee shall serve as an advisory body on ethics and interpretation of standards and professional concerns.

3. It shall consist of one member elected by each region.

4. It shall meet at least annually at the time of the Annual Conference of this Association.

Section 9

1. Each of the Committees of the Association shall consist of the Chairman of the corresponding Regional Committee with the exception of the Finance Committee, Committee on Certification and Accreditation, the Nominating Committee, and the Judiciary Committee.

2. In the event that a Regional Chairman is unable to attend a meeting of the Committee of the Association, the Region shall appoint an alternate in his stead. Should a member of the Finance Committee or Committee on Certification and Accreditation, who has been elected by the House of Delegates, be unable to attend a meeting of the Committee of the Association, that Committee is empowered to select an alternate.

Article VI
Regions

Section 1—Constitution and Bylaws

The Constitution and Bylaws of each region shall be in keeping with and shall not be in conflict with the Constitution and Bylaws of this Association.

Section 2

The names of the regions and territories of this Association shall be as listed, the boundaries of which shall be as the House of Delegates shall from time to time designate.

1. Northeast
2. Eastern
3. Mid-Atlantic
4. Southeast
5. East Central
6. South Central
7. North Central
8. Southwest
9. Pacific
10. and such other regions and territories as may be designated by the House of Delegates.

Section 3—Regional Director

Each region shall have a Regional Director who will serve on the staff of the Executive Director. He is responsible to the officers of the region and to the House of Delegates through the Executive Director. The Regional Director shall be selected by whatever means the region may elect.

Section 4—Officers

The regional officers shall consist of Chairman, Vice-Chairman, Secretary, and Treasurer.

Section 5—Regional Annual Conference

Each region shall have an annual conference which is open to all members of this Association. Those eligible to vote at such conference shall be.

A. All certified supervisors in the region;

B. One representative from each affiliated seminary in the region;

C. One representative from each accredited institution, agency or parish in the region;

D. Members at large, the number to be determined by the region.

Section 6

The Committees of each region shall consist of:

A. *Regional Standards Committee*

1. It shall, through its chairman, who is a member of the House of Delegates Standards Committee, help to determine the standards for programs of clinical pastoral education.

2. It shall interpret the standards to the region and shall facilitate the carrying out of these standards in any way feasible in that region.

B. *Regional Committee on Certification and Accreditation*

1. It shall be available for consultation to any supervisor in the region at his request on the admission of students to advanced clinical pastoral education.

2. It shall provide consultative evaluation to candidates for supervisory training and to centers offering supervisory training.

3. It shall review candidates and may grant them the status of "Acting Supervisor."

4. It shall visit institutions, agencies, and parishes that request accreditation of a clinical pastoral education program.

5. It may grant admission to the status of "provisional accreditation" to an institution, agency, or parish.

6. It shall review annually all program requests from centers within the region and recommend their listing in the annual "Training Opportunities" brochure.

C. *Regional Finance Committee*

1. The Regional Finance Committee shall be charged with the responsibility of formulating the financial policies and procedures of the region.

2. It shall raise funds and recommend disbursement in accordance with the purposes of this association and the financial need of the region in keeping with the Constitution and Bylaws of this Association.

D. *Regional Development Committee*

1. It shall be the responsibility of the Regional Development Committee to further the growth and development of this Association as it relates to communications with individuals, institutions, seminaries, ecclesiastical bodies, and the general public.

2. It shall develop and carry out suitable projects for the promotion of the regional operations of this Association and when desired in consultation with the National Development Committee.

E. *Regional Research Committee*

It shall be the Regional Research Committee's responsibility to stimulate interest in research; to facilitate communications between researchers and centers promoting research activities according to the purposes of this Association.

F. *Regional Historical Committee*

It shall be the responsibility of the Regional Historical Committee to encourage appropriate gathering of historical documents and to encourage writing on historical issues, personalities, and influences in the clinical pastoral education movement.

G. *Regional Nominating Committee*

1. This Committee shall make nominations for all officers and committee members to the annual business session of the regional conference.

2. The Nominating Committee for the following year shall be nominated from the floor at the annual regional business session.

Article VII
Periodical

Section 1

The publication of the *Journal of Pastoral Care* shall be the responsibility of the Board of Managers.

Section 2

The Board of Managers shall consist of five members, appointed by the House of Delegates, who shall manage, control, and publish said periodical.

Section 3

The Board of Managers may create and appoint committees and members of such committees as are necessary to publish said journal.

Article VIII
Fiscal Year

Section 4

Fiscal year of the Association shall be the calendar year.

Section 2

Any change in the Fiscal Year shall be determined by the Executive Committee with the approval of the House of Delegates.

Article IX
Amendments to Bylaws

Section 4

These Bylaws may be amended at the Annual Meeting of the House of Delegates or at a special meeting called for said purpose by a two-thirds vote of the delegates present and voting.

Section 2

Amendments to these Bylaws must be presented in writing to the Secretary of the House of Delegates two weeks prior to the Annual Meeting or a special meeting called for the purpose of amending the Bylaws. The Secretary shall then forward them to the Executive Committee for study and recommendation. The Executive Committee shall then report said recommendation to the House of Delegates.

notes

PREFACE

[1] Paul Halmos, *The Faith of the Counsellors* (New York: Schocken Books, 1966), p. 7.

[2] *Ibid.*, p. 20.

[3] Harrop A. Freeman, *Counseling in the United States* (Dobbs Ferry, New York: Oceana Publications, 1967), pp. 123-24.

CHAPTER I

[1] Seward Hiltner, *Preface to Pastoral Theology* (Nashville: Abingdon Press, 1958), p. 55.

[2] William Goulooze, *Pastoral Psychology: Applied Psychology in Pastoral Theology in America* (Grand Rapids: Baker Book House, 1950).

[3] American Association of Theological Schools. Bulletin No. 0, 1918, pp. 4-5.

[4] *Ibid.*, Bulletin No. 5, 1926.

[5] *Ibid.*, Bulletin No. 6, 1928, p. 35.

[6] *Ibid.*, Bulletin No. 8, 1932, pp. 16-46.

[7] R. L. Kelley, *Theological Education in America: A Study of 161 Theological Schools in the U. S. and Canada* (New York: Geo. H. Doran Co., 1924), pp. 220, 224-25.

[8] *Ibid.*, pp. 229-30, 219, 57-58.

[9] Van Cleve Morris, *Philosophy and the American School* (Boston: Houghton Mifflin, 1961), p. 356.

[10] *Ibid.*, pp. 358-64.

[11] Abraham Flexner, *Medical Education in the United States and Canada,* a report to the Carnegie Foundation for the Advancement of Teaching, I (New York, 1910), 8-9.

[12] Richard C. Cabot, M.D., *Adventures on the Borderlands of Ethics* (New York: Harper, 1926), p. 20.

[13] Richard C. Cabot, M.D., *Social Service and the Art of Healing* (New York: Moffat, Yard and Co., 1915), p. 63.

[14] W. Kenneth Cauthen, *The Impact of American Religious Liberalism* (New York: Harper, 1962), p. 6.

[15] *Ibid.*, p. 172.

[16] Anton T. Boisen, *Out of the Depths* (New York: Harper, 1960), pp. 177-78.

[17] Flexner, *Medical Education*, I, xi-xiii.

[18] John T. McNeill, "Historical Types of Method in the Cure of Souls," *The Crozer Quarterly*, July, 1934, p. 227.

[19] William Adams Brown, *Ministerial Education in America*. Vol. I of *The Education of American Ministers*, Ed. Mark A. May, 3 vols. (New York: Institute of Social and Religious Research, 1934), p. 93. See also: Mark A. May, *The Profession of the Ministry*. Vol. II of *The Education of American Ministers*, Ed. Mark A. May, pp. 173-75.

[20] *Ibid.*, I, 192.

[21] Charles F. Kemp, *Physicians of the Soul: A History of Pastoral Counseling* (New York: Macmillan, 1947), pp. 155-56, citing Eastman, *Men of Power*, IV (Nashville: Cokesbury, 1939), 203-7.

[22] Paul E. Johnson, *Psychology of Religion* (New York: Abingdon-Cokesbury, 1945), p. 20.

[23] John I. Smith, "Historical Perspective of the Institute of Pastoral Care," *Clinical Pastoral Training's Contribution to Theology* (1963 Fall Conference, Institute of Pastoral Care), p. 1, citing Karl R. Stolz, unpublished manuscript, Andover Newton Theological School.

[24] Kelley, *Theological Education in America*, pp. 145-51, 367.

[25] *Clinical Pastoral Training*, Ed. Seward Hiltner (Published by the Commission on Religion and Health, Federal Council of the Churches of Christ in America, 1945), p. 137.

[26] Kelley, *Theological Education in America*, pp. 21-22.

[27] Herbert H. Stroup, *Social Work: An Introduction to the Field* (New York: American Book Co., 1953), p. 55.

[28] Cabot, *Adventures on the Borderlands of Ethics*, pp. 2-5.

[29] *Ibid.*, pp. 6-7.

[30] Franz G. Alexander, M.D., and Sheldon T. Selesnick, M.D., *The History of Psychiatry* (New York: Harper, 1966), p. 11.

[31] Smith, "Historical Perspective of the Institute of Pastoral Care," p. 1.

[32] Max Rosenbaum and Milton Berger, *Group Psychotherapy and Group Function* (New York: Basic Books, 1963), pp. 109, 113.

[33] Anton T. Boisen, "The Consultation Clinic," *Pastoral Psychology*, May, 1954, p. 56.

[34] Carl J. Scherzer, "The Emmanuel Movement," *Pastoral Psychology*, February, 1951, p. 33.

[35] *Ibid.*, pp. 32-33.

[36] Correspondence from Russell L. Dicks, Pastoral Counseling Center, Greensboro, N.C., January 16, 1960. Dicks credits this opinion to Dr. James Means, professor of Medicine at Harvard Medical School, with whom Dicks discussed the Emmanuel Movement.

[37] Nina Ridenour, *Mental Health in the United States: A Fifty-Year History*. (Published for the Commonwealth Fund by Harvard University Press, Cambridge, 1961), pp. 23-24, 37-38.

[38] Dunbar's classic work, *Emotions and Bodily Change*, resulted from this year of study. Kemp, *Physicians of the Soul*, pp. 272-73.

[39] Dunbar, "A Few Words as to the General Significance of the Newly Established Council for the Clinical Training of Theological Students," First Annual Report to the Directors of the Council for the Clinical Training of Theological Students, September 29, 1930, p. 2. (Mimeographed.)

[40] Archibald MacLeish, "There Was Something About the Twenties," *Saturday Review*, December 31, 1966, p. 11.

[41] Frederick Lewis Allen, *Only Yesterday* (New York: Bantam Books, 1959), pp. 83, 77.

[42] *Ibid.*, pp. 146, 140, 141.

[43] *Ibid.*, pp. 200, 226.

[44] MacLeish, "There Was Something About the Twenties," p. 11.

[45] Morris, *Philosophy and the American School*, p. 366.

CHAPTER II

[1] Mark A. May, *The Institutions That Train Ministers*. Vol. III of *The Education of the American Ministers*, p. 217.

[2] Anton T. Boisen, *Religion in Crisis and Custom: A Sociological and Psychological Study* (New York: Harper, 1945, 1955), p. 111.

[3] Arthur M. Schlesinger, Jr., *The Crisis of the Old Order, 1919-1933* (Boston: Houghton Mifflin, 1957), pp. 132-33.

[4] Joseph F. Fletcher, "The Development of the Clinical Training Movement Through the Graduate School of Applied Religion," *Clinical Pastoral Training*, 1945, p. 1.

[5] Angus Dun, Jr. and Ted Thornton, "Applied Religion, Theological and Social," *The Union Review*, December, 1941, p. 21.

[6] May, *The Institutions That Train Ministers*, p. 217.

[7] Correspondence from W. C. Seitz, Professor of Homiletics and Religious Education, Bexley Hall, Gambier, Ohio, February 27, 1960: previous historical references to the 1923 Summer School credit Dr. Keller with the initiative in soliciting the interest and cooperation of the dean of Bexley Hall. Dr. Seitz of Bexley Hall says that Dean Mercer took the initiative toward Dr. Keller.

[8] *Ibid.*

[9] Fletcher, "The Development of the Clinical Pastoral Training Movement," p. 1.

[10] Correspondence from W. C. Seitz.

[11] *Ibid.*

[12] May, *The Institutions That Train Ministers*, pp. 217-18: Some questions exist as to whether or not the program was operative during the summers of 1925 and 1926. Dr. Seitz said, "I can find no record of any sessions during the summers of 1925 and 1926." The discussion in the proceedings of the first National Conference on Clinical Training in Theological Education held in June, 1944, refers to the "continuous operation" of the summer school for twelve years prior to 1935. In the absence of conclusive evidence to the contrary, I am assuming that the school enjoyed continuous operation during the years in question.

[13] *Ibid.*, p. 217.

[14] Dun and Thornton, "Applied Religion," p. 19. For details of the School's administration and growth see Fletcher, "The Development of the Clinical Pastoral Training Movement," pp. 31-36.

[15] Fletcher, "The Development of the Clinical Pastoral Training Movement," pp. 2-3, 32-33.

[16] Dun and Thornton, "Applied Religion," p. 20.

[17] Fletcher, "The Development of the Clinical Pastoral Training Movement," p. 4.

[18] Correspondence from Seward Hiltner, September 14, 1967: the findings reported here are based on Hiltner's memory of the visit to Cincinnati made during 1936, or 1937, not upon a written report made at the time.

[19] Russell L. Dicks, *Pastoral Work and Personal Counseling: An Introduction to Pastoral Care* (New York: Macmillan, 1951), p. 37.

[20] Rollin J. Fairbanks, "Richard C. Cabot," *Pastoral Psychology*, March, 1954, pp. 27-32.

[21] Everett C. Herrick, "The Place of Clinical Training in the Theological Curriculum as Theological Educators See It," *Clinical Pastoral Training*, 1945, p. 80.

[22] Boisen, *Out of the Depths*, p. 175.

[23] Richard C. Cabot, M.D., and Russell L. Dicks, *The Art of Ministering to the Sick* (New York: Macmillan, 1936), pp. 323-24. See also, Richard C. Cabot, *Case Teaching in Medicine* (Boston: D. C. Heath & Company, Publishers, 1906), pp. viii-x.

[24] Cabot and Dicks, *Art of Ministering to the Sick*, p. 324.

[25] *Ibid.*, p. 99.

[26] *Ibid.*, p. 101.

[27] Cabot, "Clinical Training on the Earhart Foundation," *The Institution Bulletin: Andover Newton Theological School*, October, 1935, pp. 3-4.

[28] *Ibid.*, pp. 4-5.

[29] *Ibid.*, pp. 5-6.

[30] *Ibid.*, pp. 6-7.

[31] Correspondence from Russell L. Dicks.

[32] Boisen, *Out of the Depths*, pp. 143-49.

[33] Personal interview with Anton T. Boisen, October 30, 1959.

[34] Boisen, *Out of the Depths*, p. 167.

[35] *Ibid.*, p. 171.

[36] Cabot, "Psychotherapy and Its Relation to Religion," in *Religion and Medicine*. Publication No. 5 (New York: Moffat, Yard & Co., 1908), pp. 14-31.

[37] Cabot and Dicks, *The Art of Ministering to the Sick*, pp. 155-56.

[38] Boisen, *Out of the Depths*, pp. 163, 171.

[39] Correspondence from Russell L. Dicks.

[40] *Ibid.*

[41] *Ibid.*

[42] *Ibid.* For an appraisal in depth see the Russell L. Dicks Memorial Issue of *Pastoral Psychology*, December, 1966.

[43] Cabot, *Adventures on the Borderlands of Ethics*, p. 10.

[44] Evidence supporting this claim will become more clear in the chapter on Boisen. A comparison of the central purpose of clinical pastoral education as stated in the Constitutions of the Council for Clinical Training, the Institute of Pastoral Care, and the present Association for Clinical Pastoral Education provides interesting corroboration of my thesis, however.

CHAPTER III

[1] Ernest E. Bruder and Marian L. Barb, "A Survey of Ten Years of Clinical Pastoral Training at Saint Elizabeth's Hospital," *Journal of Pastoral Care*, Summer, 1956, p. 86.

[2] Boisen, *Out of the Depths*, p. 201.

[3] *Diagnostic and Statistical Manual, Mental Disorders* (Published by American Psychiatric Association, Washington, D.C., 1952), pp. 26-27.

[4] Anton T. Boisen, *The Exploration of the Inner World: A Study of Mental Disorder and Religious Experience* (New York: Harper, 1936, 1952), p. 9.

NOTES

⁵ *Out of the Depths.*
⁶ *Ibid.,* pp. 195-96.
⁷ *Ibid.,* pp. 51, 150.
⁸ *Ibid.,* pp. 157-58, 166.
⁹ See Anton T. Boisen, "Cooperative Inquiry in Religion," *Journal of Pastoral Care,* Spring, 1951, which is a reprint from the September-October issue of *Religious Education;* also Anton T. Boisen, "The Present Status of William James' Psychology of Religion," *Journal of Pastoral Care,* Fall, 1953, pp. 155-57.
¹⁰ Paul W. Pruyser, "Anton T. Boisen and the Psychology of Religion," *Journal of Pastoral Care,* December, 1967, p. 218.
¹¹ *Ibid.,* p. 219.
¹² *Ibid.*
¹³ Fred Eastman, "Father of the Clinical Pastoral Movement," *Journal of Pastoral Care,* Spring, 1951, p. 5. For additional information about the founding of the Council see Philip Guiles, "Andover Newton and Clinical Training," *Andover Newton Theological School Bulletin,* December, 1947, pp. 3-4.
¹⁴ *Ibid.* Some details of this historic meeting are not firmly established. Russell L. Dicks says in personal correspondence that it occurred in the home of Dr. Richard C. Cabot. There are two accounts of those who were present. Fred Eastman gives one list and Anton Boisen gives another. Boisen's list is in the "First Annual Report to the Chicago Council for the Training of Theological Students, 1933," p. 3. (Mimeographed.)
¹⁵ *Ibid.,* p. 5.
¹⁶ Boisen, "First Annual Report, 1933," p. 3.
¹⁷ *Ibid.* The four schools were Chicago Theological Seminary, Western Theological Seminary, the University of Chicago Divinity School, and Presbyterian Theological Seminary. In addition Boisen had recruited representatives from the medical profession and from churches in the Chicago area.
¹⁸ "Man of the Month: Donald C. Beatty," *Pastoral Psychology,* February, 1955.
¹⁹ Boisen, *Out of the Depths,* p. 185.
²⁰ The Council for Clinical Training, Inc., Minutes and Reports, 1933-49, December 15, 1947, and May 16, 1949.
²¹ Interview with Anton T. Boisen.
²² Anton T. Boisen, "Clinical Training in Theological Education: The Period of Beginnings," *The Chicago Theological Seminary Register,* January, 1951, p. 3.
²³ Seward Hiltner, "The Heritage of Anton T. Boisen," *Pastoral Psychology,* November, 1965, p. 6.
²⁴ Boisen, *Out of the Depths,* p. 39.
²⁵ Boisen, *Religion in Crisis and Custom,* p. 244.
²⁶ Boisen, "Period of Beginnings," p. 3.
²⁷ Boisen, *Religion in Crisis and Custom,* pp. 201, 200.
²⁸ Anton T. Boisen, "In Defense of Mr. Bryan: A Personal Confession by a Liberal Clergyman," *American Review,* May-June, 1925 (reprint).
²⁹ Cauthen, *The Impact of American Religious Liberalism,* pp. 26-146.
³⁰ Pruyser, "Boisen and the Psychology of the Religion," p. 216.
³¹ Carroll A. Wise, "Clinical Pastoral Training—The Early Years," *Concerns: Clinical and Theological Education* (1965 Fall Conference, Institute of Pastoral Care, Inc.), p. 17.
³² *Ibid.,* pp. 16-19.
³³ "Man of the Month: Francis L. Strickland," *Pastoral Psychology,* October, 1953.
³⁴ Communication with leaders of clinical pastoral education.

[35] Hiltner, "The Heritage of Boisen," p. 7.

[36] Ernest Becker, *The Revolution in Psychiatry: The New Understanding of Man* (New York: The Free Press, 1964).

[37] Thomas S. Szasz, M.D., *The Myth of Mental Illness: Foundations of a Theory of Personal Conduct* (New York: Harper, 1961).

[38] Becker, *The Revolution in Psychiatry.*

[39] Boisen, *Religion in Crisis and Custom,* p. xi.

[40] No better example has appeared of the wealth to be mined by reading human documents more deeply, that is, by reading the ordinary as well as the extraordinary realms of religious experience, than the following: Paul W. Pruyser, *A Dynamic Psychology of Religion* (New York: Harper, 1968).

CHAPTER IV

[1] Minutes of the Board of Governors, September 22, 1934. The Council for the Clinical Training of Theological Students, Inc., Book 2 (1933-41).

[2] Correspondence from Russell L. Dicks and interview with Anton T. Boisen.

[3] Guiles, "Andover Newton and Clinical Training," p. 13.

[4] Boisen, *Out of the Depths,* pp. 154, 160.

[5] Communication with leaders of clinical pastoral education.

[6] Foundation Proposal, the Council for Clinical Training, Inc., 1941, p. 2.

[7] Communication with leaders of clinical pastoral education.

[8] Guiles, "Andover Newton and Clinical Training," p. 16.

[9] Correspondence with Russell L. Dicks.

[10] Wise, "Clinical Pastoral Training—The Early Years," pp. 26-27.

[11] *Ibid.,* pp. 22-24.

[12] Correspondence with Russell L. Dicks.

[13] Guiles, "Andover Newton and Clinical Training," p. 17.

[14] Correspondence from Robert A. Preston, February, 1960.

[15] Guiles, "Andover Newton and Clinical Training," p. 11.

[16] Foundation Proposal, Council, 1941, p. 2.

[17] David R. Hunter, "The Development of the Clinical Training Movement through the New England Group," *Clinical Pastoral Training,* 1945, p. 6.

[18] Austin Philip Guiles, "The 1935 Summer School in Clinical Experience." *The Institution Bulletin,* October, 1935, p. 7.

[19] Communication with leaders of clinical pastoral education.

[20] Correspondence from Dwight W. Cumbee, Associate Professor of Psychology and Pastoral Counseling, Bangor Theological Seminary, Bangor, Maine, March 13, 1968.

[21] Minutes of the Board of Governors, December 7, 1948. The Institute of Pastoral Care, Inc. (Archives of the Institute of Pastoral Care, Inc., in the library of Boston University School of Theology.)

[22] Communication with leaders of clinical pastoral education.

[23] John E. Bell, "A Plan for the Training Center of the Council for Clinical Training at the University of Michigan Hospital" (unpublished doctoral dissertation, Teachers College, Columbia University, 1942), p. 23. Also, Foundation Proposal, Council, 1941, Exhibit III.

[24] *A New Opportunity in Theological Education: A Description of the Policy and Program of the Council for the Clinical Training of Theological Students* (revised and approved for 1934), pp. 8-11. In the Minutes of the Annual Meeting

of the Board of Governors, September 28, 1936, the Council reported accepting 56 students out of nearly 200 applicants.

[25] Fifth Annual Conference, Council for the Clinical Training of Theological Students, September 28, 1934. (Mimeographed.) Dunbar develops the same themes in an article entitled, "The Clinical Training of Theological Students," *Religion in Life,* 1935, pp. 376-83.

[26] *A New Opportunity in Theological Education,* p. 10.

[27] The Council for the Clinical Training of Theological Students, Inc., 1935, p. 3. (Mimeographed.)

[28] Correspondence from Robert A. Preston.

[29] For further information see Wayne E. Hunter, "A Survey and Report Indicating Possible Development of a Religious Program at the U. S. Industrial Reformatory, Chillicothe, Ohio," September, 1936. (Mimeographed.) Also, Theodore E. Bachmann, "Religion in a Reformatory," *The Lutheran Church Quarterly,* April, 1937, pp. 3-12. Also, Annual Reports to the Fall Conferences of the Council for the Clinical Training of Theological Students, Inc., from 1936.

[30] The Council for the Clinical Training of Theological Students, Theological Supervisor's Conference, Fall, 1936, pp. 4-5. (Mimeographed.)

[31] Robert E. Brinkman, "Standards for a Full-Time Program in the Light of the Experience of the Council for Clinical Training," *Clinical Pastoral Training,* 1945, p. 24.

[32] Seward Hiltner, "Clinical Pastoral Training and the Schools," *To Do and To Teach: Essays in Honor of Charles Lynn Pratt* (Lexington, Kentucky: The College of the Bible, 1935), pp. 120-21.

[33] American Association of Theological Schools. Bulletin No. 9, 1934, pp. 68-80.

[34] American Association of Theological Schools. Bulletin No. 11, 1936, p. 53.

[35] *Ibid.*

[36] Correspondence from Seward Hiltner.

[37] Personal interview with Robert E. Brinkman, May 31, 1968.

[38] Communication with leaders of clinical pastoral education.

[39] Interview with Brinkman.

[40] Eugene L. Smith, "The Contributions of Clinical Training to the Counseling Resources of the Clergyman" (unpublished doctoral dissertation, School of Education of New York University, 1945), p. 13, citing a paper by Robert E. Brinkman read at a Conference of the Protestant Chaplains in Federal Penal and Correctional Institutions, Lewisburg, Pa., May 17, 1940. In an interview with Maria Brick about 1946, Brinkman interpreted the purposes of the Council in the same way, showing a consistent perspective during the forties. See Maria Brick, "Some Clinically Trained Ministers and the Program of Their Churches" (unpublished doctoral dissertation, Teachers College, Columbia University, 1947), p. 3.

[41] Communication with leaders of clinical pastoral education.

[42] Correspondence from Reuel L. Howe, February, 1960.

[43] Minutes of the Administrative Committee, 1936-41. The Council for Clinical Training, Inc.

[44] The appeal to the seminaries was endorsed by Albert W. Beaven, Arlo A. Brown, Highell E. W. Fosbroke, F. H. Cosgrave, John A. Mackay, Lewis J. Sherrill, Luther A. Weigle, and Abdel Ross Wents. The American Association of Theological Schools gave official endorsement also by action of their Executive Committee, December 14, 1960. See Foundation Proposal, Council, 1941. Exhibits.

[45] American Association of Theological Schools, Bulletin No. 15, 1942, pp. 50-51,

[46] Minutes of the Administrative Committee, 1936-41. Council.

[47] *Ibid.,* April 24, 1941.

271

[48] *Ibid.*, June 6, 1941, to July 10, 1941.

[49] Interview with Brinkman.

[50] Communication with leaders of clinical pastoral education.

[51] Thomas J. Bigham, Jr., "The Development of the Clinical Training Movement through the Council for Clinical Training," *Clinical Pastoral Training*, 1945, p. 11.

[52] *Ibid.*

[53] Brick, "Some Clinically Trained Ministers," p. 184.

[54] Bell, "A Plan for the Training Center of the Council for Clinical Training at the University of Michigan Hospital," pp. vii, 12, 85.

[55] Ernest E. Bruder conducted such a program at the Rochester State Hospital in collaboration with Colgate Rochester Divinity School in the summer of 1941. Bruder and Robert Morris participated as Council supervisors in the New Plan of Theological Education at the Philadelphia Divinity School from 1942 to 1944. See Ernest E. Bruder, "The Council for the Clinical Training of Theological Students," *The Colgate-Rochester Divinity School Bulletin*, December, 1941, pp. 97-105.

CHAPTER V

[1] Guiles, "Andover Newton and Clinical Training," pp. 18, 20.

[2] Rollin J. Fairbanks, "The Origins of Clinical Pastoral Training," *Pastoral Psychology*, October, 1953, pp. 15-16.

[3] Hunter, "The Development of the Clinical Training Movement through the New England Group," pp. 5-6.

[4] A. Philip Guiles, "Suggestions from Recorded Experience for a Clinical Psychology of Religion," Conference of Teachers, Pastors and Students of Clinical Work, June 2-4, 1941 (Archives of the Institute), p. 1.

[5] *Ibid.*, p. 3. David Eitzen commented on the role of the Cabot Club in stimulating the need for professional organization.

[6] Conference of Supervisors, 1936 (Archives of the Institute), pp. 21, 24-25, 27-30.

[7] Conference of Teachers, 1941, Institute.

[8] "Man of the Month: Rollin J. Fairbanks," *Pastoral Psychology*, March, 1954. Also correspondence from Paul E. Johnson, April 9, 1969.

[9] "Man of the Month: Paul E. Johnson," *Pastoral Psychology*, March, 1951.

[10] Minutes of the Board, February 6, 1945. Institute.

[11] Correspondence from Johnson to Guiles, July 15, 1944 (Archives of the Institute).

[12] James H. Burns, "The Institute of Pastoral Care," *Pastoral Psychology*, October, 1953, p. 21

[13] "General Discussion of the Place of Clinical Training in the Theological-Curriculum," *Clinical Pastoral Training*, 1945, p. 101. Hiltner stated that a group of fifteen or twenty persons had been working on the matter of publishing a journal for two or three years. This suggests that the idea probably originated at the 1941 New England Supervisor's Conference.

[14] Memo from Johnson to Hiltner, December 10, 1943 (Archives of the Institute).

[15] Minutes of January 13, 1944 (Archives of the Institute).

[16] Hunter, "The Development of the Clinical Training Movement through the New England Group," p. 7.

[17] Rollin J. Fairbanks, "Standards for Full-Time Clinical Training in the Light of the New England Experience," *Clinical Pastoral Training*, 1945, p. 38.

[10] Minutes of the Board, February 6, 1945. Institute.

[19] Correspondence between Johnson and Fairbanks, January 29, 1946 (Archives of the Institute).

[20] Conference of Supervisors, 1946 (Archives of the Institute).

[21] Seward Hiltner, "Summary and Review," *Clinical Pastoral Training*, 1945, p. 162.

[22] Robert D. Morris, "The Essential Meaning of Clinical Pastoral Training," *Clinical Pastoral Training*, 1945, p. 93. See aslo, A. Philip Guiles, "Clinical Training and Classroom Pastoral Courses," *Clinical Pastoral Training*, 1945, p. 113.

[23] Hiltner, "Summary and Review," p. 162.

[24] See Seward Hiltner, "Pastoral Theology in the Schools," *Clinical Pastoral Training*, 1945, p. 145.

[25] See Smith, "Contributions of Clinical Training," and Brick, "Clinically Trained Ministers." See also, *The Smith College Studies in Social Work*, December, 1947, pp. 152-57.

CHAPTER VI

[1] *Clinical Education for the Pastoral Ministry*. Proceedings of the Fifth National Conference on Clinical Pastoral Education, November 9-11, 1956. Edited by Ernest E. Bruder and Marian L. Barb (published by the Advisory Committee on Clinical Pastoral Education, 1958), p. ix.

[2] *Ibid.*, pp. v-vi.

[3] *Ibid.*, p. vi.

[4] Personal interview with Edward J. Mahnke, Ocotber, 1959.

[5] *Ibid.*

[6] *Ibid.*

[7] *Ibid.*

[8] "Lutheran Advisory Council on Pastoral Care," A Statement of Purpose and Minimum Standards, n.d. (Mimeographed.)

[9] *Clinical Education for Pastoral Ministry*, 1956, p. v.

[10] Charles C. Bachmann, "The Development of Lutheran Pastoral Care in America" (unpublished doctoral dissertation, Boston University School of Theology, 1949).

[11] "The Practical Field in Theological Education with special reference to pastoral care and counseling," Report of Conference, April 23-24, 1948 (the Department of Pastoral Services, National Council of the Churches of Christ in the U.S.A.).

[12] *Ibid.*, p. 6.

[13] Personal interview with Frederick C. Kuether, October, 1959. See also Maurice C. Clark, *CPT's Contribution*, 1963, pp. 10-20.

[14] Minutes of the Board, December 13, 1948, Council.

[15] Interview with Kuether.

[16] Minutes of the Board, October 22, 1947, Council.

[17] Minutes of the Board, March 30, 1948, Council.

[18] Memorandum for the Record, October 26, 1948, in the Minutes of the Board, Council.

[19] Interview with Kuether.

[20] Conversation with many Council for Clinical Training supervisors supports this interpretation. The phrase "fraternity of rebels" comes from Maurice C. Clark, *CPT's Contribution*, 1963, p. 19.

[21] Minutes of the Executive Committee, October 25, 1948, and December 13, 1948, Council for Clinical Training, Inc. Minutes and Reports, 1933-49.

[22] Preliminary report of the subcommittee to study the function and structure of the Council for Clinical Training, Inc., January 21, 1949, in the Minutes of the Board, Council.

[23] *Ibid.*

[24] Minutes of the Board, April 18, 1949, and May 16, 1949, Council. Also interview with Kuether.

[25] Minutes of the Executive Committee, November 15, 1948, Council. Also Memorandum, November 3, 1948, in the Minutes of the Board, Institute of Pastoral Care, Inc. (Archives of the Institute).

[26] Minutes of the Executive Committee, December 13, 1948, Council.

[27] Minutes of the Board, October 24, 1949, Council.

[28] Minutes of the Board, March 27, 1950, Council.

[29] Minutes of the Board, September 25, 1949, and January 16, 1950, Council.

[30] Reports of the proceedings of some of these conversations are to be found in the following sources: Report to the Deans of Seminaries of the Protestant Episcopal Church, April 1, 1950, Minutes of the Board, Council. Minutes of the Board, December 15, 1950, Council. Joint Conference on the Relations Between Clinical Pastoral Training and Theological Education, November 27-28, 1953, Minutes of the Board, Council.

[31] Interview with Kuether.

[32] Minutes of the Board, October 24, 1949, Council.

[33] Standards of the Council for Clinical Training, Inc., April, 1952.

[34] Standards of the Council for Clinical Training, Inc., November, 1957.

[35] Report to the Annual Meeting of the Board of Governors, Council for Clinical Training, Inc., of the Meeting held in Chicago, October 12 and 13, 1953, in the Minutes of the Board, Council.

[36] Minutes of the Board, April 6, 1948; November 30, 1950; February 6, 1951, Institute.

[37] Minutes of the Board, December 2, 1947, Institute.

[38] Minutes of the Board, June, 1948, Institute.

[39] Minutes of the Board, October 15, 1948, and December 7, 1948, Institute.

[40] Minutes of the Board, December 6, 1949, Institute.

[41] Minutes of the Board, October 10, 1951, and December 4, 1951, Institute.

[42] Minutes of the Board, February 3, 1948, Institute.

[43] Minutes of the Board, June 10, 1947, and October 7, 1947, Institute.

[44] Minutes of the Board, October 15, 1948, Institute.

[45] *Ibid.*

[46] Minutes of the Board, December 2, 1947, Institute. This interpretation of the minutes has been confirmed by conversations with leaders of clinical pastoral education.

[47] Minutes of the Board, November 7, 1949, Institute.

[48] Minutes of the Board, June, 1948; December 7, 1948; November 7, 1949; December 6, 1949; February 6, 1950; and February 14, 1950, Institute.

[49] Minutes of the Board, December 6, 1949; February 6, 1951; October 6, 1953; and December 1, 1953, Institute.

[50] Minutes of the Board, May 4, 1950; June 6, 1950; November 30, 1950; and February 6, 1951, Institute.

[51] Minutes of the Board, February 6, 1951, Institute.

[52] *Ibid.*

[53] Minutes of the Board, June 5, 1951, Institute.

[54] *Ibid.*

[55] Minutes of the Board, October 10, 1951 and December 4, 1951, Institute.

[56] Minutes of the Board, December 6, 1949, Institute.

[57] Minutes of the Board, December 2, 1952, Institute.

[58] Minutes of the Board, February 3, 1953, Institute; also Meeting of the Special Committee of the Institute of Pastoral Care, Inc., November 3, 1953, in the Minutes of the Board, Institute.

[59] Statement by the Executive Secretary of the Institute of Pastoral Care, Inc., September 16, 1953 (Archives of the Institute).

[60] Minutes of the Board, October 6, 1953, Institute.

[61] Meeting of the Special Committee of the Institute, November 11, 1953, in the Minutes of the Board, Institute.

[62] The Committee of Twelve, Buckhill Falls Conference (verbatim transcription from an electronic recording of the Conference, April 25-26, 1952). See also Appendix B for a copy of the Standards for Clinical Pastoral Education, adopted by the National Conference on Clinical Pastoral Training, October 13, 1953.

CHAPTER VII

[1] *Clinical Education for Pastoral Ministry*, 1956, p. vii.

[2] Minutes of the Committee of Twelve, April 28-29, 1956, Chicago, Ill. The name suggested for a national organization at the time was "College of Clinical Pastoral Education."

[3] *Clinical Education for Pastoral Ministry*, 1956, p. 130.

[4] Minutes of the Committee of Twelve, March 1-2, 1957, Chicago, Ill.

[5] Personal correspondence from Samuel Southard to John M. Price, Jr., October 23, 1957. See also, Minutes of the Advisory Committee on Clinical Pastoral Education, October 18-19, 1957, New York City.

[6] Report of the Committee on Procedures, February 15, 1958, in Minutes of the Advisory Committee.

[7] Minutes of the Advisory Committee, February 27-28, 1959, Louisville, Ky.

[8] Minutes of the Advisory Committee, February 14-15, 1960, Columbus, O.

[9] Minutes of the Board, October 25, 1960, Institute.

[10] Personal participation on the Steering Committee of the Advisory Committee of the National Conference on Clinical Pastoral Education, representing the Southern Baptist Association for Clinical Pastoral Education, October 29, 1960.

[11] *Clinical Education for Pastoral Ministry*, 1956, pp. 124, 130.

[12] Bruder's role has been described. Richard K. Young, Director of the School of Pastoral Care, North Carolina Baptist Hospital in Winston-Salem, N.C., was a representative from the Southern Baptist Association for Clinical Pastoral Education. Young was added to the Steering Committee in 1958.

[13] For a full discussion of the Institute of Religion and the Council of Southwestern Theological Schools, Inc. see my dissertation: "A Critique of Clinical Pastoral Education" (Southern Baptist Theological Seminary, 1961), pp. 256-91.

[14] Minutes of the Advisory Committee, February 14-15, 1958, Chicago, Ill. Appendix IV A.

[15] Carroll A. Wise, "Recent Developments," *Journal of Pastoral Care*, Winter, 1956, p. 239.

[16] Annual Report of the Director of the Institute of Religion for the year June, 1959, through May, 1960, to the Board of Trustees. The Institute of Religion's second president, Thompson L. Shannon, Ph.D., has developed an inter-

faith dimension by the addition of a Roman Catholic priest to the faculty and the inclusion of a Roman Catholic Seminary in the affiliations of the Institute. New leadership is being given to the development of medical ethics and to the field of marriage counseling.

[17] Address by Frederick C. Kuether, Fall Conference of Supervisors, October 26-29, 1959, Council.

[18] Minutes of the Board, October 19, 1955, Council. See also, Report of the Accreditation Committee to the Board of Governors, November 11, 1955, Council, pp. 2-3.

[19] Address by Kuether.

[20] Earl Loomis, "Experiments in Education for Effective and Committed Ministry," *Report of the Fifth Biennial Meeting of the Association of Seminary Professors in the Practical Fields,* June 14-17, 1958, pp. 83-84.

[21] "Editorial: Psychiatry and Religion," *Pastoral Psychology,* December, 1954, pp. 8-9. The Menninger Foundation set up the Edward F. Gallahue Seminars on Religion and Psychiatry.

[22] *A Program in Religion and Psychiatry* (The Menninger Foundation, Topeka, Kansas, n.d.) , pp. 5-8.

[23] Thomas W. Klink, "Goals and Content of Advanced Clinical Pastoral Training," Fall Conference of Supervisors, October 28, 1959, St. Louis, Mo., Council.

[24] Hans Hoffman, "Instruction of Mental Health in Theological Schools" (A Report by the Director of the Harvard University Project on Religion and Mental Health, n.d.) , p. 13 (lithographed). See also "Notes and News," *Pastoral Psychology,* September, 1956, p. 57; December, 1957, pp. 57-60; November, 1958, pp. 52-56. See articles by Kobler *et al.,* "Loyola University NIMH Project on Religion and Mental Health," *Pastoral Psychology,* February, 1959, pp. 44-46; I. Fred Hollander, "The Specific Nature of the Clergy's Role in Mental Health," *Pastoral Psychology,* November, 1959, pp. 11-21.

[25] Secretary's Report, September 28, 1960, Southern Baptist Association for Clinical Pastoral Education.

[26] Report of the Executive Secretary to the Administrative Committee, March 18, 1937, Council. (Typed.)

[27] Gaines S. Dobbins, "An Historical Description of the Developing Program of Pastoral Care," A Tenth-Year Report: Curriculum Development, Department of Psychology of Religion and Pastoral Care, Southern Baptist Theological Seminary, Louisville, Ky., November, 1953, p. 4. (Mimeographed.)

[28] "The Man of the Month: Wayne E. Oates," *Pastoral Psychology,* May, 1951.

[29] *Ibid.,* p. 65.

[30] Personal interview with Wayne E. Oates, January, 1959.

[31] *Ibid.*

[32] Wayne Oates, "Our Mission to the Sick," *The Tie,* November, 1947, p. 4. Oates was appointed instructor in Psychology and Clinical Training in 1945, Assistant Professor in 1948, Associate Professor of the Psychology of Religion in 1953, and full Professor in 1955.

[33] The program at Central State Hospital was under the direction of Clarence Y. Barton, assisted by John H. McClanahan. The supervisor at Louisville General Hospital was John H. Boyle, and both the Norton Infirmary Psychiatric Unit and the Family Relations Center were under Edward E. Thornton. For a more detailed study of the clinical pastoral education program at Southern Baptist Seminary see my doctoral dissertation, "A Critique of Clinical Pastoral Education," pp. 176-83, 228-42, 250-51, 291-318.

[34] Report of the Department of Pastoral Care to the Board of Trustees, North Carolina Baptist Hospital, for the year 1959; the statistics for 1957 come from a chart of comparative figures for the years 1953-58.

[35] Personal correspondence from John M. Price, Dean, School of Religious Education, New Orleans Baptist Theological Seminary, New Orleans, La., April 16, 1960. Price was made Director of the Religious Education Division and Assistant Professor of Religious Psychology and Counseling in 1948; Associate Professor in 1949; Dean of the School of Religious Education and Professor of Counseling and Clinical Pastoral Education during the period 1952-58. He has continued as Dean of the School of Religious Education to the time of this writing.

[36] Minutes of Committees on Standards, Centers and Approval, September 29, 1959, Southern Baptist Association for Clinical Pastoral Education.

[37] Minutes of the Annual Meeting, September 28-29, 1959, Southern Baptist Association for Clinical Pastoral Education. See also evidence of the problem created for the Council for Clinical Training by this delay in accepting national standards: Minutes of the Board, November 22, 1957, Council.

[38] For a detailed discussion of additions to the national standards see the section on the Southern Baptist Association in the next chapter.

[39] Minutes of the Annual Meeting, September 26-27, 1960, Southern Baptist Association for Clinical Pastoral Education.

[40] Beginning July 1, 1954, an Advisory Committee began study. Their reports were made under the following titles: H. Richard Niebuhr, *The Purpose of the Church and Its Ministry: Reflections on the Aims of Theological Education* (New York: Harper, 1956); H. Richard Niebuhr, Daniel Day Williams, and James M. Gustafson, *The Advancement of Theological Education* (Harper, 1957). A series of monographs was published also for theological educators. Derived from the momentum of the study came a third volume, *The Ministry in Historical Perspectives*, edited by H. Richard Niebuhr and Daniel D. Williams (Harper, 1956).

[41] Niebuhr, *The Purpose of the Church and Its Ministry*, pp. 126, 132-33.

[42] Niebuhr et al., *The Advancement of Theological Education*, p. 128.

[43] Reuel L. Howe, "Christian Group Life in Theological Education" (Report of the Fifth Biennial Meeting of the Association of Seminary Professors in the Practical Fields, June 14-17, 1958).

[44] See Hiltner, *Preface to Pastoral Theology;* Carroll A. Wise, *Psychiatry and the Bible* (New York: Harper, 1956). Paul E. Johnson, *Personality and Religion* (Nashville: Abingdon Press, 1957). William E. Hulme, *Counseling and Theology* (Philadelphia: Muhlenberg Press, 1956). Wayne E. Oates, *Religious Dimensions of Personality* (New York: Association Press, 1957).

[45] Minutes of the Board, April 5, 1960, and October 25, 1960, Institute.

[46] Minutes of the Board, April 4, 1956; October 2, 1956; and December 4, 1956, Institute.

[47] Minutes of the Board, February 10, 1959, Institute.

[48] Minutes of the Board, February 12, 1955, Institute.

[49] Minutes of the Conference of Supervisors, January 30-31, 1959, St. Louis, Mo., (Archives of the Institute).

[50] Minutes of the Board, February 3, 1953, and February 2, 1960, Institute.

[51] Minutes of the Conference of Supervisors, January 30-31, 1959, St. Louis, Mo., (Archives of the Institute).

[52] Minutes of the Board, April 27, 1954, Institute.

[53] Minutes of the Board, October 5, 1954, Institute.

[54] Summary, Chaplain Supervisor's Conference, February 12, 1955, Chicago, Ill., (Archives of the Institute).

[55] Minutes of the Board, April 4, 1956, Institute.

[56] Minutes of the Board, December 9, 1958, Institute.

[57] Minutes of the Board, December 1, 1959, and June 7, 1960, Institute.

[58] Minutes of the Board, December 10, 1957, Institute.

[59] Minutes of the Board, October 1, 1957, and February 4, 1958, Institute.

[60] Minutes of the Conference of Supervisors, January 30-31, 1959, St. Louis, Mo. (Archives of the Institute).

[61] *Clinical Pastoral Education* (Fall Conference, Chaplain Supervisors, Institute of Pastoral Care, October 5-9, 1959, Farmington, Mass.), p. 35.

[62] *Ibid.*, p. 33.

[63] Paul R. Swanson, "Clinical Pastoral Education in the Institute of Pastoral Care," *Clinical Pastoral Education* (1959 Fall Conference, Institute of Pastoral Care, Inc.), p. 18.

[64] Minutes of the Board, December 6, 1960, Institute.

[65] Minutes of the Board, February 26, 1954, Council.

[66] *Ibid.*

[67] Minutes of the Fall Conference of Supervisors, October 17-21, 1955, Council. In January, 1956, Virginia Theological Seminary became the first active member seminary in the Council. In March, 1956, Garrett Biblical Institute, Episcopal Theological Seminary of the Southwest, and Columbia Theological Seminary of Decatur, Georgia, were added to the active list, and Westminster Theological Seminary became an associate member. See Minutes of the Board, January 27, 1956, and March 23, 1956, Council.

[68] Minutes of the Board, January 11, 1954, Council.

[69] Minutes of the Board, November 22, 1957, Council.

[70] Statistics were compiled from Minutes of the Board. A full summary for the years 1934-53 is contained in the Minutes of the Board, February 26, 1954, Council.

[71] See particularly: Minutes of the Board, March 23, 1956, Council; also the annual audits appended to Minutes of the Board.

[72] Report of the Curriculum Committee to the Board of Governors, November 11, 1955, Council.

[73] Procedures and Criteria in Accreditation, January 24, 1958, in Minutes of the Board, Council.

[74] Kenneth Stanley Crofoot, "A Survey of Programs of Clinical Pastoral Education in the Protestant Denominations of the United States as a Preparation for Pastoral Counseling" (unpublished doctoral dissertation, George Washington University, Washington, D.C., 1959).

[75] Minutes of the Board, January 27, 1956, Council; See also Minutes of the Executive Committee and Regional Representatives, July 20, 1956, Council.

[76] The record of the Bruder-Wise conflict may be found in the Minutes of the Board and of the Executive Committee from June 13-14, 1958, to October 17, 1960, Council. See also papers presented to the Fall Conference of Supervisors, October 26-29, 1959, St. Louis, Mo., Council.

[77] *The Church and Clinical Pastoral Education.* Proceedings of the Sixth National Conference on Clinical Pastoral Education, Plymouth, Mass., 1958 (published by the Advisory Committee on Clinical Pastoral Education), pp. iii, vi.

[78] Address by Carroll A. Wise to the Fall Conference of Supervisors, October 26-29, 1959, St. Louis, Mo., Council.

CHAPTER VIII

[1] Seward Hiltner, "Clinical Pastoral Education: An Appraisal 1960," *Trends in C.P.E.: Objectives-Methods-Standards.* Proceedings of the Seventh National Conference on Clinical Pastoral Education (published by the Advisory Committee on Clinical Pastoral Education, n.d.), pp. 2, 5-6.

[2] *Ibid.,* p. 11.

[3] *Ibid.,* pp. 20, 29.

[4] *Ibid.,* pp. 26-28.

[5] Charles V. Gerkin, "Objectives of C.P.E." *Trends in C.P.E.,* 1960, p. 85.

[6] Edward E. Thornton and Charles D. Flory, "Professional Education in Ministry: Program of Human Development at Crozer Theological Seminary." *Report of the Tenth Biennial Meeting of the Association of Seminary Professors in the Practical Fields,* June 13-18, 1968, Fontbonne College, St. Louis, Mo., p. 57.

[7] Alfred Alschuler, "Psychological Education: a new focus for training in the Guidance Area" (Harvard Graduate School of Education, January, 1967), p. 5. (Mimeographed.) Alschuler addressed his remarks to guidance counselors in elementary and secondary education. Clinical pastoral educators have anticipated these concerns by several decades introducing psychological education into theological education in an explicit way as early as the thirties.

[8] Minutes of the Board, December 6, 1960, Institute.

[9] Minutes of the Board, February 24, 1962, Council; See also, Clark, *CPT's Contribution,* 1963, p. 13.

[10] Minutes of the Board, February 24, 1962, Council.

[11] John M. Billinsky, "Facing the Merger Questions," *CPT's Contribution,* 1963, p. 23.

[12] *Ibid.,* p. 24.

[13] Judson D. Howard, "Supervisors' Conference: Its Relationships," *Levels of Clinical Pastoral Training* (1961 Fall Conference, Institute of Pastoral Care, Inc.), p. 14.

[14] John I. Smith, "Issues Involved in a Closer Relationship of the Council for Clinical Training and the Institute of Pastoral Care," *Theological Education and Clinical Pastoral Training* (1962 Fall Conference, Institute of Pastoral Care, Inc.), pp. 66-67.

[15] Andrew D. Elia, M.D., "A Physician's View of the Inter-Relationship Between the Clinically Trained Minister and the Medical Profession," *Theological Education and CPT,* 1962, p. 27.

[16] Seward Hiltner and Jesse H. Ziegler, "Clinical Pastoral Education and the Theological Schools," *Journal of Pastoral Care,* Spring, 1961, pp. 129-43.

[17] President's Report, February 6, 1962, in Minutes of the Board, Institute.

[18] Minutes of the Board, February 10, 1961, Institute.

[19] Smith, "Issues Involved in a Closer Relationship of the Council for Clinical Training and the Institute of Pastoral Care," pp. 72-73.

[20] Richard J. Lehman, "Facing the Accreditation: Facing the Joint Accreditation," *CPT's Contribution,* 1963, pp. 25-26.

[21] Personal interview with John I. Smith, April 26, 1968.

[22] Lehman, "Facing the Accreditation," p. 27.

[23] Personal correspondence from John I. Smith, October 4, 1968. The initial presentation to the Stone Foundation was made by Charles E. Hall, Jr., who was then President of the Council for Clinical Training, Inc., John M. Billinsky, President of the Institute of Pastoral Care, Inc., and Arthur Tingue of the American Foundation of Religion and Psychiatry.

[24] Personal participation, December 10-11, 1965, Washington, D.C.

[25] Memo on Consultation on Accreditation and Certification for C.P.E. to the Southern Baptist Association for Clinical Pastoral Education, December 10-11, 1965, Washington, D.C.

[26] Personal correspondence from Charles E. Hall, Jr., April 12, 1966.

[27] Personal participation in the Joint Structure Committee, April 30, 1966, New York City.

[28] Memo on Meeting of Joint Structure Committee, CCT-IPC, April 30, 1966, New York City, to the Southern Baptist Association for Clinical Pastoral Education from E. A. Verdery, Chairman, May 18, 1966.

[29] Personal correspondence from Kenneth R. Strom, January 26, 1967, containing a summary of the viewpoints of the chaplains representing four Federal Institutions.

[30] ACPE Newsletter, April, 1967.

[31] Constitution and Bylaws of the Association for Clinical Pastoral Education, New Thrusts in Clinical Pastoral Education (1967 Fall Conference, Association for Clinical Pastoral Education), pp. 64-82. See also Appendix D.

[32] Ibid., p. 73: Bylaws, Article I, Section 4 C.

[33] Annual Report, 1967 (the Georgia Association for Pastoral Care, Inc.).

[34] Personal correspondence from Charles V. Gerkin, October 8, 1968.

[35] Ibid.

[36] Ibid.

[37] Annual Report, 1967 (Georgia Association), pp. 3-4.

[38] Ibid., pp. 5-6, 8.

[39] Constitution and Bylaws of the Southern Baptist Association for Clinical Pastoral Education, September 30, 1958. Constitution, Article I, Section 2.

[40] Ibid., Bylaws, Article III.

[41] Minutes of the Southern Baptist Association for Clinical Pastoral Education, September 25-26, 1961.

[42] Minutes of the Association of Clinical Pastoral Educators, September 27-28, 1965, and September 26-27, 1966.

[43] Minutes of the Accreditation Committee, Southern Baptist Association for Clinical Pastoral Education, September 22-24, 1963, September 26-29, 1964.

[44] Minutes of the Southern Baptist Association, September 22-24, 1963.

[45] Minutes of the Association of Clinical Pastoral Educators, September 27-28, 1965.

[46] Minutes of the Association of Clinical Pastoral Educators, September 26-27, 1966.

[47] Minutes of the Association of Clinical Pastoral Educators, September 25-26, 1967. Two nos and nine abstentions were recorded. Eighty percent of the fifty-two members present and voting voted yes.

[48] Minutes of the House of Delegates of the Association for Clinical Pastoral Education, October 19-20, 1967.

[49] See Reports on Regional Meetings from the Joint Executive Director to the Joint Structure Committee, Spring, 1967. Lutheran supervisors were counted in the totals only when they were not certified also by the Council for Clinical Training or the Institute of Pastoral Care, in Minutes of Joint Structure Committee.

[50] Minutes of the Executive Committee, Association for Clinical Pastoral Education, November 16-17, 1967.

[51] ACPE Newsletter, March, 1968, p. 2.

[52] W. Paul Jones, "New Thrusts in Theological Education: Anatomy of an Experiment," New Thrusts, 1967, p. 28.

[53] Thomas W. Klink, "Critical Incidents in Supervision: Towards a General Theory of Learning in Practicum-Based Education," *New Thrusts*, 1967, pp. 42-47. See also case studies of critical incidents by Richard A. Bollinger, pp. 48-52; Kenneth R. Mitchell, pp. 53-58; and Leo Thomas, pp. 59-63.

[54] Freeman, *Counseling in the United States*, p. 124.

[55] *Theological Education*. Special Issue on Theological Education in the 1970's: Redeployment of Resources, Summer, 1968. See also, Supplement on Cooperative Structures for Theological Education, Summer, 1968, Supplement 1.

CHAPTER IX

[1] *Clinical Experience for Theological Students*. Worcester State Hospital, Worcester, Mass. 1928. (Mimeographed.)

[2] "Man of the Month: Donald C. Beatty," *Pastoral Psychology*, February, 1955.

[3] Boisen, *Out of the Depths*, pp. 121-26.

[4] First Annual Report to the Chicago Council (1933), pp. 5-6.

[5] Anton T. Boisen, "The Service of Worship in a Mental Hospital: Its Therapeutic Significance," *Journal of Clinical Pastoral Work*, Summer, 1948, p. 21.

[6] *Ibid.*, pp. 22-24.

[7] Anton T. Boisen, "The Minister as Counselor," *Journal of Pastoral Care*, Spring, 1948, p. 22.

[8] Anton T. Boisen, "Group Therapy: The Elgin Plan," *Pastoral Psychology*, March, 1954, pp. 33-38.

[9] Boisen, *Out of the Depths*, p. 212.

[10] *Ibid.*, pp. 163-64.

[11] Report on the Clinical Training of Theological Students in the Worcester State Hospital Under the Auspices of the Council for the Clinical Training of Theological Students in Cooperation with the Worcester State Hospital, Summer of 1933, by C. A. Wise, September 8, 1933, in the Council for the Clinical Training of Theological Students Reports of Conferences and Activities, Summer of 1933, pp. 45-52.

[12] The Elgin State Hospital Report in the Third Annual Conference of the Council for the Clinical Training of Theological Students, Worcester State Hospital, Worcester, Mass., 1932, p. 2. See also, *An Adventure in Theological Education and Pastoral Service*, 1937, p. 1.

[13] Guiles, "Andover Newton and Clinical Training," p. 7, citing the First Annual Report to the Directors of the Council for the Clinical Training of Theological Students, Anton T. Boisen, Secretary, 29 September 1930. See also, The Elgin State Hospital Report in the Third Annual Conference, 1932, p. 2.

[14] Guiles, "Andover Newton and Clinical Training," pp. 3-4.

[15] Paul E. Johnson, "Clinical Pastoral Training at the Crossroads," *Levels*, 1961, pp. 55-57.

[16] Personal interview with John I. Smith, October 22, 1968.

[17] Minutes of the Board, June, 1948, Institute.

[18] Minutes of the Board, December 2, 1952, Institute.

[19] Interview with Smith, October 22, 1968.

[20] Summer School in Clinical Pastoral Education, Worcester State Hospital, 1968.

[21] *Ibid.*

[22] Interview with Smith, October 22, 1968.

[23] Summer School (Worcester, 1968).

[24] *Ibid.*

[25] *Ibid.*

[26] John I. Smith, "Philosophy and Methods of Clinical Pastoral Education," *Clinical Pastoral Education*, 1959, p. 32.

[27] Interview with Smith, October 22, 1968. See also, Andover Newton Theological School, Clinical Pastoral Education, Description of Center and Programs, by John I. Smith, Training Supervisor, August, 1968.

[28] Interview with Smith, October 22, 1968.

CHAPTER X

[1] Edward E. Thornton, "The Place of Clinical Pastoral Education in New Plans of Theological Education," *Journal of Pastoral Care*, March, 1966, pp. 16-23.

[2] Seward Hiltner, "Clinical Training as an Integral Part of the Curriculum of a Theological Seminary," 1936. (Typed.)

[3] Personal interview with Leon R. Robison, Jr., August 20, 1968. It is noteworthy that after pioneering as a supervisor, 1933-35, Robison entered the American Baptist pastorate. In 1967 he re-entered the field of clinical pastoral education, taking refresher work with Chaplain Kent D. Smith of Delaware State Hospital before reinstatement as a full supervisor (1968) and resumption of functioning as a chaplain supervisor.

[4] Correspondence from Howe.

[5] Reuel L. Howe, "The Development of the Clinical Training Movement through the Philadelphia Divinity School," *Clinical Pastoral Training*, 1945, p. 13.

[6] *Ibid.*, pp. 13-14; supplemented by correspondence from Howe.

[7] *Ibid.*, pp. 14-16.

[8] Correspondence from Howe.

[9] Howe, "The Development of the Clinical Training Movement," pp. 15-16.

[10] Reuel L. Howe, "Clinical Training in Relation to Classroom Teaching," p. 119.

[11] *Ibid.*, p. 125.

[12] Howe, "The Development of the Clinical Training Movement," p. 16.

[13] Howe, "Clinical Training in Relation to Classroom Teaching," p. 121.

[14] *Ibid.*, p. 118.

[15] Howe, "The Development of the Clinical Training Movement," p. 16.

[16] Brick, "Clinically Trained Ministers," citing correspondence from Seward Hiltner, April 7, 1947.

[17] Correspondence from Howe.

[18] *Ibid.*

[19] The Philadelphia Divinity School Supplement to 1967-68 Catalogue. 4205 Spruce Street, Philadelphia, Pa. 19104.

[20] *Theological Education in the American Baptist Convention*, Digest Report: Committee of Seventeen, June, 1962.

[21] Personal interview with Stewart G. Cole, January 14, 1968.

[22] *Ibid.*

[23] Principles of Curriculum Re-Making, Crozer Theological Seminary, January, 1935, pp. 3-8.

[24] File on the Franklin-McNutt affair in the Archives of the Crozer Theological Seminary Library.

[25] William Roy McNutt, "Some Phases of Practical Theology," *Bulletin*, Crozer Theological Seminary, October, 1928, pp. 174-85.

[26] Written Memories, etc., of William Roy McNutt, p. 13.

[27] Correspondence from President Franklin to Professor William R. McNutt, June 4, 1942. This was reaffirmed at Franklin's insistence in June, 1943, in order to block the introduction of new courses by McNutt (Archives of Crozer Theological Seminary).

[28] Report to President Franklin and Board of Trustees, by William R. McNutt, December 26, 1942 (Archives of Crozer Theological Seminary).

[29] Report to President Franklin and Board of Trustees, by William R. McNutt, April 14, 1943 (Archives of Crozer Theological Seminary).

[30] Feilding, "Education for Ministry," p. 173.

[31] For a more systematic analysis of the program of human development at Crozer Theological Seminary including the results of a three-year pilot program completed in 1967, see the following: Edward E. Thornton and Charles D. Flory, "Professional Education in Ministry: Program of Human Development at Crozer Theological Seminary," *Report of the Tenth Biennial Meeting of the Association of Seminary Professors in the Practical Fields*, June 13-18, 1968, Fontbonne College, St. Louis, Mo., pp. 53-72.

[32] Lowell G. Colston, "Seminaries and Clinical Pastoral Education," an unpublished paper, 1967, p. 1.

[33] See Appendix D.

[34] I have discussed this problem more fully, suggesting a way to extract the essence of clinical pastoral education for theological seminaries in my article, "Clinical Pastoral Education in New Plans," 1966, pp. 16-23.

[35] Peggy Way, "Community Organization and Pastoral Care: Drumbeat for Dialogue," *Pastoral Psychology*, March, 1968, p. 25.

[36] Gibson Winter, "The Pastoral Counselor Within the Community of Faith," *Pastoral Psychology*, November, 1959, p. 21.

[37] Notable among many experiments offering clinical pastoral education in parish settings is the program of the Menninger Foundation for which Hiltner has long served as consultant.

[38] Seward Hiltner, "Ten Years of Pastoral Psychology," *Pastoral Psychology*, January, 1960, p. 10.

[39] Henry Babcock Adams, "Consultation: An Alternative to Supervision," *Developments* (published by the Department of Ministry, National Council of Churches, 475 Riverside Drive, New York, N. Y. 10027, June, 1968), pp. 1-7.

[40] Alschuler, "Psychological Education," 1967.

[41] Freeman, *Counseling in the United States.*

[42] Harry Emerson Fosdick, "The Minister and Psychotherapy," *Pastoral Psychology*, February, 1960, p. 11.

bibliography

Books

Alexander, Franz G., M.D. and Selesnick, Sheldon T., M.D. *The History of Psychiatry*. New York: Harper, 1966.

Allen, Frederick Lewis. *Only Yesterday*. New York: Bantam Books, 1959.

Becker, Ernest. *The Revolution in Psychiatry: The New Understanding of Man*. New York: The Free Press, 1964.

Boisen, Anton T. *Out of the Depths*. New York: Harper, 1960.

———. *Religion in Crisis and Custom: A Sociological and Psychological Study*. New York: Harper, 1945, 1955.

———. *The Exploration of the Inner World: A Study of Mental Disorder and Religious Experience*. New York: Harper, 1936.

Cabot, Richard C., M.D. *Adventures on the Borderlands of Ethics*. New York: Harper, 1926.

———. *Case Teaching in Medicine*. Boston: D. C. Heath & Company, Publishers, 1906,

———. *Religion and Medicine*. Publication No. 5. New York: Moffatt, Yard & Co., 1908.

———. *Social Service and the Art of Healing*. New York: Moffat, Yard & Co., 1915.

———, and Dicks, Russell L. *The Art of Ministering to the Sick*. New York: Macmillan, 1936.

Cauthen, W. Kenneth. *The Impact of American Religious Liberalism*. New York: Harper, 1962.

Diagnostic and Statistical Manual, Mental Disorders. Published by the American Psychiatric Association, Washington, D.C., 1952.

Dicks, Russell L. *Pastoral Work and Personal Counseling: An Introduction to Pastoral Care*. New York: Macmillan, 1951.

Dittes, James. *The Church in the Way*. New York: Scribner's, 1967.

Flexner, Abraham. *Medical Education in the United States and Canada: A Report to the Carnegie Foundation for the Advancement of Teaching*. New York: The Carnegie Foundation, 1910.

Freeman, Harrop A. *Counseling in the United States*. Dobbs Ferry, New York: Oceana Publications, 1967.

Goulooze, William. *Pastoral Psychology: Applied Psychology in Pastoral Theology in America.* Grand Rapids: Baker Book House, 1950.

Halmos, Paul. *The Faith of the Counsellors.* New York: Schocken Books, 1966.

Hiltner, Seward. *Preface to Pastoral Theology.* Nashville: Abingdon Press, 1958.

Hulme, William E. *Counseling and Theology.* Philadelphia: Muhlenberg Press, 1956.

Johnson, Paul E. *Personality and Religion.* Nashville: Abingdon Press, 1957.

————. *Psychology of Religion.* New York: Abingdon-Cokesbury Press, 1945.

Kelley, R. L. *Theological Education in America: A Study of 161 Theological Schools in the U. S. and Canada.* New York: Geo. H. Doran Co., 1924.

Kemp, Charles F. *Physicians of the Soul: A History of Pastoral Counseling.* New York: Macmillan, 1947.

May, Mark A. *The Education of American Ministers.* 3 vols. New York: Institute of Social and Religious Research, 1934.

Morris, Van Cleve. *Philosophy and the American School.* Boston: Houghton Mifflin, 1961.

Niebuhr, H. Richard. *The Purpose of the Church and Its Ministry: Reflections on the Aims of Theological Education.* New York: Harper, 1956.

————, Williams, Daniel Day, and Gustafson, James M. *The Advancement of Theological Education.* New York: Harper, 1957.

Oates, Wayne E. *Religious Dimensions of Personality.* New York: Association Press, 1957.

Pruyser, Paul W. *A Dynamic Psychology of Religion.* New York: Harper, 1968.

Ridenour, Nina. *Mental Health in the United States: A Fifty-year History.* Published for the Commonwealth Fund by Harvard University Press, Cambridge, 1961.

Rosenbaum, Max, and Berger, Milton, Eds. *Group Psychotherapy and Group Function.* New York: Basic Books, 1963.

Schlesinger, Arthur M., Jr. *The Crisis of the Old Order, 1919-1933.* Boston: Houghton Mifflin, 1957.

Stroup, Herbert H. *Social Work: An Introduction to the Field.* New York: American Book Co., 1953.

Szasz, Thomas S., M.D. *The Myth of Mental Illness: Foundations of a Theory of Personal Conduct.* New York: Harper, 1961.

The Ministry in Historical Perspectives. Edited by H. Richard Niebuhr and Daniel D. Williams. New York: Harper, 1956.

Wise, Carroll A. *Psychiatry and the Bible.* New York: Harper, 1956.

Periodicals

Adams, Henry Babcock. "Consultation: An Alternative to Supervision," *Developments.* Published by the Department of Ministry of the National

Council of Churches, 475 Riverside Drive, New York, N. Y. 10027, June, 1968.

Bachmann, Theodore E. "Religion in a Reformatory," *The Lutheran Church Quarterly*, April, 1937, pp. 3-12.

Boisen, Anton T. "Clinical Training in Theological Education: The Period of Beginnings," *The Chicago Theological Seminary Register*, January, 1951, pp. 1-5.

————. "Cooperative Inquiry in Religion," *Journal of Pastoral Care*, Spring, 1951, pp. 17-26.

————. "Group Therapy: The Elgin Plan," *Pastoral Psychology*, March, 1954, pp. 33-38.

————. "In Defense of Mr. Bryan: A Personal Confession by a Liberal Clergyman," *American Review*, May-June, 1925. (Reprint.)

————. "The Consultation Clinic," *Pastoral Psychology*, May, 1954, pp. 55-56.

————. "The Minister as Counselor," *Journal of Pastoral Care*, Spring, 1948, pp. 13-22.

————. "The Present Status of William James' Psychology of Religion," *Journal of Pastoral Care*, Fall, 1953, pp. 155-57.

————. "The Service of Worship in a Mental Hospital: Its Therapeutic Significance," *Journal of Clinical Pastoral Work*, Summer, 1948, pp. 19-25.

Bruder, Ernest E., and Barb, Marian L. "A Survey of Ten Years of Clinical Pastoral Training at Saint Elizabeth's Hospital," *Journal of Pastoral Care*, Summer, 1956, pp. 86-94.

————. "The Council for the Clinical Training of Theological Students," *The Colgate-Rochester Divinity School Bulletin*, December, 1941, pp. 97-105.

Burns, James H. "The Institute of Pastoral Care," *Pastoral Psychology*, October, 1953, pp. 21-24.

Cabot, Richard C., M.D. "Clinical Training on the Earhart Foundation," *The Institution Bulletin: Andover Newton Theological School*, October, 1935, pp. 1-7.

Dun, Angus, Jr., and Thornton, Ted. "Applied Religion, Theological and Social," *The Union Review*. December, 1941, pp. 19-21.

Dunbar, Helen Flanders. "The Clinical Training of Theological Students," *Religion in Life*. 1935, pp. 376-83.

Eastman, Fred. "Father of the Clinical Pastoral Movement," *Journal of Pastoral Care*, Spring, 1951, pp. 3-7.

Fairbanks, Rollin J. "Richard C. Cabot," *Pastoral Psychology*, March, 1954, pp. 27-32.

————. "The Origins of Clinical Pastoral Training," *Pastoral Psychology*, October, 1953, pp. 13-16.

Feilding, Charles. "Education for Ministry," *Theological Education*, Autumn, 1966, pp. 1-258.

Fosdick, Harry Emerson. "The Minister and Psychotherapy," *Pastoral Psychology*, February, 1960, pp. 11-13.

Guiles, A. Philip. "Andover Newton and Clinical Training," *Andover Newton Theological School Bulletin*, December, 1947, pp. 1-20.

———. "The 1935 Summer School in Clinical Experience," *The Institution Bulletin: Andover Newton Theological School*, October, 1935, pp. 7-8.

Hiltner, Seward, "Ten Years of Pastoral Psychology," *Pastoral Psychology*, February, 1960, pp. 7-10.

———. "The Heritage of Anton T. Boisen," *Pastoral Psychology*, November, 1965, pp. 5-10.

———, and Ziegler, Jesse H. "Clinical Pastoral Education and the Theological Schools," *Journal of Pastoral Care*, Spring, 1961, pp. 129-43.

———. "Psychiatry and Religion." Editorial in *Pastoral Psychology*, December, 1954, pp. 8-9.

Hollander, I. Fred. "The Specific Nature of the Clergy's Role in Mental Health," *Pastoral Psychology*, November, 1959, pp. 11-21.

Kobler, F. J., *et al.* "Loyola University NIMH Project on Religion and Mental Health," *Pastoral Psychology*, February, 1959, pp. 44-46.

"Man of the Month: Donald C. Beatty," *Pastoral Psychology*, February, 1955.

"Man of the Month: Rollin J. Fairbanks," *Pastoral Psychology*, March, 1954.

"Man of the Month: Paul E. Johnson," *Pastoral Psychology*, March, 1951.

"Man of the Month: Wayne E. Oates," *Pastoral Psychology*, May, 1951.

"Man of the Month: Francis L. Strickland," *Pastoral Psychology*, October, 1953.

MacLeish, Archibald. "There Was Something About the Twenties," *Saturday Review*, December 31, 1966, pp. 10-13.

McNeill, John T. "Historical Types of Method in the Cure of Souls," *The Crozer Quarterly*, July, 1934, pp. 323-34.

McNutt, William Roy, "Some Phases of Practical Theology," *Bulletn*, Crozer Theological Seminary, October, 1928, pp. 174-85.

"Notes and News," *Pastoral Psychology*, September, 1956, pp. 57-58.

"Notes and News," *Pastoral Psychology*, December, 1957, pp. 57-60.

"Notes and News," *Pastoral Psychology*, November, 1958, pp. 52-56.

Oates, Wayne. "Our Mission to the Sick," *The Tie*, November, 1947, p. 4.

Pruyser, Paul W. "Anton T. Boisen and the Psychology of Religion," *Journal of Pastoral Care*, December, 1967.

Scherzer, Carl J. "The Emmanuel Movement," *Pastoral Psychology*, February, 1951, pp. 27-33.

The Smith College Studies in Social Work, December, 1947, pp. 152-57.

Theological Education. Special Issues on Theological Education in the 1970's: Redevelopment of Resources, Summer, 1968.

Theological Education. Supplement on Cooperative Structures for Theological Education, Summer, 1968, Supplement 1.

Thornton, Edward E. "The Place of Clinical Pastoral Education in New

Plans of Theological Education," *Journal of Pastoral Care*, March, 1966, pp. 16-23.

Way, Peggy. "Community Organization and Pastoral Care: Drumbeat for Dialogue," *Pastoral Psychology*, March, 1968, pp. 25-36.

Winter, Gibson. "The Pastoral Counselor Within the Community of Faith," *Pastoral Psychology*, November, 1959, pp. 26-30.

Wise, Carroll A. "Recent Developments," *Journal of Pastoral Care*, Winter, 1956, p. 239.

Proceedings and Miscellaneous Publications

American Association of Theological Schools. *Bulletin* No. 0 (1918), No. 5 (1926), No. 6 (1928), No. 8 (1932), No. 9 (1934), No. 11 (1936), No. 15 (1942).

ACPE Newsletter, April, 1967.

ACPE Newsletter, March, 1968.

A New Opportunity in Theological Education: A Description of the Policy and Program of the Council for the Clinical Training of Theological Students. Revised and approved for 1934.

A Program in Religion and Psychiatry. The Menninger Foundation, Topeka, Kansas, n.d.

Clinical Education for the Pastoral Ministry. Proceedings of the Fifth National Conference on Clinical Pastoral Education, November 9-11, 1956. Edited by Ernest E. Bruder and Marian L. Barb. Published by the Advisory Committee on Clinical Pastoral Education, 1958.

Clinical Pastoral Education. Fall Conference, Chaplain Supervisors, Institute of Pastoral Care, October 5-9, 1959, Farmingham, Mass.

Clinical Pastoral Education. 1959 Fall Conference, Institute of Pastoral Care, Inc.

Clinical Pastoral Training. Edited by Seward Hiltner. Published by the Commission on Religion and Health, Federal Council of the Churches of Christ in America, 1945.

Clinical Pastoral Training's Contribution to Theology. 1963 Fall Conference, Institute of Pastoral Care, Inc.

Concerns: Clinical and Theological Education. 1965 Fall Conference, Institute of Pastoral Care, Inc.

Levels of Clinical Pastoral Training. 1961 Fall Conference, Institute of Pastoral Care, Inc.

New Thrusts in Clinical Pastoral Education. 1967 Fall Conference, Association for Clinical Pastoral Education.

Report of the Fifth Biennial Meeting of the Association of Seminary Professors in the Practical Fields, June 14-17, 1958, the Boston University School of Theology, Boston, Mass.

Report of the Tenth Biennial Meeting of the Association of Seminary Professors in the Practical Fields, June, 1968, St. Louis, Mo.

The Church and Clinical Pastoral Education. Proceedings of the Sixth National Conference on Clinical Pastoral Education, Plymouth, Mass.,

1958. Published by the Advisory Committee on Clinical Pastoral Education, n.d.

Theological Education and Clinical Pastoral Training. 1962 Fall Conference, Institute of Pastoral Care, Inc.

Theological Education in the American Baptist Convention, Digest Report: Committee of Seventeen, June, 1962.

The Philadelphia Divinity School Supplement to 1967-68 Catalogue. 4205 Spruce Street, Philadelphia, Pa. 19104.

Trends in C. P. E.: Objectives-Methods-Standards. Proceedings of the Seventh National Conference on Clinical Pastoral Education. Published by the Advisory Committee on Clinical Pastoral Education, n.d.

Unpublished Materials

Alschuler, Alfred. "Psychological Education: a new focus for training in the Guidance Area." Harvard Graduate School of Education, January, 1967.

An Adventure in Theological Education and Pastoral Service: A Statement of the Aims and Accomplishments of the Council for the Clinical Training of Theological Students in the Chicago Area, 1937.

Andover Newton Theological School, Clinical Pastoral Education, Description of Center and Program by John I. Smith, Training Supervisor, August, 1968.

Annual Report, The Georgia Association for Pastoral Care, Inc., 1967.

Annual Report of the Director of the Institute of Religion for the year June, 1959, through May, 1960, to the Board of Trustees.

Bachmann, Charles C. "The Development of Lutheran Pastoral Care in America." Unpublished doctoral dissertation, Boston University School of Theology, 1949.

Bell, John E. "A Plan for the Training Center of the Council for Clinical Training at the University of Michigan Hospital." Unpublished doctoral dissertation, Teachers College, Columbia University, 1942.

Brick, Maria. "Some Clinically Trained Ministers and the Program of Their Churches." Unpublished doctoral dissertation, Teachers College, Columbia University, 1947.

Clinical Experience for Theological Students. Worcester State Hospital, Worcester, Mass., 1928.

Colston, Lowell G. Seminaries and Clinical Pastoral Education. Unpublished paper, 1967.

Conference of Supervisors, 1936. Archives of the Institute of Pastoral Care, Inc.

Conference of Supervisors, 1946. Archives of the Institute of Pastoral Care, Inc.

Conference of Teachers, Pastors and Students of Clinical Work, June 2-4, 1941. Archives of the Institute of Pastoral Care, Inc.

Constitution and Bylaws of the Southern Baptist Association for Clinical Pastoral Education, September 30, 1958.

Correspondence between Johnson and Fairbanks, January 29, 1946. Archives of the Institute of Pastoral Care, Inc.

Council for Clinical Training, Inc. Minutes of the Administrative Committee, 1936-41.

Council for Clinical Training, Inc. Minutes and Reports, 1933-49.

Council for Clinical Training, Inc. Minutes of the Board of Governors, n.d.

Council for the Clinical Training of Theological Students, Inc. Minutes of the Board of Governors. Book 2, 1933-41.

Crofoot, Kenneth Stanley. "A Survey of Programs of Clinical Pastoral Education in the Protestant Denominations of the United States as a Preparation for Pastoral Counseling." Unpublished doctoral dissertation, George Washington University, Washington, D.C., 1959.

Dobbins, Gaines S. "An Historal Description of the Developing Program of Pastoral Care," A Tenth-Year Report: Curriculum Development, Department of Psychology of Religion and Pastoral Care. Southern Baptist Theological Seminary, Lousiville, Ky., November, 1953.

Fall Conference of Supervisors, October 28, 1959, St. Louis, Mo. Council for Clinical Training, Inc.,

Fifth Annual Conference, Council for the Clinical Training of Theological Students, September 28, 1934.

File on the Franklin-McNutt Affair. Archives of the Crozer Theological Seminary Library.

First Annual Report to the Directors of the Council for the Clinical Training of Theological Students, September 29, 1930.

First Annual Report to the Chicago Council for the Clinical Training of Theological Students, 1933.

Foundation Proposal, the Council for Clinical Training, Inc. 1941.

Hiltner, Seward. "Clinical Training as an Integral Part of the Curriculum of a Theological Seminary," 1936.

Hoffman, Hans. "Instruction of Mental Health in Theological Schools," a report by the Director of the Harvard University Project on Religion and Mental Health, n.d.

Hunter, Wayne E. "A Survey and Report Indicating Possible Development of a Religious Program at the U. S. Industrial Reformatory, Chillicothe, Ohio," September, 1936.

Joint Conference on the Relations Between Clinical Pastoral Training and Theological Education, November 27-28, 1953. The Council for Clinical Training, Inc.

Lutheran Advisory Council on Pastoral Care. A statement of Purpose and Minimum Standards, n.d.

Memo from Johnson to Hiltner, December 10, 1943. Archives of the Institute of Pastoral Care, Inc.

Memo on Consultation on Accreditation and Certification to the Southern Baptist Association for Clinical Pastoral Education, December 10-11, 1965, Washington, D.C.

Memo on Meeting of Joint Structure Committee, CCT-IPC, April 30, 1966, New York City, to the Southern Baptist Association for Clinical Pastoral Education, from E. A. Verdery, Chairman, May 18, 1966.

Minutes of the Accreditation Committee, Southern Baptist Association for Clinical Pastoral Education, 1962-67.

Minutes of the Annual Meeting, Southern Baptist Association for Clinical Pastoral Education, 1957-64.

Minutes of the Annual Meeting, Association of Clinical Pastoral Educators, 1965-67.

Minutes of January 13, 1944. Archives of the Institute of Pastoral Care, Inc.

Minutes of the Advisory Committee on Clinical Pastoral Education, 1957-60.

Minutes of the Board of Governors, Institute of Pastoral Care, Inc., 1944-62. Archives of the Institute of Pastoral Care, Inc.

Minutes of the Committee of Twelve, 1952-56.

Minutes of the Committees on Standards, Centers and Approval, Southern Baptist Association for Clinical Pastoral Education, 1957-61.

Minutes of the Conference of Supervisors, January 30-31, 1959, St. Louis, Mo. Institute of Pastoral Care, Inc. Archives of the Institute of Pastoral Care, Inc.

Minutes of the Executive Committee, Association for Clinical Pastoral Education, Inc., 1967-68.

Minutes of the House of Delegates, Association for Clinical Pastoral Education, Inc., 1967-68.

Minutes of the Joint Structure Committee, 1966-67.

Principles of Curriculum Re-Making, Crozer Theological Seminary, January, 1935.

Reports of Conferences and Activities, Summer of 1933. The Council for the Clinical Training of Theological Students, Inc.

Report of the Department of Pastoral Care to the Board of Trustees, North Carolina Baptist Hospital, for the year 1959.

Report of the Executive Secretary to the Administrative Committee, March 18, 1937. Council for the Clinical Training of Theological Students, Inc.

Reports on Regional Meetings from the Joint Executive Director to the Joint Structure Committee, Association for Clinical Pastoral Education, 1967-68.

Report to the Deans of Seminaries of the Protestant Episcopal Church, April 1, 1950. Council for Clinical Training, Inc.

Secretary's Report to the Southern Baptist Association for Clinical Pastoral Education, 1959-60.

Smith, Eugene L. "The Contributions of Clinical Training to the Counseling Resources of the Clergyman." Unpublished doctoral dissertation, School of Education of New York University, 1945.

Standards, 1968. Association for Clinical Pastoral Education, Inc.

Standards for Clinical Pastoral Education. Adopted by the National Conference on Clinical Pastoral Training, October 13, 1953.

Standards of the Council for Clinical Training, Inc., April, 1952.

BIBLIOGRAPHY

Standards of the Council for Clinical Training, Inc., November, 1957.

Statement by the Executive Secretary of the Institute of Pastoral Care, Inc., September 16, 1953. Archives of the Institute of Pastoral Care, Inc.

Summer School in Clinical Pastoral Education, Worcester State Hospital, 1968.

The Committee of Twelve, Buckhill Falls Conference. Verbatim transcription from an electronic recording of the Conference, April 25-26, 1952.

The Council for the Clinical Training of Theological Students, Inc., 1935.

The Council for the Clinical Training of Theological Students, Theological Supervisor's Conference, Fall, 1936.

The Practical Field in Theological Education with special reference to pastoral care and counseling. Report of Conference, April 23-24, 1948. The Department of Pastoral Services, National Council of the Churches of Christ in the U.S.A.

Third Annual Conference of the Council for the Clinical Training of Theological Students, Worcester State Hospital, Worcester, Mass., 1932.

Thornton, Edward E. "A Critique of Clinical Pastoral Education," unpublished doctoral dissertation, the Southern Baptist Theological Seminary, Louisville, Kentucky, 1961.

Written Memories, etc., of William Roy McNutt.

index

Ackerly, Spafford, 203
Advisory Committee on Clinical Pastoral Education, 143-47, 158, 171, 188
Allentown State Hospital, 89
American Association of Pastoral Counselors, 94, 139, 150, 193, 229
American Association of Theological Schools, 88, 103, 106, 143, 158, 177, 180, 182, 195
American Foundation of Religion and Psychiatry, 106, 114, 149, 170
American Medical Association, 78, 85
American Protestant Hospital Association, 115, 117
American Psychiatric Association, 115
American Sociological Society, 60
Anderson, Lloyd, 194
Anderson, Orwoll O., 194
Andover Newton Theological School, 27, 40, 46, 57, 68, 76-82, 99-100, 109, 114, 133, 205, 208, 212, 223, 228
Andrew, William, 63, 117, 154
Association for Clinical Pastoral Education
  forerunners, 131, 145, 175-79, 187
  formation of, 179-84, 191-95, 200, 229, 232

Association for Clinical Pastoral Educators (former SBACPE), 189, 190
Association of Mental Hospital Chaplains, 115
Association of Seminary Professors in Practical Fields, 116, 119-21, 158, 164
Assumption College, 209
Augustana Hospital (Chicago), 133

Bachman, Charles, 116, 118, 163
Ballinger, Malcolm, 134, 135
Bangor State Hospital, 82
Bangor Theological Seminary, 82, 99
Barton, Walter E., 134
Bates, Sanford, 86
Beatty, Donald, 59, 62-63, 89, 94, 110, 200, 201, 205, 209
Beaven, A. W., 88
Belgum, David, 134
Berkeley Divinity School (Episcopal), 43
Bexley Hall Plan, 31, 32, 41-46
Bibace, Roger, 207
Bigham, Thomas J., 96, 110, 115, 122, 123, 167
Billinsky, John M., 114, 115, 116, 133, 134, 135, 176, 180, 194, 207
Bixby, F. Lovell, 86

Boisen, Anton T., 28, 32, 34, 41, 50-51, 55-71, 77, 79, 89, 94, 106, 107, 108, 109, 120, 121, 142, 154, 195, 199-204, 210, 222, 230
Bonacker, Ralph, 122, 154
Bond, Earl D., 91, 109, 214-15
Boston City Hospital, 99, 223
Boston Psychopathic Hospital, 50, 91
Boston University School of Theology, 27, 31, 67-68, 91, 99, 100, 103, 109, 114, 120, 130, 133
Brinkman, Robert E., 80, 87, 91, 105, 109, 110, 115, 121, 223
Brinkman tradition, 83-98, 100, 108, 114, 120, 155
Brooks, Henry C., 194
Brown, William Adams, 65, 66
Bruder, Ernest, 115, 116, 117, 122, 123, 124, 125, 128, 134, 142, 143, 144, 165, 170-71, 186, 216
Bryan, Dawson, 146, 148
Bryan, William A., 40, 50, 62, 67, 68, 109
Burkhart, Roy, 114
Burns, James, 104, 115, 116, 129, 131-33, 134, 135, 160

Cabot Club, 100-101, 156
Cabot, Richard C., 27, 32-35, 46-54, 57, 59, 62, 69, 78-79, 99, 103, 105, 106, 108, 120, 129, 195, 203-4, 230
Cabot Trusts, 99, 103, 104-5, 130, 133
Caldwell, Joe E., 187
Campbell, Macfie, 91
Candler School of Theology, 185, 186
Cassler, Henry, 86, 109, 117
Central State Hospital (Kentucky), 155
Central State Hospital (Milledgeville, Ga.), 185
Chicago Council for the Clinical Training of Theological Students, 58, 94, 107, 121

Chicago Theological Seminary, 27, 30, 58, 59, 67-68, 89, 109, 114, 120, 121, 212
Clark, Maurice C., 167, 176
Clinical Pastoral Education
  accreditation, 128, 129, 135-36, 138-39, 140-45, 162, 166, 177-79, 189
  context, 24, 26, 27, 30, 31, 35, 37
  fees for, 122, 124, 170-71, 183-84
  goals, 42, 48-49, 54, 64-65, 75, 93, 101, 104-5, 118, 136-39, 140, 167-70, 172-75, 205, 216, 224-27, 229-36
  interpretation of, 37, 39, 40, 54, 58, 59, 68, 70, 75, 83, 90, 97, 107-10, 113-15, 119-20, 126, 128, 139, 140-42, 158, 167-68, 170, 172-75, 194-96, 199, 208-12, 217-18, 223-24, 227-29, 229-36
  methods, 47, 58, 64, 102, 200-208, 215-18, 221, 224-27
  professional education for ministry, 199-236
  psychiatric vs. pastoral orientation, 79, 100, 104, 108, 129-30, 132, 160, 167-68
  standards, 78, 85, 87, 90, 115-16, 123, 126-28, 134-35, 136-39, 149, 151, 157, 161-62, 189-90, 234-36
  structure, 49, 116-19, 121-29, 134-36, 150, 155-57, 170-71, 182-84, 191-94, 213-14
Clinical Pathological Conference, 47
Coe, George Albert, 59, 65
Cole, Stewart G., 220-22
Collin, L. H., 194
Colston, Lowell G., 194, 231
Columbia Theological Seminary, 185
Committee of Twelve, the, 115-16, 118-19, 128, 132, 134-39, 142-45, 158
Community mental health centers, 211-12, 226

Concordia Theological Seminary, 114-17
Conservatism, 67
Consultation, 234
Cook County Hospital (Chicago), 121
Cooperative inquiry, 67, 202
Corely, Don, 156
Council for Clinical Training, Inc., 83, 102, 103, 106, 107, 108, 110, 115, 116, 118, 121-29, 130, 131, 134-36, 137, 144, 145, 146-47, 148, 149, 152, 154, 155, 157, 158, 160, 164-71, 175-79, 182, 183, 185, 186, 188, 189, 192-95, 223
Council for the Clinical Training of Theological Students, Inc., 46, 61-63, 68, 75-98, 108
Council of Southwestern Theological Schools, 146, 148
Crozer-Chester Medical Center, 223, 226
Crozer Theological Seminary, 200, 219-29

Danielson Foundation, 162
Danielson Pastoral Counseling Center, 114, 130
Department of Institutional Chaplaincy and Clinical Pastoral Education, Lutheran Council in the USA, 118, 180, 181. See also Lutheran Advisory Council
Dewey, John, 26, 41, 69
Dicks, Russell L., 46, 50, 52-53, 78-79, 80, 83, 99, 102, 108, 109, 110, 114-15, 121, 142, 146, 204
Dobbins, Gaines S., 153, 154
Dodd, Alexander, 59, 82, 101, 110, 200
Duke Theological School, 114, 146
Dunbar, Helen Flanders, 36-37, 75, 76-82, 83, 90, 107, 109, 214-15, 230
Dykens, James W., 194

Earhart Foundation, 76-82, 99, 104

Eastern Maine General Hospital, 82
Eastman, Fred, 109
Ecumenicity, 109, 187, 190, 205, 230
Eden Theological Seminary, 117, 121
Eichorn, Herman, 166
Eitzen, David, 102
Elgin State Hospital, 57, 62-63, 86, 121, 154, 201, 203
Eliot, Samuel A., 62
Emmanuel Church (Boston), 130
Emmanuel Hospital (Portland), 133
Emmanuel Movement, 34-35
Emory University School of Medicine, 186
Episcopal Hospital (Philadelphia), 216
Episcopal Theological School (Cambridge), 33, 43-45, 51, 100, 102, 114, 132, 204
Evans, Allan, 109, 214-15
Existentialism, 113

Fairbanks, Rollin J., 102, 103, 104-5, 109, 115, 124, 129, 131, 160, 194
Federal Bureau of Prisons, 86
Federal Council of Churches, Commission on Religion and Health 36, 85, 86, 90, 104, 106, 119, 130, 218
Field education, 89, 214, 226, 233
Fielding, Charles, 227
Fletcher, Joseph F., 44-45, 105-6, 107, 110, 116, 134
Flexner Reports, 27
Flory, Charles D., 225
Flower, Birdwell N., 194
Fosdick, Harry Emerson, 38, 66, 236
Foxborough State Hospital, 81
Freudianism, 32, 69, 92, 113

Garrett Theological Seminary, 31, 114
Gavarin, Miriam, 207

General Service Foundation, 134, 162

General Theological Seminary, 31, 122

Georgia Association for Pastoral Care, 184-87, 188, 190

Georgia Baptist Hospital, 185, 186, 190

Georgia Department of Public Health, 186

Georgia Mental Health Institute, 186

Georgian Clinic (Atlanta), 186

Gerkin, Charles V., 185, 194

Glenn Mills School (Pa.), 226

Graduate School of Applied Religion, 41-46, 106, 114

Grady Memorial Hospital (Atlanta), 185

Greene, Al, 130, 204

Greystone Park State Hospital, 92, 108, 223

Guiles, A. Philip, 40, 50, 52-53, 59, 61-62, 76-82, 99, 100, 101, 103, 105, 107, 108, 109, 110, 114, 115, 129, 131, 133, 142, 200, 209, 214, 223

Hahnemann Medical College (Philadelphia), 226

Hall, Charles E., Jr., 178, 180, 193, 194

Handspicker, Meredith B., 208

Hartford Theological Seminary, 29

Hartl, Emil M., 194

Harvard Divinity School, 57, 99, 100, 132

Healing, 108, 137-39, 156, 159, 163, 210, 229

Healy, William, 91

Herrick, Everett C., 76, 109

Hill, Lewis B., 109, 203

Hiltner, Seward, 23, 45, 64, 69, 70, 82, 87, 89, 102, 104, 106, 107, 109, 110, 114, 119, 131, 142, 153, 159, 172-74, 214-15, 218, 233

Hiltner tradition, 83-98, 99, 108

Hoffman, Hans, 151

Holt, Arthur E., 57, 59, 109

Homiletics, 214

Howard, Judson D., 194

Howe, Reuel, 93, 109, 110, 126, 159, 200, 215, 218-19, 222

Hulme, William E., 159

Hunter, David R., 81, 99, 100, 102, 110

Hunter, Wayne, 59, 86

Institute of Pastoral Care, 82, 102, 103, 104-5, 106, 108, 115, 116, 118, 124, 129-36, 137, 144, 145, 147, 152, 157, 158, 159-64, 171, 175-79, 182, 183, 189, 191-93, 200, 204

Institute of Religion, 146, 148, 187, 188

Interdenominational Theological Center, 186

James, William, 26, 59-61

Jernigan, Homer L., 194

Johnson, Paul E., 68, 102, 103, 105, 109, 114, 115, 116, 134, 138, 143, 144, 159, 164, 204

Jones, W. Paul, 195

Jorjorian, Armen, 146, 194

Journal of Clinical Pastoral Work. See Periodicals

Journal of Pastoral Care. See Periodicals

Judge Baker Foundation, 91

Keidel, Keith, 168

Keller, William S., 32, 41-46, 59, 69, 106, 107, 109, 199-204

Kentucky Baptist Hospital, 154, 155

Kentucky State Hospital, 153

Klinke, Thomas W., 143, 144, 151, 195

Knight, Augustus S., 91, 96, 109

Krumbholz, Clarence, 117

Kuether, Frederick, 59, 86, 94, 109, 110, 115, 116, 117, 121-29, 131, 142, 154, 165, 166

Lehman, Richard J., 163, 178
Leslie, Robert, 115, 131-33, 135, 177
Liberalism, 27-28, 41, 64, 65, 66, 70, 228
Loomis, Earl, 150
Lutheran Advisory Council (CPE), 116-19, 137, 144, 151-52, 160, 164, 180, 181, 192-93. *See also* Department of Institutional Chaplaincy and Clinical Pastoral Education
Lyman, Eugene W., 66

McDill, Thomas H., 186
McGregor, Daniel, 215
McNutt, William Roy, 222-24
Madden, Myron C., 155, 156
Mahnke, Edward J., 114, 117
Massachusetts Council of Churches, 104, 133
Massachusetts General Hospital, 27, 46, 52, 79, 82, 99, 102, 103, 104-5, 121, 129, 133, 204
Maxfield, Otis, 160
May, Rollo, 222
Mead, George, 67
Medicine, 24, 28, 31-34, 36
Menninger Foundation, 150
Mental hygiene movement, 35, 78, 95
Mental illness, 55-58, 60-61, 66-67, 69-70
Mercer, Samuel A. B., 40, 42, 109
Morris, Robert, 122, 125, 216
Mowrer, O. Hobart, 69-70
Moyle, Henry B., 203
Mystical religious experience, 69-70

Nash, Norman B., 103
National Conferences on Clinical Pastoral Education
first, 82, 106
second, 134, 158
fourth, 116
fifth, 143, 188
sixth, 144, 171
seventh, 145, 172

National Council of Churches, 135, 143, 180, 181, 182
National Institutes of Mental Health, 151
New England Group, 76-82, 85, 99-110, 161
New England Theological School Committee on Clinical Training, 81, 100, 102, 103
New Orleans Baptist Theological Seminary, 156
New Plan of Theological Education, 89, 110, 214-19
Newton, Louie, 185
New York Academy of Medicine, 77
Niebuhr, Richard, 158
Norristown State Hospital, 216
Norstad, Frederic, 116, 117
North Carolina Baptist Hospital, 155
Norton Infirmary (Louisville), 154
Noyes, Arthur P., 215

Oates, Wayne E., 114, 153-58, 159

Pastoral care, 108, 208, 214
Pastoral counseling, 88, 100, 101, 106, 108, 114, 129-30, 134, 150, 170, 186, 202, 208, 214
Pastoral Psychology. See Periodicals
Pastoral theology, 108, 159, 173, 230
Patten, John, 187
Pennsylvania Hospital of Philadelphia, 82, 216
Periodicals
Journal of Clinical Pastoral Work, 103, 124, 131
Journal of Pastoral Care, 82, 103, 114, 124, 131, 133, 136
Pastoral Psychology, 114
Religion and Health, 114
Perkiomen, Pennsylvania, Conference, 123, 126
Philadelphia Divinity Theological School, 89, 120, 200, 214-19, 228
Pittsburgh City Home and Hospitals, 89

Plack, Carl, 115, 116, 122, 142, 143
Preston, Robert A., 80, 86, 223
Price, John, 156, 157, 158
Princeton Theological Seminary, 90
Progressive education, 26, 29, 39, 42-46, 113, 220, 228
Pruyser, Paul W., 60-67
Psychological education, 174-75, 213-36
Psychology of religion, 30, 58-61, 211
Psychotherapy, 34, 70, 80, 105, 174, 230, 235
Purdie, J. Arnold, 215

Rablen, Richard, 207
Randolph, George, 133
Rauschenbusch, Walter, 66
Reichian psychoanalysis, 92
Religion and Health. See Periodicals
Religious education, 214
Rhode Island State Hospital, 81
Rice, Otis, 110, 115, 116, 122, 123, 125
Richards, J. McDowell, 186
Riseling, Maurice, 122
Roberts, David, 116
Robison, Leon R., Jr., 214-15
Rubinow, R. S., 95
Rutledge, Aaron L., 155

St. Charles School for Boys, 121
St. Elizabeths' Hospital (Washington, D.C.), 181, 186
St. Louis City Hospital, 117, 121
St. Luke's Hospital (Houston), 147
St. Paul's Cathedral (Boston), 129
Schwenksville, Pennsylvania, Conference, 125, 132
Seminaries, 24-26, 28-29, 87, 93, 95, 108, 114, 117, 119-21, 122, 123, 125-26, 135, 137, 142, 158-59, 165-66, 173-75, 177, 184, 194-95, 213-32
Shaw, Don, 128
Shedron, Mark, 86

Shepherding, 108, 137-39, 156, 159, 163, 202, 210, 229, 230
Sherrill, Lewis J., 121
Sieck, Louis J., 117
Smith, John I., 130, 134, 160, 163, 164, 176, 178, 193, 194, 200, 204-12
Social change, 29-30, 41-46, 211, 214, 232-34
Social engineering, 41-46, 58, 229
Social work, 24, 31, 36, 88, 108, 129
Sociology, Christian, 29
Southard, Samuel, 143, 156, 157, 158, 188
Southern Baptist Association for Clinical Pastoral Education, 143, 148, 151-58, 160, 164, 170, 171, 180, 181, 183, 185, 186, 187-91, 192-93
Southern Baptist Hospital (New Orleans), 156
Southern Baptist Theological Seminary, 114, 153, 155, 158
Southwestern Baptist Theological Seminary, 31
Spickler, Emily, 167
Spofford, William B., Jr., 163
State Prison Colony at Norfolk, 81
Stinnette, Charles R., 150
Stolz, Karl, 30, 156
Stone Foundation, 179
Stretch, Robert N., 216
Strickland, Francis L., 68
Strunk, Orlo, 160
Sullivan, Harry Stack, 67
Summer School in Social Service for Theological Students and Junior Clergy, 43-44
Suter, John W., 79
Swanson, Paul, 164
Swilley, Monroe, 185
Symington, Charles J., 95
Szasz, Thomas S., 69-70

Taylor, Graham, 29-30, 45
Tewksbury State Hospital, 99

Theological education. *See* Seminaries

Thornton, Edward E., 181, 189, 194, 200

Tibbs, A. E., 156

Tingue, Arthur M., 194

Topeka State Hospital, 193

Tufts School of Theology, 99

Union Theological Seminary, 27, 31

U. S. Industrial Reformatory (Chillicothe, Ohio), 86, 121

U. S. Penitentiary (Atlanta), 223

University of Chicago Divinity School, 27, 90

University of Michigan Hospital (Ann Arbor), 82, 98, 135

Verdery, E. A., 181, 185, 186, 189, 190, 194

Virginia Theological Seminary, 31, 93, 126, 219

Warner, W. Arthur, 215

Wells, Hal, 122

Wells, Ronald V., 220

Westberg, Granger, 114, 133, 134

Western Theological Seminary, 106

Whitney Foundation, 78, 95

Wiesbauer, Henry H., 129

William Allenson White Institute, 124

Williams, Allison, 186

Wind, Henry, 117

Winter, Gibson, 233

Wise, Carroll A., 59, 67-68, 79, 90-91, 108, 109, 110, 114, 142, 144, 148, 159, 164, 166, 170, 171, 203, 204

Wolberg, Lewis, 124

Wolf, Theodore, 92

Worcester, Alfred, 33

Worcester State Hospital, 40, 50-51, 57, 67, 79, 90-91, 109, 130, 200-212, 214, 227, 228

Worship, 202

Yale Divinity School, 27, 99

Young, Richard K., 154, 155, 156, 158

Zabriski, Edwin G., 81, 91